T0337542

DECOY

DECOY

ROBERT MURPHY

This book is based on true events and meticulous research.
Some scenes and characters have been altered to protect the identities
of victims or for the purposes of dramatisation.

HarperElement
An imprint of HarperCollins*Publishers*
1 London Bridge Street
London SE1 9GF

www.harpercollins.co.uk

HarperCollins*Publishers*
Macken House, 39/40 Mayor Street Upper
Dublin 1, D01 C9W8, Ireland

First published by HarperElement 2024

1 3 5 7 9 10 8 6 4 2

© Robert Murphy 2024

Robert Murphy asserts the moral right to
be identified as the author of this work

A catalogue record of this book is
available from the British Library

ISBN 978-0-00-866681-1

Printed and bound in the UK using 100%
renewable electricity at CPI Group (UK) Ltd

MIX
Paper | Supporting
responsible forestry
FSC™ C007454

This book contains FSC™ certified paper and other controlled
sources to ensure responsible forest management.

For more information visit: www.harpercollins.co.uk/green

For Ellie and my sons

FOREWORD

I first heard about this unique, incredible undercover operation two decades ago. A colleague, an old, talented newspaper hack, let rip this true-life drama of covert cops, seventies-style surveillance and the decision made by a young, brave female officer to trap a true monster. I filed it in the back of my mind: great story, but nothing to do with me or my career as a TV news reporter.

A year or so later there were developments, which you'll learn of, that involved me watching from the press bench as a courtroom drama played out. Then, a few years ago, I started moving from two-minute reports for ITV News into longform: writing books, directing films and producing podcasts. After some success with podcasts and with a book under my belt, I wanted to tell a multi-layered crime story which took me to a different era. I looked at this police inquiry, thinking it might be something of a history piece.

How wrong I was.

This story may start decades ago, but it ends in the present day. In a way in which I could never have predicted.

Such is the nature of this predator.

At its height, more than 200 officers worked on this covert operation. It was unlike anything tried before in British policing.

Over the last few years I have spoken with many of the key figures: from the original senior investigating officer in his retirement home to the decoy operatives, some still only teenagers, who put their lives on the line every night. From the young observation officers who would be so inspired by this early surveillance success that they would spend the rest of their careers in the shadows of covert policing to the detectives who were dragged from their division to a neighbouring district in which people lived in fear.

Some have been thankful for my interest – surprised that other writers haven't approached them before. Others were amused by my questions. One or two have found our conversations therapeutic. I found their recollections in turn moving, entertaining, thought-provoking and chilling. They have all been good company, a joy to get to know. I hope you find this so too, within these pages.

I have been granted access to documents kept stashed away and secrets that those involved once whispered to each other but didn't say out loud for many years. And I have managed to track down activists, journalists, politicians and students who remember the time when a cloak of fear seemed to be draped over a Bristol neighbourhood.

I also give thanks for the trust placed in me by the family of a young woman whose murder has for six decades cast a long shadow over them. It has been an honour and a privilege to draw all the strings together to create this book.

Decoy highlights everything I feel is important in a good true crime story: a team of police who show perseverance, a willingness to take risks and the determination that evil will be stopped. But more than that, it shines a light on policing then and now, on society then and now. And it highlights the importance of justice for victims, no matter how many years have passed between crime and punishment.

Robert Murphy
April 2024

PROLOGUE

BRISTOL, 1979

Is he out here tonight?

The neon lights of clubland flashed red on the Undercover Officer's face as she passed through the city, asking the same question she had been putting to herself for months. She leaned forward and turned up the car's heater, turned down the disco music on the radio and sank back into the passenger seat, resuming her gaze through the side window.

It would be 2 a.m. soon: club closing time. A few figures were already tumbling out of bar-room doors and onto the pavements.

A thin man, maybe a student, stood on the street in a tight T-shirt and enormous flares, squinting drunkenly at the officer's car. He put out his hand in a vain attempt to flag it down. A friend pushed him playfully.

'Better luck next time, matey,' said Kelvin, from behind the wheel. The Undercover Officer glanced across at him. How many decoy operatives had Kelvin Hattersley deployed over the last month or so?

Is he out here tonight? the Undercover Officer repeated to herself before closing her eyes.

One more run, then bed. One more freezing run.

Kelvin hit a stretch of road where there were neither pedestrian crossings nor traffic lights, but he didn't speed up. Instead, he kept a steady 25 miles an hour, watching as he went, glancing from side to side.

The Undercover Officer turned to her left and saw the darkened side streets beyond the street lamps: this was where all of the attacks had happened. Flicking past her, the turnings into avenues which stretched off into black.

Did the man wait down these roads? Like a spider in its web, did he set a trap and wait for a woman to fall in? Or, like a predator, did he find a victim on the main street then stalk her until he found a dark corner, where he knew he could carry out his attack unseen?

The Undercover Officer knew one thing: the main road was a safe space. Relatively. The crowds, the fights, kicking-out time, drunken men ... She could handle all of these.

But the side streets were different.

The Undercover Officer pulled down the sun visor and tried to look in the mirror on the underside.

Her eyes were dark, her skin pale.

She thought of her friends who had done this exact same job night after freezing night. Not for the first time did she ask herself: *What am I doing?*

She remembered the latest headlines in the newspapers: 'A City in Fear'; 'The Police Should Do More'; 'How Many More Women Will Be Attacked Before He Kills?'

The Undercover Officer flipped the sun visor up. She opened her coat and reached for the brick-shaped radio hanging from a strap around her neck and twisted the dial.

As her earpiece crackled, she spasmed, found the dial again and turned it down.

'You okay?' Kelvin was looking at her kindly as he pulled up to the kerbside.

The Undercover Officer nodded.

She recalled her first walk: the flash of fear and excitement, a sense of the unknown as she left the car. But that pang of nervy adventure had dulled over the weeks. This was her job tonight – the same job she had done countless times.

She opened the car door and walked into what felt like a wall of cold air.

'Subject's left the car …' she heard Kelvin say as she closed the door. The words echoed into her earpiece.

The Undercover Officer saw a set of traffic lights ahead and began walking towards them, then turned left onto the main road. A group of men walked past, shouting at each other. Guttural laughs. She slipped by them and started up the gentle incline before the steep stretch of Whiteladies Road.

This was the main strip: a broad road with wide pavements heading out of the city. Bars, clubs, shops and restaurants either side.

'Alpha One. Subject's past me,' the Undercover Officer heard in her earpiece. Glancing right, she thought she saw a pair of eyes near a pathway behind a bush.

Which observation guy had that been? she wondered. *Andy? John? Chris?*

The cold was starting to seep through her duffle coat, through her heavy jumper and was biting into her skin.

How many runs have we done over the months now? she asked herself as she started up the steeper hill.

Then, again: *Is he out here tonight?*

'Alpha Two, subject's in view,' crackled the voice through her earpiece. She had been picked up by the next observation officer on the route.

The Undercover Officer breathed out.

Across the road a young woman walked purposefully down the hill. She looked as if she was on her way to work. *Was she on a cleaning shift, or off to the hospital? Maybe a nurse, or even a doctor?*

The same thoughts flashed into the Undercover Officer's mind whenever she saw someone who held any vague likeness to herself: *Do you know what you're doing out at night? Is it really worth putting your safety at risk for the price of a cab? I have an earpiece, a microphone, a backup team and self-defence training – you have nothing.*

It was then that her thoughts were interrupted by a message in her earpiece. She couldn't quite make it out, so she stayed silent so as not to talk over the repeat. But the second time she heard it perfectly.

This was Kelvin Hattersley's voice.

'There's a man on your tail. He's in a car, a Ford Capri. Repeat, a yellow Ford Capri. He's driving behind you. Looks just like the photo-fit. Repeat, there's a man on your tail.'

Okay, she thought.

The Undercover Officer's breath pulsated out of her in clouds under the orange street lamps. Cars cruised down the hill towards her, but she could neither focus on them nor on a crowd of women just yards away by the kerb.

The Undercover Officer listened for a car behind her. Was she imagining a distant chug of an engine?

Was that him?

There had been no sound in her earpiece for a few minutes. Was it working?

Speak to me. Speak to me.

Then there was a crackle. And another voice. Not Kelvin's deep tones. This was higher-pitched.

'This is Control. We've run a check on the number plate. You're not going to believe this. He's a killer. *A killer.* Out on life licence. He also raped his victim.'

It took a few moments for the words to land in the Undercover Officer's mind.

A killer?

'You can pull out at any time. If you carry on, he has to touch you. Repeat. He has to *touch* you. But you don't have to go through with this.'

The Undercover Officer breathed out again and closed her eyes. Ahead of her was the well-lit road. He would never assault her there. To catch this man, she must lead him into those darkened side streets. There, and only there, might he attack.

What he had done to these women was brutal, life-changing … She knew this, she had read the reports. Should she put her own safety first, knowing he would almost certainly target another woman tonight? An innocent, unsuspecting woman, perhaps like the one she had just seen? Or should she put herself in the line of fire of one of the country's most wanted men? What if the backup teams didn't arrive in time? What if he had a knife? What if he took her hostage?

He had threatened to kill every single one of his victims. Now she had discovered he *had* murdered someone before.

'Do you copy?' crackled the voice in her earpiece. 'You have a killer on your track.'

Ahead of her was the well-lit road: safety. To her left were the darkened side streets: danger.

The Undercover Officer took one last breath and made up her mind.

CHAPTER ONE

THURSDAY, 29 JULY 1976

Stephanie Whittle was trying hard not to melt. The thermometer indicated a temperature in the high twenties and she
was wearing full police cadet's uniform – including tights,
leather gloves and her tunic.

The heatwave of 1976 seemed to have brought Britain to
a sticky standstill. It was all the newspapers wrote about, all
anyone talked about. There had been warnings to drink
water, stay inside, be careful of sunburn. But Steph Whittle
and 49 other cadets were in the grounds of a police training
school marching quickly in full uniform.

She looked ahead at the platform. The Chief Constable
and other members of the force's top brass stood rigidly
under the high sun, pips sparkling. How did they manage to
look so cool? Steph fought the urge to look to her right, at
her parents. Her eyes rested on something shining on the
table ahead, next to the dignitaries on the dais in front.

A small table with four silver trophies. In a few minutes
one of these would be hers.

Steph's parents would be so proud when they learned she
had won more points than any other cadet in this intake.
The swimming, the judo, the abseiling, those current affairs

exams ... She'd never read newspapers as avidly as over the last few months. But her test for today was to get through the next 15 minutes without fainting.

She looked ahead, keeping in time with the other teenage cadets, and thought about something cool.

Bloody tights. Gloves in a heatwave?

They reached their positions and Chief Constable Kenneth Steele, OBE, KPM looked down at the 50 young, sweltering cadets in front of him: 40 boys and 10 girls. In a deep, clipped baritone, he complimented the cadets on the culmination of a year's hard work. Some of them, he said, might never join the force but these teenagers would take forth the skills and learning in whatever endeavours they chose. And any employer would be delighted to obtain the services of a young worker who showed the dedication, drive and determination that they had to complete the year's cadet training.

Steph glanced left to right at the friends she had made over the last year.

Surely they were feeling the heat too?

Kenneth Steele carried on: 'But some of you will have been bitten by the policing bug. You will have seen, at least in some small measure, what it takes to be a police officer. And you will apply to join your local force.

'If you have shown that you can work for a year as a police cadet, to give up your time as a teenager to learn the skills and develop the mentality needed to be a warranted officer, it will put you in great stead for any force. You will make exemplary candidates. And now, we will have a short presentation to celebrate those of you who have shown particular dedication and success.

CHAPTER ONE

'First of all, the Norman Frost Baton. This is for the outstanding male cadet of the year ...'

Steph felt the 40 boys alongside her take a collective intake of breath.

'This cadet is enthusiastic and hard-working. He has shown aptitudes in both the academic and physical elements of his cadet training. He can follow orders but also comes up with imaginative ways to overcome everyday and extraordinary problems. He is a team player but also a leader.

'The winner of the Norman Frost Baton is Christopher Gould.'

Steph glanced around and saw Chris's short, slender figure leaping from the lines of cadets, up onto the platform, his ginger hair cropped close under his cap. She saw Kenneth Steele lean in to say something. They smiled. Chris received the trophy, beaming.

'Now, the Kathleen Twist Salver, which is awarded to the female cadet of the year. This young lady has shown great leadership, particularly in a very dangerous situation during a snowstorm on Exmoor. This cadet has excelled at sport and her studies throughout the year. She is highly motiv-ated, popular and intelligent.

'The winner of the Kathleen Twist Salver is ... Stephanie Whittle.'

The penny dropped: Steph had won. She had been expecting to win the trophy for the most points scored over the year. That was in the bag. But a second trophy?

She moved through the ranks and up to the platform. As she reached the top step and moved towards Kenneth Steele, the Chief offered a broad grin, his white military moustache spread wide over his mouth.

'Very well done, Cadet Whittle. You will have made your family very proud. Are your mother and father here?'

She nodded, grinning.

'They must be so happy. You would be a great asset to the police force.'

The Chief handed Steph a wide silver inscribed plate. He congratulated her once more and she returned to the ranks below.

Steph found her spot and felt a wave of pride wash over her. To her right was Chris. He seemed to be glowing. Perhaps it was the heat? Possibly pride? Maybe a mixture of both. She looked ahead. The Chief Constable was talking about something …

Cadet of the Year?

What an achievement!

'Stephanie Whittle,' she heard the Chief say in the distance. The other prize.

She had won the award for most points scored. Steph wondered if she should leave her salver in her place, but she took it with her.

There was an awkward moment on the dais when the Chief tried to shake her hand, but she had the salver and was also running out of limbs with which to carry her trophies and press flesh with Kenneth Steele.

She looked down at her fellow cadets. Some looked back at her with smiles beaming from their faces, others seemed deeply unimpressed.

* * *

Afterwards, Steph, Chris and her fellow cadets marched away, three abreast. She didn't notice the heat as much now; it was as if she were floating above the brown-burnt lawn.

There were photographs with Steph's parents, with her sister (who had been a cadet trainer) and with her friends in uniform.

Steph heard an instructor shout. It was time for the practical displays. Could all the visitors gather round?

She, her family and a crowd were called to watch a judo demonstration. Mats had been laid out to create a makeshift dojo on the grass. Chris Gould and six other lads waited for the visitors to arrive and quieten down.

Chris bowed to another cadet, who seemed nearly a foot taller. They stepped towards each other and tentatively started gripping each other's lapels.

'Are the girls not doing judo?' Steph heard one of the other parents ask their daughter. She watched as, in a thrusting movement, Chris parried, twisted, squatted and threw the larger boy over onto his back with a thwack.

The crowd clapped.

'What are the girls doing instead …?'

'I don't want to do this,' Steph heard one of the other girls say.

It was half an hour later and she was in her accommodation block with the nine other female cadets. The instructor was out of earshot. Steph was convinced the protest would never have been made if the instructor could hear.

'I don't want to do this and I don't want to wear *that*,' a second girl protested.

'This is humiliation,' continued the first cadet.

Steph glanced at the frog-green leotard in her hands, then looked up at the second girl who was complaining.

'What the hell has *this* got to do with policing?' groaned a third girl.

Steph looked out at the field from inside the accommodation block. Everyone was there: her mother, father and sister, all the other parents, the Chief Constable, other top brass and members of the police authority. The boys had finished their judo display and were standing with the others, forming a large square on the grass. She could hear her instructor's voice projecting.

'We hope you enjoyed the male cadets and their judo display. There you have seen how we have trained them with the rudiments of self-defence. But being a cadet, as well as being a police officer, is about how one carries oneself in public. It is about poise, professionalism and *character-building*. In a way it is about grace and performance, and to that end I am proud to introduce to you the cadet's Grace and Movement display.

'Girls, please …'

Steph shuffled out of the accommodation block and made her way with the nine other girls to the empty square of grass surrounded by the crowd.

The boys looked at the girls in their frog-green leotards. Some were grinning, others were trying not to. Some were looking at her with expressions of genuine support.

You've just got to get through this, you've just got to get through this, she told herself. *You've been practising this for a year, keep smiling through the humiliation.*

The girls formed two lines of five in the grass and from somewhere a tinny loudspeaker started playing 'December, 1963 (Oh, What a Night)' by Frankie Valli & The Four Seasons.

Steph clutched a scarf and started wafting it in the air. And they pranced and they danced while Steph smiled as widely as she could bear. Any flicker of doubt would be magnified, she knew. To the crowd she was grace and elegance personified. Really, she wanted the field to open up and swallow her whole.

As the sun shone down on the tumbling, leaping, scarf-throwing girls in leotards, Steph reflected on what her friend had said as they left the accommodation block.

'What the hell has *this* got to do with policing?'

JUNE 1977

Had Chris Gould's teenage dreams been realised, he would not have been an award-winning cadet, a probationary police officer and then standing in the rain next to the wreckage of a car crash in Bristol, late at night. He would have been in a classroom in Australia, teaching kids about the finer points of grammar and language before sloping off to the beach after school. But life has a habit of throwing up challenges.

Chris's family had been 'Ten Pound Poms', migrating Down Under following the Second World War on the Australian government's assisted package scheme when he was just nine years old. The purpose of this scheme being to enlarge the country's population while supplying workers for Australia's growing economy and industry.

There, Chris led a charmed life. In school he had been top of each top set and he enjoyed the outdoors life, but most of all he loved the sports: boxing, martial arts and swimming. His school loved him too. He was destined for great things, the headmaster said. And Chris wanted to help young people realise their potential. But when Chris was 15, his father had got homesick so he'd found himself in an all-boys grammar school in Weston-super-Mare in Somerset, where his new academic standing was middle-to-low.

After becoming increasingly angry and frustrated at English schooling, he had flunked his exams. The sixth form had been arduous. Thankfully, A-levels were now in mixed classes with students from the nearby girls' school. He had met Steph Whittle, who was something of a kindred spirit: sporty and competitive.

Teaching was no longer on the cards – Chris would never have gained the exam results needed. He was struggling in his retakes, but even so he had answered an advert for the police cadets. The academic requirements were lower, the physical demands would be great and the job looked like genuine fun.

After excelling as a cadet, winning the award and securing a job as a probationary police constable, now Chris stood in the rain on a summer's night in central Bristol. The water flicked off the crushed metal of what was once a pristine Datsun Violet before the driver skidded on wet cobbles and wrapped it into a shopfront.

A pub on the opposite side of the road had been playing The Buzzcocks, The Slits and The Sex Pistols but now the music was cut and Chris heard a loud peel of a bell followed by a collective groan. They were starting to filter out. Some of the teenagers who stumbled out of the door had Mohicans, others were skinheads. Most had piercings, a few sported tattoos. Some pointed and laughed at Chris standing in the rain by the wrecked Datsun.

'Oy, you, Rozzer …' shouted a girl with green hair, ripped jeans and a biker's jacket.

Chris noticed a flashing light reflect off a shop window before a tow truck rounded the corner, pulling up between the wreckage of the car and the pub. The driver jumped out. He and Chris said hello and the guy started connecting chains to the Datsun.

The pub seemed to be fully emptying now and a stream of punk rockers was laughing and jostling. Chris noticed a friend from school. A straight-A student with ambitions for university. Now he wore a ripped white T-shirt and had a line of piercings down his left ear.

'Alright, Chris?' the friend half-shouted.

Chris detected a look of embarrassment from him. He nodded back as a marked police car arrived. A sergeant got out, swearing at the rain as he made his way over to Chris.

'Ah, good. The tow truck's here,' said the officer.

Chris turned and saw the truck pulling the car from the shopfront onto the back of the recovery vehicle. Oil gushed from underneath, melting into a stream of rainwater on the cobbles. There was a crunch and a crack, and Chris glanced at the smashed window of the shop. Hopefully, a glass firm would soon be here to board it up.

The recovery man appeared from the back of the truck.

'All done, matey.'

The man held out his hand to shake Chris's before climbing back into his truck and juddering away along the wet cobbles.

Chris looked down at the palm of his hand and saw a £5 note folded inside. His brain was just computing its appearance when the sergeant leaned over.

'That's great, Chris. I'll take that. Cheers.'

The sergeant reached down and plucked the note from Chris, leapt into his car and sped off. Chris briefly wondered whether the sergeant was heading for the next car crash, recovery vehicle and £5 bribe. He turned back and stood by the shopfront's smashed glass. A small overhang prevented most of the rain from landing on him, but fat drips of water continued to fall down his forehead and cheeks as he watched the final punk rockers hurry from the pub, running up the cobbled streets to the warmth of their homes.

Australia might be the other side of the planet, but it seemed even further away that night.

CHAPTER TWO

Chris Gould had only just started as a probationary police constable when the first attack occurred.

Steph Whittle would take her first steps as a rookie in the weeks to come.

It was early in the morning of Saturday, 16 July 1977 and at 27, Alice Matthews was older than most of the other women who would later fall victim to the attacker. She was married too. But she was in Bristol for work, away from her husband, who was renovating their home in the West Midlands.

She had been at Platform One nightclub, near Clifton Down railway station. The night had ended with the current number one, 'So You Win Again' by Hot Chocolate, the crowd swaying gently, left to right. Alice had managed to dodge a couple of blokes making a final attempt at copping off with a woman before the club's lights went up.

Earlier, she'd been transfixed by the rhythmic thumping of one song's electronic beat. Her friend said it was called 'I Feel Love' by someone called Donna Summer.

There was an Our Price in the city centre, she really should buy that single.

Alice walked alone on Whiteladies Road. She passed Marsh Department Store. A toy shop's window was packed with action figures for a James Bond film about to be released. Everywhere, there were signs for *The Spy Who Loved Me*.

Alice walked south for just a block on the main street before heading west onto Alma Road. This was bedsitland: grand Victorian mansions, which had been divided up. Brief flights of staircases to the front doors of four-storey brick houses. Entrances to basement flats underneath, behind small pockets of front gardens. There was a short parade boasting shops, two cafés and a launderette. The only light was from the moon and the orange of the sodium street lamps.

Alice could hear footsteps behind her, but when she turned, no one was there. She felt a sharp pang of fear. As she continued, the footsteps started again behind her. She felt trapped. It was still 10 minutes to the flat her firm had arranged for her. If she was being followed, she would have to lose the man now.

Alice reached the junction with Pembroke Road, a broad avenue with large, beautiful houses. She turned the corner and jumped into a front garden, hiding in the bushes.

Everything happened so quickly. He just appeared. Placing both hands around her throat, he dragged her towards him and whispered, 'Don't scream or I'll kill you.'

Alice wasn't from Bristol, but she had spent enough time there now to know the accent well. And this man spoke with gruff, short vowels – he came from somewhere up north.

CHAPTER TWO

The man sexually assaulted her.

After the attack, Alice found a phone box and, through tears, managed to dial 999.

As a policeman and woman arrived and whisked her to the police station, she started telling herself off for not fighting back. Surely she would have? For years, in the back of her mind she had even had a plan for what to do if she found herself alone and under attack.

'Grab your keys, Alice, use them as a weapon. Punch him where it hurts,' she'd always told herself.

But tonight, when she thought she might be assaulted, even though she'd had time to mentally prepare after hearing his steps behind, nothing could ready her for the moment when he appeared. And, as she sobbed, she was furious with herself. Utterly furious.

'This is my fault,' she said to herself. 'I should have been quicker, smarter. I can't believe I just *froze*.

'Why didn't I fight? I'm a clever woman. Why couldn't I just follow my plan,' she asked herself. 'My body refused to move. What happened to my arms and legs. Why didn't I struggle? Or even run away? Did I try to shout? I don't think I even spoke.'

As she silently berated herself, Alice was interviewed by the woman police constable (WPC), to whom she gave her account before being taken to the force's on-duty doctor. She was given a standard-issue gown and her clothes were taken. Alice looked at the pile: skirt, jumper and boots, and now it all made sense to her. 'That's right, maybe that skirt is too short. Maybe I provoked him. What was I doing walking alone? And was I drunk? Yes, I had had a couple more than

I should. Walking home in a short skirt drunk, what was I expecting? What will my husband think? Can I ever tell him?'

The shame of it.

Then Alice was taken to a photographer. The man told her to lie on a bed in different positions while he click-clicked away. Afterwards, the photographer didn't address Alice, but spoke directly to the WPC, telling her when the pictures would be ready.

The WPC told her that the chances of finding the man were slim. She might never see justice. They would hope to get his blood grouping from samples on her clothes.

Then Alice went back to her empty flat.

Soon after, she was called in by the police to try to produce a composite sketch of the attacker. As she swapped images of one pair of eyes for another, one type of hair for another, Alice tried her best to remember what he looked like. Slowly, a picture of the man's likeness appeared in front of her.

He was white, in his late twenties or early thirties, she thought. The image which emerged on the table in front of her had a big, thick mane of black shoulder-length hair, parted near the centre. He had a large handlebar moustache, dark, almost black eyes and unblemished skin. His lips were thin, his nose neither large nor small.

The image stared back at Alice.

That was him. That was the man.

She looked at the picture of the man and felt nothing. 'What's going on?' she asked herself. 'This man has attacked you, but you are more angry at yourself than you are at him. Why? Why is that?' She couldn't understand why she was questioning everything at the moment. Why couldn't she wear what she wanted? Why couldn't she drink as she pleased?

Why couldn't she walk safely at night?

Alice couldn't understand these feelings. He'd attacked her, but in her mind, she was to blame.

There were no reports of Alice's attack in the *Bristol Evening Post* that week. It was just another sexual assault on a woman, another street assailant.

Alice felt the chances of catching her attacker were equal to the number of column inches devoted to him in the papers: zero.

There was neither a Rape Crisis centre nor a police support service. Victim Support had been set up a couple of years earlier in Bristol, but Alice wasn't sent there. She was left to continue her life as a survivor of a sex attack on her own or with the help of those she chose to tell.

The second attack happened three days later, in the early hours of Tuesday, 19 July.

Patsy Delaney had been at Tiffany's nightclub at the top of Whiteladies Road. Just 18, she was the youngest victim. She was born in Bristol, had lived her entire life in the city and knew its streets well.

A little after 1 a.m., she left the lights and bustle of the main street and turned down dark, quiet Alma Road. Patsy didn't hear the man – the first she knew of her attack was when she felt a pair of hands around her throat and heard a beer-soaked voice whisper something about being killed if she screamed.

After dragging her into the doorway of a house, he asked her if she had been raped before. When she said 'No,' he told her she would be now. Patsy just froze. She could understand what was happening to her, but she seemed unable to do anything about his prolonged sexual assault. He disappeared into the night.

Patsy ran to a phone box and called her boyfriend. He sped over in his car and they drove around, trying to find the attacker.

It was now 2 a.m. on the Tuesday and there was hardly anyone around, let alone anyone who looked like Patsy's attacker. At one point they spotted a yellow Ford Capri in the distance but anyone could have been driving.

Patsy went through the same procedure as Alice Matthews: she went to the police station, where she had a short wait while a female officer was found from somewhere. This WPC interviewed her and she was taken to the force's on-call doctor and then the photographer.

The WPC told Patsy that if the sample contained enough semen, scientists should be able to get her attacker's blood type. This might help find him.

Patsy felt lost. What would a blood type do? She was only young, had never paid any attention to the sciences in school, but she knew millions of people had each blood type.

They'd never catch him.

Then she went home, traumatised, depressed and angry. She called her work the following day, said she was sick, went to her bedroom and wouldn't come out.

She didn't tell her parents what had happened. They put her 'mood' down to 'boy trouble'.

The day after Patsy's assault, the first news article about the attacks appeared. It featured on page seven of the *Bristol Evening Post*, between a report warning of how the cost of school meals was crippling Avon County Council and a feature about a 97-year-old wood carver.

Just seven paragraphs, the headline read: 'Warning after two sex attacks'. The report said: 'neither of the women was hurt but police describe the attacks as "serious".

'Today they [the police] issued a warning to young women walking by themselves in the area to carry a torch, walk in the centre of the pavement and if attacked, run to a lighted area and create a commotion by screaming.'

Later, Patsy found herself sitting with a man who said he made composite sketches for the force. They looked down at a table, building a picture of the face of the man who had attacked her.

He was white, in his late twenties or early thirties, with a thick mane of dark-nearly-black hair, which reached his shoulders. He had a chunky handlebar-style moustache. His eyes were dark and seemed to frown from the image back at Patsy, as if he were asking a question of her.

The images were not circulated in the press. The media was so busy with big stories: Jim Callaghan's Labour government seemed in a permanent state of crisis, a young mother had been murdered in a town near Bristol and fire crews had just spent two days putting out a blaze at a large factory in the city centre.

There seemed little interest in publicising what seemed to be a couple of 'indecent assaults', which was how Alice and Patsy's attacks were classified; the police could not write them up as 'rape', based on the legal definition at the time. But those who had heard directly from the two young women had no doubt of the depravity and horror of the assaults they had been forced to endure.

Around the time the attacks started, Stephanie Whittle was called for an interview for the post of woman police constable at Avon and Somerset Police.

Dressed in a police uniform, she caught the bus from her home in Weston-super-Mare, a resort town 25 miles away on the Somerset coast. She found her way to the decrepit Central Police Station, known as The Bridewell, and went to the reception. The secretary to the Deputy Chief Constable guided Steph through a door into the bowels of the building.

As the winner of not one but two awards, Steph stood as good a chance as anyone of getting one of the jobs as probationary officer. She was confident, but only as much as anyone can be when they are 18 years old, walking through ancient, intimidating corridors past smoke-filled inquiry rooms, interview suites and makeshift cells.

They reached an office, the secretary showed Steph in, sat behind her typewriter and smiled. She buzzed the Deputy Chief and beamed back at Steph: 'He'll see you now.'

Steph stood up and made her way through a frosted-glass door. Sat behind his desk, the Deputy Chief gazed up from a file as Steph walked towards him. She stopped, saluted and made a soft smile.

The Deputy raised a finger.

'Get. Out.'

CHAPTER TWO

Steph wasn't sure if she had heard him correctly. She stood there for a moment, looking at him.

'Did you hear what I said?' growled the Deputy. 'GET. OUT.'

Steph wondered what she had done. She had never met the Deputy before, could never have said anything to slight or belittle him. *What was happening?* She turned around and made the 10 or so steps back to the secretary's office.

Steph could feel tears welling in the backs of her eyes, but she fought with herself not to cry.

'What's up?' asked the secretary.

'He's thrown me out.'

'Oh no, not again! Just go back in.' The secretary nodded to the frosted-glass door.

Thoughts flashed through Steph's mind: what should she do? She wanted not to speak with the Deputy, but to punch him. But she also wanted the job.

She turned, opened the door and walked back into the office. The Deputy was sitting behind his desk in exactly the same position as moments earlier.

Steph stopped a few paces away. Any thought of tears had gone, she was feeling pure anger now. Her fist was clenched, but she managed to raise it in a salute.

The Deputy got up, offered his hand and shook hers.

'I'd like to welcome you to Avon and Somerset Police, Cadet Whittle. As a probationary officer, you won't have your sister looking after you now …'

Steph looked at him, questioning whether to accept the job or tell him to fuck off.

* * *

Chris Gould, in the meantime, was starting to shed his long-held ambitions to be a teacher in Australia. He had been bitten by the policing bug and was learning to love his new job.

Avon and Somerset was divided into force areas: A-Division was based at the crumbling Bridewell station, the scene of Steph Whittle's interview humiliation. That covered the heart of Bristol's ancient city centre and docks. B-Division looked after the south of the city; C-Division controlled the north and west of Bristol, including the Clifton, Redland and Westbury-on-Trym neighbourhoods. D-Division took care of the eastern sprawl. But the force stretched further over what was – and still is – something of a contrasting geographical patch. Away from the urban challenges of Bristol and the nearby city of Bath, it extended across great swathes of the West Country where the misdeeds were unlikely to be murders, sex attacks and youth crime. More often, officers would face sheep rustling, drink driving and theft from farms. Other divisions spread across the towns, villages and hamlets: Frome, Taunton, Weston-super-Mare and Yeovil. Also, Glastonbury, Shepton Mallet, Dulverton and even the poetically-named-but-completely-lacking-in-crime Nempnett Thrubwell.

Chris had been posted to C-Division. This covered the grand Georgian neighbourhood of Clifton, which boasted Bristol's most expensive and elegant properties. Nearby was Redland, named after the rose-coloured stone quarried for the Victorian mansion houses. Many of these were now sub-divided into bedsits housing Bristol University's student population.

CHAPTER TWO

The dividing line between Clifton and Redland was Whiteladies Road, a long, broad main street which was home to some of Bristol's busiest pubs, bars and nightclubs. This part of C-Division was policed from Redland Police Station, an old, three-storey Victorian detached red-brick building with a stone porch and awkwardly shaped rooms.

C-Division was run by Malcolm Popperwell. Chief Superintendent Popperwell was short in both stature and disposition. He should have worn a uniform, but preferred to dress in a suit with a trench coat, which he wore year-round, along with a pork-pie hat. It didn't matter what the weather or if he was inside or out, the trenchcoat and pork-pie hat were permanent fixtures. He ran C-Division as a tight ship. It was an efficient and effective police area, but Popperwell paid little attention to his junior officers, Chris included.

Chris was starting to make a name for himself. Okay, he was still a probationary officer, but he was beginning to work on operations in which constables would usually be invited to take part after many years of service.

He was going undercover. Almost unheard of for a rookie.

His first taste of covert operations was sparked by a 12-year-old schoolboy. The boy attended Clifton College, Bristol's most expensive private school. When he wasn't in lessons, he frequented a brothel.

It was run by an agency which called itself Magic Fingers. The boy spent £10 on a 'massage'. Afterwards he pulled out a gun and demanded his money back from the terrified sex worker. She was used to threats, intimidation and even physical abuse, but she had never had the muzzle of a gun

31

pressed to her face by a schoolboy. After she had returned the £10 to the boy, she called the police.

With Magic Fingers' cover story as a 'reputable' massage parlour, perhaps she felt it was unlikely that detectives would probe deeply into the types of rub-downs on-offer. But they became very interested in its properties across the city, in the women who worked shifts and the men who would go there as clients.

Chris was drafted in to help find out more. He started by calling up Magic Fingers, pretending to be a punter in need of a massage before gently enquiring whether any other services were on offer. The women at the end of the line were cagey and would never explicitly say that a massage could, for a fee, develop into anything sexual.

Hour upon hour, he sat in cars, watching men leave, before following them on foot to their homes. He and the teams would stop them and ask them what they'd just done. Chris and his teams would also follow the women after their shifts to find out where they lived, to discover more about their background. They were building up a picture.

Then Chris took a bigger step: he started actually going into the flats, pretending to be a punter. The apartments were a strange mix: some were grotty, run-down bedsits with faded carpet and ripped wallpaper. Others were elegant apartments on Bristol's finest streets. Chris noticed that all of the women were struggling: gaunt, drawn, desperate characters. He soon learned that 'massage' could indeed mean something more.

Chris loved the thrill of acting. Wearing an outfit, inhabiting a character, knowing this was a performance in which he could not fluff his lines. There were no second-takes. He found it exhilarating. Plus, he was gaining experience and an education. He could never have predicted quite where those early, tentative steps dressed in someone else's clothes would lead. An extraordinary operation beckoned. But not for months to come.

CHAPTER THREE

21 NOVEMBER 1963

Kathleen Heathcote kisses George goodnight.

Her fiancé has a night shift at the colliery to get to. George gets on his motorbike and speeds off in the rain, into the dark.

Kathleen stays with George's mother until it's time for her bus to arrive, says goodbye, pulls out her blue umbrella and heads out into the storm.

She boards the bus at 10.25 p.m.

It's a six-mile route from Selston to Mansfield and on this 30-minute trip, perhaps she thinks of where her life is heading. She and George have agreed they'll wait until he's 20 before they get married. Kathleen's a year older. She likes her job in the shop. She's also doing extra shifts to help with their savings. How long will it be before they'll have enough to set up home by themselves?

Christmas is just a month away but she's been organised and has already bought and wrapped presents for her three nephews.

The rain is heavy tonight.

Kathleen knows her mother will be worried. Her mum often waits at the end of the road to greet Kathleen as she gets off the bus. But surely this storm will deter even her?

The bus pulls up at her stop near Princes Street, Mansfield, shortly before 11 p.m. Kathleen gets off the bus, opens her umbrella and heads towards a stretch of wasteland past which she must walk to get home.

It's a short distance from the bus stop to her house: just 400 yards.

The bus pulls away.

It's late on a wintry Thursday and there are few cars on the road, but Kathleen is the sole person on the pavement. In the distance behind her, a car's headlamps emerge from the darkness. The car seems to be swerving slightly.

Kathleen walks closer to home. She is passing the wasteland now.

The car, a yellow hatchback, reaches her and slows. It pulls up ahead of her and the passenger window is wound down.

'Alright? Do you want a lift?'

'No, thanks.'

'Come on. Can I take you home?'

'No. I live just near here.'

'I really want to take you home.'

Kathleen can smell something in the crisp, wet night: 'You're drunk.'

'Let me take you home.'

'Leave me alone.'

The car pulls over and The Driver's door opens. Kathleen looks at The Driver and wonders just what he wants from her.

CHAPTER FOUR

SEPTEMBER 1977

It would be more than two months before the attacker struck again.

Alice Matthews and Patsy Delaney were adjusting to life in their new normal. They had a time before their attacks and a time after them. Even though Alice was married, she felt she had lost an innocence about her. Patsy broke off her relationship with her boyfriend. She didn't say why: that she felt utterly worthless for the first time in her life. He was devastated.

The seven-paragraph news report in the *Bristol Evening Post* had been forgotten by most of the people who had read it, while the inquiries into the first two attacks had drawn complete blanks. The school summer holidays had been and gone. Soon, university students would be descending on the city en masse.

At 33 years old, Denise Turner was the oldest of the survivors. She was a guitarist and had come to the city for a trial gig with a folk band. The concert had been okay: a city centre pub, the other players – a singer and another guitarist – performed together more regularly and had seemed to coordinate better. Denise felt a bit of an outsider, but no one in the pub seemed to mind. She had noticed crowds getting smaller these days. Rock, disco and punk were all the young-sters cared about. Folk tunes with melodies were a dying thing.

After her concert, she had a half-pint of a Bristol ale, collected her paltry earnings and started walking slowly up Whiteladies Road, swinging her guitar case. It was nearly 11 p.m. when she turned off the main road into the darkened side streets towards her lodgings near the heart of Clifton Village.

As she neared her flat, Denise's arm started to ache. She had no knowledge of what had happened to two women in this very block months earlier. And tonight, the attacker used the same method: he approached silently. Placing both hands around her throat, he said that he would kill her if she screamed. He dragged her into the doorway of one of the mansions, where he began his assault. Perhaps it was the shock, but she said something to the man about not damag-ing her guitar, rather than not hurting her.

He looked at her, disbelieving.

Denise tried to get as good a look at the man as possible. She noticed he was wearing a dark anorak. Clean-shaven, he had dark, wiry hair. He also smelt of alcohol – beer, in particular. The few words he spoke were in an accent Denise couldn't quite identify, but she knew it was not Bristolian, the vowels were too short. Having gigged around the coun-try, she would have put him as coming from Yorkshire or the East Midlands.

At one point, Denise noticed a doorbell nearby and she lunged to press it, but the attacker blocked her hand and pulled her away. Afterwards, he told her that he knew where she lived and if she told anyone about the attack, he'd find her and kill her. Then he disappeared.

Denise grabbed her guitar case, held it close to her body, ran onto Whiteladies Road, found a phone box and dialled 999. A police officer, a man, arrived within minutes and took her to Redland Police Station. There, she waited for a female officer to turn up. She gave a brief description of what had happened and she heard that a few patrol cars were told to look for the attacker.

Denise saw a doctor – a man. He took samples. She then saw a photographer – another man. He took pictures. Then she gave a fuller description of the attack to the woman officer.

Denise was dropped back at her lodgings. She stood under her shower, stunned, until the hot water ran cold.

The following day, Denise met with a man who called himself a composite image expert. His desk was littered with pieces of faces – like a child's board game, she thought. She tried her best to recall what he looked like, but none of the rectangles with eyes or cut-off triangles with mouths seemed quite right. Hours later, when she was finished with the artist, she picked up her suitcase and guitar case and she left Bristol.

After detectives linked the three attacks, the Clifton Sex Attacker made the front page of the *Bristol Evening Post* for the first time, on Saturday, 1 October 1977. It was a short article, just nine paragraphs entitled 'Warning On Sex Attacker'.

Twenty officers were now working on the inquiry. Denise Turner's composite image of the man was printed above it. It showed a round, shaved face; big jowls and wide grin. He seemed happy, jovial – a bit like a stand-up comic or a darts player. There seemed little resemblance to the earlier photo-fits produced by Alice Matthews and Patsy Delaney.

The inquiry was now elevated to Detective Chief Superintendent Brian Theobald, who was in charge of the Criminal Investigation Department (CID). Theobald was the same rank as Malcolm Popperwell. He was tall, slim, with greying hair, something of a silver fox. His reputation was business-like but not bossy. If a junior officer approached him, he would listen without biting their heads off. He was urbane, calm, thoughtful and extremely well dressed.

Brian Theobald was one of The Gods, the detectives. They were a different breed to uniformed cops. And Theobald was the Chief God.

It was Theobald who assembled the team of detectives to look at the sex attacker inquiry. They had three photo-fits: two were similar, but the third was quite different. Scientists had been able to get a blood type from semen samples. But the blood type was a common one, found in 35 per cent of the population, meaning its use was limited. However, the attacker's behaviour had the same chilling hallmarks: how he approached the women, his accent, what he said to them. The double-handed throat grip …

The Clifton Sex Attacker was on Theobald's patch and it was his job to catch him.

There was some discussion about what they should even call him – the attacker still hadn't committed a 'rape' in the eyes of the law. And Theobald would not have this man being given an incorrect moniker.

Theobald's team set up lines of inquiry: to Trace, Interview and Eliminate suspects. It was known as TIE.

One of the detectives working on the case acquired a list of sex offenders living in the area. He went through, looking at their ages, where they were from and PDFs (Personal Descriptive Forms). Detectives studied the attacker's characteristics: a northern accent, 5'9" or taller, dark hair, had a moustache until recently but maybe shaved it off in the last month.

Soon, Theobald's orders started cascading down the ranks. He, Theobald, was in charge of the detectives and the investigation. He asked Chief Superintendent Popperwell, who ran the district, to set up another strand to the inquiry: students were starting to arrive in Bristol for the 1977/78 academic year and the last thing Malcolm Popperwell needed was for half the population to be terrified to go out at night.

He called in the Task Force.

Each police division had a Task Force: a sergeant and five or six uniformed officers. They had a big van with Avon and Somerset livery. If there was a football match which needed law-enforcement muscle, a demonstration planned in Bristol city centre, a raid on one of the district's drugs dens, or even a visit from HM The Queen and HRH The Duke of Edinburgh, the Task Force was called. Now, they were needed to deal with a rapist, or an indecent assaulter, as Popperwell corrected his men, some calling him a 'fucking pedant' under their breath.

The head of C-Division's Task Force was Sergeant Kelvin Hattersley. He was 29 years old, married with two daughters and had 10 years' policing experience under his belt. Kelvin was called to the CID offices in the attic-space of Redland Police Station along with the seven or eight heads of the other Task Forces. On the wall were the three photo-fits produced by Alice Matthews, Patsy Delaney and Denise Turner, the top two so strikingly similar with the big black hair and the Mexican moustache. The third – the round, clean-shaven face – seemed so different. Next to this was a map showing central and north Bristol. The room was full of men. Like the CID, the Task Force was not a place where women got involved.

'Okay, gents. We're going big on this sex attacker, we're gonna flood the streets,' announced Popperwell, pointing to the images. 'We think he's the same man – he's probably shaved. So far, we know of three attacks. There may be more we haven't been told about or ones we haven't linked. Could be in other parts of the city. None of the girls have put up a fight. They've all been compliant, done what he's said. He's threatened to kill 'em all. My concern is if one screams or fights back, what'll he do? We need to catch him before these attacks develop into something worse. These points here ...'

Popperwell pointed to three pins on different parts of the map.

'These points are where the victims spent their evening. Platform One nightclub, Tiffany's Club and a pub in the city centre. I think it unlikely he'd been in all these places but all of the girls walked along the same stretch of Whiteladies Road.'

Popperwell then pointed at lengths of red string tied between each of the pins.

'All the girls turned west down one of these side streets and he pounced in the same place, more or less.'

All three strands of string were tied to pins near each other by Alma Road.

'We're doing house-to-house, we're looking at sex attackers who've been released from the nick. We're looking at who lives here. But we've got a couple of thousand students turning up in a week and we need you boys out to reassure women.

'Look out for this man,' Popperwell concluded, pointing to the photo-fits.

Kelvin Hattersley looked at the photo-fits and wondered how they could ever find this man. Maybe a handlebar moustache? Maybe clean-shaven? Like half the men in the city …

The Task Force operation started the following night. Sergeant Kelvin Hattersley and his men patrolled Whiteladies Road. Four of his team went out in pairs and he buddied up with the fifth. There was still just enough sunlight for it to feel like late summer – autumn was yet to beckon.

'Remember, lads,' he said, 'you might see a few students walking home but apart from them, the only people out at midnight are villains and police. If they're not wearing a uniform, or if you don't recognise them as a detective, check them out. Remember the A, B, C of policing: Assume nothing, Believe no one, Challenge everything. Don't take their word for what they're up to.'

Over the next few weeks, Hattersley's men walked the city in their uniforms. They stopped street thefts and burglaries from bedsits and shops. They were called to fights. They walked drunken students home and took abuse from punters at throwing-out time.

Some of the Task Force teams brought up from rural Somerset managed to get lost in the city's side streets. The detectives at Redland Police Station loved that: 'carrot crunchers', they called the rural teams.

No woman was attacked. They didn't spot any man lurking who remotely resembled the images.

After three weeks, Chief Superintendent Popperwell received a frantic call from the head of B-Division in the south of the city.

'For fuck's sake, Malcolm, I need my Task Force back! All your burglars have moved down here, you've frightened them out of C-Division. All the robbers we've nicked say they can't do business off Whiteladies Road 'cause it's crawling with cops. This is out of order!'

With no success in finding the Clifton Sex Attacker, Sergeant Kelvin Hattersley and his team were called off the high-visibility patrols, along with the force's other Task Forces. The city resumed its old rhythm of policing – until a night that changed everything.

CHAPTER FIVE

10 NOVEMBER 1977

Hélène Baur had been in Bristol for just over a month. Aged 21, she had come from a village near Vienna to study English at the University. She liked her new city, but there was a lot about it that seemed strange to her.

Hélène understood English well, but she struggled with the dialect of some of the locals in Bristol – they seemed to add an unnecessary 'l' to words ending with a vowel. She wondered what 'That's a good ideal' meant until an English friend explained the idiosyncrasy: 'That's a good idea.' She also heard people in the city saying 'Where's that to?' and wondered what it meant. But she was genuinely starting to find funny the phrase city folk shouted when disembarking a bus: 'Cheers, drive [driver].'

Hélène wanted to teach. She liked children and could see herself standing in front of a classroom of eager-to-learn teens as she guided them through the peculiarities and pitfalls of the English language. When they started their courses, they would be novices, but by the end, they would speak English as well as she did. Perhaps even with a gently lilting West Country accent.

Another thing Hélène did not understand was the

English way of drinking. On Wednesday, 9 November, she had been in a pub in a side street near Whiteladies Road. She had managed to nurse a half-pint of lager for three hours while chatting with her friends. Her friends, even the more refined girlfriends, managed to drink at least three pints each.

At closing time, Hélène walked her friend back home. Josie was a bit unsteady on her feet and she was slurring. She saw Josie into her flat, had a cup of tea and they laughed about some of the things one of the boys had said in the pub earlier. Then, a little after midnight, Hélène said goodbye.

It was a short walk, maybe half a mile. And most of it was along Whiteladies Road, which was well lit. At the top of this main road, she turned north-east along Grove Road. Hélène approached a phone box, in which she saw a man standing, the receiver strapped to his ear. As she passed, he turned and she caught a glimpse of the whites of his eyes. In a moment, she took in what she could of him: he was tall, stocky and had a thick mop of black hair. He was wearing a blue tracksuit top with white stripes down the arms.

Hélène carried on walking and heard the gentle crunch of what might have been the closing of the phone box's door. She heard footsteps. Moments later, she felt two hands around her throat. A man was whispering, his beer-soaked breath in her ear: 'Don't scream or I'll kill you.'

Hélène found herself being dragged. At first, she thought he would pull her into a garden, but he carried on and on. As his hands tightened around her neck, her terrified mind raced: *Will I live? Will I die? Will I see my parents again? What does this man want with me?*

Still they continued, his hands around her neck. They reached a small wall and she was bundled over it. Behind was a small red-brick building. The attack lasted for more than an hour. Afterwards, Hélène couldn't remember where she was or what she should do. She had never thought she might need to call the police in England and hadn't researched emergency procedures.

Dazed, she stumbled around the suburban streets before realising a man was looking at her. He seemed shocked at her appearance but after mentioning something about calling the police, he ran away.

Perhaps he went to that phone box?

Moments later, a female officer in a dark blue uniform arrived, asking her questions. She was driven to a red-brick building a couple of streets away. There, the officer asked more questions, including what the man looked like.

There was a doctor and an examination and a photographer and pictures taken. Then there were more questions before she was driven home.

The following day, there was a man who called himself a police artist. Could she describe the attacker? He might have been in his late twenties, possibly early thirties, said Hélène. There was the thick black hair. His nose? It was neither small nor large.

Did he have a moustache? No.

What about his voice? Could she determine if he spoke with a Bristolian accent or not? She didn't think he did.

* * *

John O'Connor was a 24-year-old detective constable who'd been a police officer for two years. He sat in the smoke-filled CID room in the attic at Redland Police Station and wondered what would happen if Chief Superintendent Malcolm Popperwell ever took off his pork-pie hat.

John normally worked on A-Division and had just spent the last few months monitoring the newly formed direct-action pressure group, the Animal Liberation Front (ALF). Who was in it? Where did they meet? Was it a terrorist outfit? Who would be its targets? But now he had been seconded over from animal activists to investigate these attacks.

John was medium-height with brown hair and a handle-bar moustache. He was never happier than when swapping cop stories of blundering burglars, covert ops gone wrong or top brass being embarrassed. John was observant, popular, fun and extremely clever. Now, he watched Popperwell as the Chief Superintendent checked his watch, waited for detectives to file into the attic room and scowled at those who were already there.

His face was nearly puce.

'If you're early, you're on time. If you're on time, you're late,' Popperwell bellowed at two detectives, who scurried in before finding seats at the back of the room. The Chief Superintendent took in the team of detectives gathered in the smoke-filled CID room before announcing: 'He's gone and done it. His first rape. He's getting rougher each time. Hélène Baur was compliant, like the other victims. If she'd screamed or struggled, I'm sure we'd have a corpse on our hands. The Chief Constable's furious. He's due to retire next year and he doesn't want to go while this man's still out attacking women.'

Popperwell then checked himself.

'And, of course, what this man does is terrible. The press will have a field day, they'll say we've not done enough. This attack changes everything. He's gone too far this time. We're gonna have more house-to house, more publicity, more pressure. This guy we're dealing with, he's not a man, he's a monster.

'I've got lines of enquiry, I'll tell you where you're going and what you're doing. Before that – any questions about the attacks?'

There was silence.

Then John O'Connor raised his hand and said softly: 'Guv, this man's been attacking here on C-Division for what, five months now?'

'Yes.'

'The geography and the type of attacks are the same? Same location, more or less?'

'Yes.'

'What about the timings? He went away for months, then he returned. Then he vanished for another six weeks then he came back. Where do you think he's been?'

'Could be anywhere. Could have been away for work. Might have been abroad. We've checked the prisons and no one matching his description's been nicked in between time.'

'Yeah, but Guv, there were big police operations on in between the attacks. The streets were flooded with cops. We were all the way up and down Whiteladies Road,' John continued.

'Yes.'

'But he didn't attack then. He waited until it was safe, until the Task Force was stood down. He seemed to know what was happening, to be one step ahead.'

'What's your point?'

John waited for a half-beat and said gently: 'Do you think he could be a cop?'

Steph Whittle had now been in service for nearly four months. She lived on Belgrave Road, just off the Whiteladies Road, with another rookie cop. The building had once been a large villa, but was now divided into flats. And these flats had seen better days. The carpet was threadbare, the walls were brown, the windows did nothing against the chill autumnal air. The Victorians might have known how to build sturdy homes, but their glazing technology left much to be desired, Steph thought. The landlord had no interest in updating the windows into something more suitable for the late seventies.

Storage heaters removed some of the chill but December was fast approaching and Steph feared they wouldn't be up to the job of keeping her warm when winter really bit. She and her friend rented a television and they sat watching as Avon and Somerset Police made an impassioned appeal for people to help find the man now known as 'The Clifton Rapist'.

The news report began with a reconstruction.

A man, clearly a detective, was dressed in a blue tracksuit top with stripes down the arms. He had a big mop of light-brown hair and a handlebar moustache. He wore wide flares which flapped as he walked from Whiteladies Road onto Grove Road then he jumped over the small wall of an electricity substation.

A man who looked like a senior detective then stood next to the cop-copy of the attacker. He pointed to a printout of Hélène Baur's photo-fit image – a picture of a man without a moustache – and described how someone like the image or like the man in the tracksuit top was the rapist. He warned women not to go out alone at night in Clifton, Redland or Whiteladies Road. They shouldn't do it anymore, he said. They would not be safe.

Steph raised an eyebrow as she watched this interview.

The news report then cut to a grand wood-panelled office. Chief Constable Kenneth Steele sat at a desk with a middle-aged flunky nodding at files. Then Steele started being interviewed by the news reporter.

'Well, we think he's a young man aged between 25 and 30. I expect he's single. We suspect he might live alone, we're trying to build up a picture from what he says and how he behaves. He's obviously pretty fit. He obviously associates late at night in clubland or licensed premises because he's always out late at night. And he obviously knows the area very well. So, I suspect he lives in or near the Clifton area because he knows the district so well.'

The reporter asked a question: 'In the latest rape he dragged a woman for nearly 100 yards. Just how determined is he to get what he wants?'

'That's an indication to get what he wants, in spite of the blandishments of the women to leave them alone. He's a selfish man, he's a pig of a man.'

The report continued with a police warning saying women should not go out alone after dark. They should be chaperoned or go around in pairs.

Steph and her friend looked at each other. Why should women be terrified to go out at night? Why should they be subjected to rape? What faith could they have that this small army of detectives was going to find the predator? And why was the Chief Constable so clear about the attacker's profile? A single man? A man who lived near the rapes? A night-clubber?

How could he be so sure?

CHAPTER SIX

Sally Difazio glanced at the teenage girl in the corner of the room. It struck her that she could almost be looking at a mirror image of herself. There must have been only 18 months between them, probably a school year apart. Except Sally was wearing a policewoman's uniform and the girl wore a miniskirt and a look of complete disdain.

And the girl's parents were furious.

'You've got to kick her out. You've got to tell her. She's a disgrace … a disgrace to our family. We didn't raise her to be like this – out at all hours, doing god knows what with god knows who.'

The girl's father went on and on. He wore a smart shirt, beautifully pressed. His trousers were immaculate, with razor-sharp pleats at the front, but his comfy slippers didn't quite seem to work with the whole semi-formal get-up. Until now, it had been the mother who had done all the shouting but she had stormed off into the kitchen, which was show-home gleaming, doubtless to take a break before continuing the verbal battering she was giving their 17-year-old daughter.

Sally Difazio was 19, only a few weeks into the job. She was tall, sporty and terrified of saying or doing the wrong thing. She thought as quickly as she could.

'Listen, I'm a policewoman, I'm not a counsellor. You know, it's not my place to get involved in family arguments. There's not been a crime here.'

'A crime? A crime!' came a shrill shout from the show-home kitchen. The girl's mother stormed back past the hallway's grand staircase, through the mock Tudor door and into the sitting room, where no one had the slightest intention of doing what the name suggested.

They were standing and they were furious.

'A crime?' repeated the mother. She had a glamorous trouser suit, flared at the bottom, and a big red belt, which Sally thought was pretty trendy for a woman who must be in her early forties.

'A crime?' she continued. 'Get her to take a drugs test, see what she's been smoking. What's the point of a police force if you don't *enforce* the law? She had a curfew – A CURFEW. We discussed it. Eleven o'clock sharp. Do you know what time she turned up? Twelve thirty. In the morning! In the MORNING – a.m!'

The girl remained with her arms crossed, although Sally noticed her look of disdain was calming to something closer to boredom. Perhaps she'd been given this lecture many times before.

'We told her if she can't live by the rules of this house, she'll have to find a place for herself. She's on her own. We'll get the police in and get her out. And she was on a final warning.'

Woman Police Constable Sally Difazio might not have had much experience, but what she lacked in hours on the beat, she made up for with a soft, kind demeanour. She smiled at the girl. Then she looked back at the parents in their expensive clothes in their fine house – they looked like they were in a magazine shoot.

'Listen, your name's Emma, isn't it? Emma?'

The girl nodded.

'Give me five minutes with your mum and dad, Emma.'

The girl with the folded arms and the miniskirt slinked out of the room; Sally heard her padding up the stairs.

'This isn't a police matter. Your daughter hasn't broken the law. If you're struggling with her … well, that must be hard. But teenagers will be teenagers.'

Sally thought for a moment. She herself was still nine months away from turning 20.

'Look, it's dangerous out there at the moment. Have you heard about these attacks, in Clifton and Redland? There's a guy doing awful things to women. The city's not safe. And yes, she may have come back a bit late one too many times but if she was to move out, you would have no control over her whatsoever. No say, no influence on her life. If you let her carry on here, at least you could continue providing her with a safe, stable place to be – at least until she finishes her exams. She's doing A-levels?'

The couple nodded.

'I'm not going to take her into care – I can't. This is a domestic matter and no one's in danger, although Emma might be put in danger if she's thrown out.'

Sally outlined other options which she thought could have been kinder and safer avenues than simply kicking out their daughter: a severe grounding, cutting down or cutting off altogether her allowance or perhaps, why not give Emma some responsibilities? A Saturday job, volunteering, joining the police cadets as she had. She wouldn't have the time to party until 12.30 a.m.

The parents harumphed and glowered, but they also seemed appeased.

As Sally Difazio left the grand mansion in Stoke Bishop, she got into the car, joining her probationary tutor.

'How'd it go?' asked the middle-aged uniformed constable.

'Okay, I think. It was like talking to my parents. Except they listened to me because I was wearing this uniform.'

The man started the patrol car, muttering something about the uniform doing strange things to a person's mind.

4 MARCH 1978

The DJ in Platform One changed the record and the club seemed to erupt. Hands flew into the air, men put down their pint glasses and sped to the dancefloor, while women who had been grooving around their handbags grinned at each other.

Everyone seemed to love ABBA's 'Take a Chance on Me'.

Except for Joanna McGarry.

She was stuck behind the bar. It had been a hellish shift – the first Friday night since payday, the worst night of any month. And she had grown to gently despise the song – it had been at number one for five weeks now. She had heard it enough.

It was nearly the end of her shift, but she still had to try to eject the mass of dancing, parading, pointing twenty-somethings from the sticky club. As the dancefloor of club-bers rocked their hips and protruded their arms in occasional spasms, she began washing glasses.

A bouncer came over.

'You okay, Jo?'

She nodded. Tony was nice. One of the security guys who hadn't made a pass at her. He was tall, well built, with the same dark hair and handlebar moustache that so many men seemed to have at the time. Joanna didn't understand why men couldn't shave. It was as if they were hiding something behind their facial hair.

She caught a glimpse of herself in the mirror behind the optics: she was tired. She had had enough of night shifts, she could never sleep in the days. Only three more months of this and then, finally, she would have enough money to go travelling.

This wasn't where she should have been at the age of 23. She'd worked hard for her law degree, she had made her parents proud. But she had realised that she didn't just dislike the idea of working in the legal profession, she despised the whole concept, so she had taken a year out.

Her friends from university had secured placements at prestigious companies and were starting to earn good money. When she caught up with them, they spoke a lot about money and very little about their jobs. It was as if they were embarrassed at how dull their working life was, she thought. None of them ever asked Joanna about either her wages or her job, she noticed. It was as if they found it demeaning. But she was happy and she had six months planned in Greece and Italy.

Joanna had never seen herself as a free spirit, but the option of a career in law had made her one.

Now, 'Take a Chance on Me' was over and the DJ was telling the dancefloor the night was over. If they wanted to come back tomorrow night, it would be Super Saturday at Platform One. And don't forget, girls get in for free in the month of March.

Tony was chaperoning women out of the club, rounding up groups of men and occasionally quietly persuading a few of the more reluctant ones that it was time to leave with some gentle physical pressure. Joanna and the other bar staff cleared the glasses, washed them, emptied the ashtrays, mopped the sticky tiles of the dancefloor.

'You want a drink, Jo?' asked Tony.

'Just a Coke, I'm driving.'

He brought a glass over as she carried on mopping the floor.

'These shifts are meant to finish at three, but it's nearly four. We don't get paid for this,' complained one of the other bar staff.

Joanna thought about having to spend all day in an office looking at legal files and thought, *I'd still rather do this for free than that for money*.

The staff sat around a table and finished their drinks. They talked about a member of their team who had not turned up for her shift, about passes that had been made at them and about some of the outfits they had seen: skirts were getting shorter, heels higher, flares wider. Some of them were going back to one of their flats for more drinks, but Joanna said no.

Joanna found something comforting in the unchallenging conversation of her colleagues. All her bar staff friends seemed to worry about was earning enough to pay the rent and for food, fashion and fun. Joanna wasn't like them, but she admired their uncomplicated lives.

'You're not walking?' Tony looked genuinely concerned.

'No, I've got my car.'

Joanna had read news reports of the Clifton Rapist and seen the photo-fit images. She had always walked the mile-trip back home but had started to use her battered car since the headlines about the attacks began.

'I'll walk you down,' he offered.

Joanna went to the staffroom and found her coat, Tony led all the bar staff out. A small crowd headed towards the city centre.

Joanna checked her watch: 4.15 a.m.

'This is me,' she said, smiling at Tony when they reached a Morris Marina parked in a space on the northbound Whiteladies Road.

'Okay, drive safely,' he smiled from behind his large moustache.

She got into her car, turned the ignition and it clicked. Joanna sighed. When she tried again, the engine fired. She wound down her window, waved, indicated and pulled the car away from the parking spot into the carriageway. She turned on the radio. The announcer said: 'Well, this next tune has been selling really well this week. Word is, it might even knock the mighty ABBA from the top spot …'

Damn well hope so, Joanna thought.

'It's a new artist – she's 19, she's from London and she's called Kate Bush. This is "Wuthering Heights" …'

A strange screeching sound came from the car.

What now? thought Joanna. Then she realised it was the song, not her car in distress. She turned the radio off and noticed how empty the streets were.

But in the distance behind her was a set of headlamps.

She reached the top of Whiteladies Road, where the traffic lights were turning red, and she stopped. The car behind slowed to a halt.

Joanna had little interest in vehicles, but she could see it was yellow and quite sporty. She couldn't make out clearly what the driver looked like, but she was sure it was the silhouette of a man.

As the traffic light turned from red to green she hit the accelerator a bit quicker than she should. Her car stalled. Joanna swore, pulled the handbrake, turned the ignition and moved off. She wondered if the car behind might beep, but it didn't.

At the top of Whiteladies Road she filtered into a small one-way system by Durdham Down, which led to her home street. The yellow car was still behind her. As she pulled over by her flat, she didn't know why her senses were so alert, but she was on edge.

She saw the yellow car drive past.

Joanna got out of her car, closed and locked its door and half-walked, half-jogged up her front garden to her flat.

The man appeared from behind some bushes. He told her not to scream. If she did, he would kill her, he said. He then dragged her further into the garden, where he attacked her.

Joanna McGarry did not make a sound; she did not put up a fight. The attack was long and brutal. Afterwards he fled from the scene and Joanna noticed the same yellow car driving away at speed. Joanna called police and a female officer came to collect her, taking her to Redland Police Station. There was a doctor for her injuries. A photographer too. Both men, both nice to meet in normal circumstances, but not like this.

After the examination and the photos, Joanna was interviewed. She tried to remember the snatched images and senses in her mind, like a slideshow: getting out of her car, the man appearing from behind the bushes, his large hands around her throat, the smell of his beer-soaked breath as he snarled, 'Don't scream or I'll kill you.' Being dragged and doing every dark thing he asked her and feeling empty, humiliated, as he ran from the scene.

Joanna didn't catch the name of the female officer, but she noticed her eyes widened as she gave her statement. If Joanna wasn't mistaken, she also spotted a tear running down the policewoman's cheeks. But then came the anger. She couldn't stop it – she knew this woman was here to help, but something inside Joanna McGarry flipped like a switch and she found herself shouting at the young woman officer.

'What difference is this going to make? You've got no proof. What am I? His third victim, or fourth or fifth? Like you lot are going to catch him – he's hardly a criminal fucking mastermind! Look, I studied law. I studied what you do. What's your job? To protect life and property? Fucking clueless, you are absolutely fucking clueless!'

She saw the young officer silently shrink somehow.

CHAPTER SIX

The following day, Joanna met a police artist and an image of a man formed on the blank sheet of paper. He was white, in his late twenties or early thirties, with a thick mop of dark hair, parted at the side.

And a handlebar moustache.

No, she didn't recognise him. He wasn't like anyone she knew. It all happened in such a blur, she wasn't sure what was going on. He was so distinctive, Joanna told the police artist. Why couldn't they have caught him yet?

The following Friday night, Platform One nightclub was almost as busy as the week before. 'Take a Chance on Me' was no longer number one, it had indeed been replaced by Kate Bush's debut single. But 'Wuthering Heights' was not the kind of tune they played here. So, the DJ put on the ABBA favourite again. As the dancefloor began to fill, few realised that the intelligent-looking woman behind the bar wasn't there as usual. Apart from Tony, the bouncer, who really quite liked Joanna McGarry. She hadn't showed for her shifts that week. He didn't know how to contact her, but he hoped she was okay.

The team of detectives had grown to 40, all permanently looking for this man. There were house-to-house inquiries either side of Joanna McGarry's flat which continued all the way down her road. For days afterwards, she felt her neighbours must have known that she, Joanna McGarry, was the Clifton Rapist's latest victim. She wondered if people were looking at her differently now.

Detective Chief Superintendent Brian Theobald sent Sergeant Kelvin Hattersley and his Task Force out again –

more high-profile patrols to calm nerves. There was another appeal on television. The same detective who had dressed as the attacker put on another tracksuit and was filmed again walking the streets for the television news.

There had been a small incident room at Redland nick, but this was moved to a larger police station – at Southmead – to accommodate the bigger team of detectives. They received calls: 50 people said they had seen a man like that out in Bristol in the early hours of 4 March. Each call was followed up and sightings chased down.

The inquiries led to nothing.

Steph Whittle was sent to Bristol University to help a middle-aged detective try to connect with students. He spoke to the Students' Union. Some of them looked concerned, others seemed bored.

Some asked why the police weren't doing more. One student, a forthright girl in a pair of blue dungarees, asked the DC how a man could attack five times in less than a year, each of his victims gave good descriptions, he was operating on the same, short stretch of road, yet he was completely free to carry on.

How hard could it be?

Something deep inside Steph Whittle agreed with her.

CHAPTER SEVEN

Michelle Tighe knew she shouldn't have gone into the pub alone but she really hadn't much choice. She had been on patrol on Bristol's Gloucester Road soon before closing time and her partner – her probation tutor – had disappeared. He was in the habit of vanishing. So, when she heard in her radio that there was a fight in the Robin Hood's Retreat pub, the rookie cop decided to go.

When Michelle opened the door, she thought two things: One: *Oh, this is a big fight*. Two: *Perhaps I shouldn't have gone into the pub alone*.

The Retreat was a favourite of Bristol Rovers' fans – 'Gasheads', as they called themselves. The fight could have been sparked by anything from someone looking the wrong way at a diehard Gashead to the arrival of a Bristol City fan. Whatever the cause, as WPC Michelle Tighe opened the pub door, she saw a table being turned over, two groups of men punching each other and a pint glass flying across the room.

How am I going to deal with this? she thought.

But Michelle was a little bit older than most of the other probationary officers. She was 23 and had worked in pubs and holiday parks for years. With a strange mix of this limited experience, assertion, naivety and cool, she managed to calm the riot.

One of the ringleaders was a man in his early twenties. He wore a Bristol Rovers shirt and was missing a couple of front teeth but Michelle noticed he had a spider's web tattoo on his elbow, which she knew suggested he'd spent some time behind bars.

He looked at Michelle before flashing a glance at a group of men by the bar.

'Go, man!' one of them shouted. Michelle clocked they hadn't used his name.

The pub, which only moments ago had been a chaotic cacophony of smashing glass, punches and yelps of pain, fell silent. Michelle felt that every pair of eyes was either on her or the thug. And he was about to run away: humiliation.

'Do … Not … Move …' Michelle didn't know where she found either the calmness or the authority to say it but her voice was deep, controlled and had just the right amount of menace.

The tattooed, toothless thug seemed frozen.

'Hear that siren? That's my backup coming,' Michelle said.

The silence continued, inside and outside the pub. The man seemed to strain his ears.

She was in the middle of the room, by the central bar. He was near the door, just a few short steps from liberty.

Michelle glanced at the mirror behind him: an old one with a brand of whisky painted across it in green letters. Framed in the glass, she could see herself face to face with this villain. He was wiry, but probably had a low cunning. She was perhaps the same age as him but looked younger: tall, dark curly hair, in her dark uniform, her tie slightly askew from pulling two fighters apart.

Thoughts flashed through Michelle's mind: her fold-up truncheon was in her bag, but she couldn't use it in a pub like this. It'd take her five minutes to get it out, he'd flee and she was worried that a police officer with a weapon would spark another riot. Call for backup? Well, she'd already done that and it would look as if she was panicking. Cuff him? No chance. He was the ringleader and it would all kick off again.

'They'll be here in 30 seconds, matey,' Michelle told the man, who seemed to be going through his own tortured questioning. 'You're going to stay exactly there until they turn up.'

The man looked at the door and then he looked back at Michelle.

'One move and we'll add resisting arrest to the charge sheet and you'll be back inside for longer this time. Hear the siren?'

There was no siren.

He shook his head gently.

Then, in the distance, Michelle heard a distinctive whine of a patrol car racing towards the pub. She tried not to show any sense of relief. The doors burst open and a team of five police constables stumbled through. They stopped, stared at Michelle in this face-off with the thug. One of them recognised her: 'Oh, alright, Michelle? Where's your probation tutor?'

After the arrests, the tutor turned up. Michelle thought she could see a dusting of doughnut sugar around his mouth and some crumbs on his uniform.

'You shouldn't have gone in there alone, Michelle. Anything could have happened. You might have been injured. And you, a woman? A WPC in a pub fight like that alone? I'm going to have to mark you down for that – it was improper procedure.'

Michelle Tighe was one of Avon and Somerset Police's few new starters who was not from the force area. She had grown up in Nottinghamshire and even though she'd moved with her parents to Dorset a few years earlier, she still had a strong East Midlands accent.

As a nine-year-old, she had got lost at the Goose Fair in Nottingham. Craning her neck, young Michelle realised she had become separated from her parents, looked desperately among the crowd for them and began to cry. A policeman saw her sobbing, knelt down and asked what the matter was. Within 20 minutes she was reunited with her mum and dad. The incident had fired the spark in Michelle to join the force. After school, she had a few pub jobs and worked in holiday clubs before she decided to take the leap and join Avon and Somerset Police – she got an interview.

Michelle was keen to go from working in bars to putting criminals behind them.

She made it to the final interview stage. As she sat outside a big door, waiting for her interview, a female superintendent walked by – Michelle didn't know there were female superintendents in 1978.

'What are you doing?' asked the woman in the uniform.

'I've got a job interview.'

The superintendent looked down at Michelle, studying her like a scientist might examine a sample. Then she said: 'Well, good luck. But remember one thing: the police is not a marriage bureau.'

Michelle passed the interview, got the job, did her training and was put on shifts. If she was to go out to a crime scene, she would have to find a male officer to accompany her. In those days it wasn't deemed appropriate for two female officers to go out together.

Michelle was put on earlies, lates and nights. The overnight shifts were the worst. Only the men would be permitted to leave the confines of Redland Police Station. Michelle was allowed to *man* the front desk on a night shift – a term which caused her to inwardly groan. If that job was taken, she was sent to the control room – the streets were no place for a woman.

The only time a sergeant might ask for a woman was if they needed a female officer for something: a job involving women or children. Then, and only then, was Michelle allowed out on a night shift. An arrest of a woman, a case of domestic abuse, or a vulnerable child or a rape victim: then the top brass would call for Michelle, Steph Whittle or Sally Difazio, or one of the other women who were starting to populate the ranks.

Women could be in the police force, that was accepted. Typists, canteen ladies, definitely. Officers, potentially. Detectives, no.

Uniforms only for women. One woman had secured a place on Redland's CID team, but she acted like a man, according to the young female officers who saw her at work. The new starters might have been able, clever and determined, but they also needed to be realistic: they would not become detectives, they would not run inquiries, they had very little hope of climbing the ranks.

CHAPTER EIGHT

The Driver looks down at the girl. She is limp, but he is sure she is alive. He is sure she is breathing.

He told her not to scream – but she had. So, it was *her* fault. He really had little choice: he gave her the option, she made an informed decision.

The girl is on her back, her eyes closed. She has mud all over her coat from the ground and her hair is sticky from the rain. He looks down and sees his trousers are soaked and covered in grime from the wasteland. What a place.

The roads are still empty, not a single car has come past. How long have they been here? Ten minutes?

His car is next to the girl's body and he reaches for the handle of the back door. He presses a button and the door pops open. He turns around, lifts the girl up and puts her in the back seat. She's going to get mud all over the inside of his car.

He runs a hand through his hair – it's wet like he's been swimming.

He walks round to the driver's door, opens it and gets inside. Shit, he got lost in the moment with the girl and left the passenger window open. There's water all over his passenger seat as well.

What'll his wife say?

The Driver turns the ignition and pulls off the wasteland onto the road. The wipers flick quickly as he heads past the red-brick terraces and out of town.

What should he do with her? Hospital? How will he explain it? Police station? Not likely. Leave her somewhere?

He's in the countryside now. Once every few moments he looks in the rear-view mirror. He can't see her, she's too low in the seat. He can just see the black of the night behind him, a corner of his eye and a few strands of his wet, thick black hair. He checks his upper lip – he's been trying to grow a moustache, but he's only young and it's taking longer than he would like. It's wispy. Pathetic.

He misses the bend in the road, the steering wheel spins, flying from his hand; he makes a grab for it, slamming his foot on the brakes. The car whips round quicker on its wheels, finally seeming to sink into something and stop.

This is all he needs.

The windscreen wipers are still flicking big drops of rain away: left, right, left, right. His headlamps show only a few metres ahead: there's some long, rough grass but he can make nothing else out. He turns the ignition and throws the gearstick into first. The engine whines loudly, he can feel the wheels spinning underneath him.

He's going nowhere.

He opens the door, looks behind and tries to drive off again. His wheels are throwing back great clumps of mud as his car judders left to right.

Reverse? Perhaps he should reverse out?

Same thing. It seems like the car is actually starting to sink.

He takes a breath and gets out. His foot seems to squelch down into a soft bog of some kind. These are new shoes … There are no street lights, but he can just about make out the main road – he must have skidded about 20 yards off the carriageway. He looks back at his car and heads to the road. He pulls up his coat and waits: he can hear something coming in the distance, it's rounding a corner.

A car. Another car. He puts out his hand, thumb up, hitchhiker style.

The car whizzes by.

He swears.

Something else is coming. This sounds bigger, louder.

Now a truck rounds the corner, its large headlamps cutting two slashes of blinding yellow through the rain.

He holds out his hand.

The truck speeds around the corner.

How's he going to get out of this?

He looks around, takes a breath and then goes back to his car. He opens the boot, goes to the rear seat and drags the girl out. She's only slight, quite light. He carries her around to the boot and puts her inside.

He doesn't check her breathing.

He slams the boot door shut and feels a bit better – it's as if he's closed a part of his mind off, as if it's not quite so real, now that he can't see her. He glances again at his wheels: they look as though they've sunk further into the mud. He shrugs and walks into the wet night.

The Driver doesn't know how long he's walked, he just knows he's wet through and feels thoroughly miserable. It's miles to his home and he's really not sure he knows where he is. He tries a turning off the main road and finds himself in one of the new housing estates, which the local authority put up soon after the war.

He just needs to find a phone box.

If he sees a light on in a house, should he knock on the front door?

He rounds a corner and lets out a quiet 'Hallelujah!' A man is working in his home garage, the door is up, a light is on. He approaches.

He goes up the short drive and sees a car on a jack and a man underneath.

'Hello?' he hears himself saying.

The man pushes himself out from under the car, looks up and then gets up.

He looks at The Driver, horrified.

'You alright, mate? Look like you've seen a ghost. Look at the state of you.'

'No, no – I've just broken down. Been walking for miles.'

He looks down at his mud-soaked trousers. 'I tried fixing it meself, but I don't know one end of a car from another. Could I borrow yer phone?'

'Yeah, course.'

He's shown into a small front room, where there's a green phone on an ornate stand. He takes off his shoes and pads over the carpet to pick up the receiver. The man follows him in, picks up a Yellow Pages, looks up 'garages' and reads out a number.

The Driver dials it, but no one answers.

'You'll be lucky to get 'owt at this time, matey,' says the homeowner.

'You got the number for Mansfield cop shop?'

The man flicks through the pages and reads out a second number.

The Driver silently thinks twice, then dials.

A man answers: 'Nottinghamshire Police?'

'Hello. I wonder if you can help? It's an emergency. My car has broken down and I'm having to walk home. I wonder if you can get an officer to give my wife a knock? We ain't got a phone, yer see. Tell her I'll be back late?'

The Driver gives his name, his wife's name, the address and hangs up. He asks the homeowner for directions to where he lives, thanks him, turns before pulling his collar up and walking back into the storm.

CHAPTER NINE

After months of working earlies, lates and nights, Michelle Tighe transferred to the C-Division Police Women's Unit (PWU). The male top brass had set up the PWU to deal with everything 'female': women prisoners, sex workers, care cases, domestic abuse and vulnerable mothers and children.

It was run by Sergeant Carol Curnock. Like the proverbial iron fist in a velvet glove, Curnock was tough, soft and not to be messed with. She was only 38, but seemed from a different generation from the team of teens and twenty-somethings. She joined the former City of Bristol force in 1958, so by March 1978 she had been a police officer for longer than some of her charges – like Steph Whittle – had been alive. No one ever said it to her face, but she was called 'Mother Hen'. And she was as protective as she was particular.

While the male detectives ran their CID departments like boys' clubs – feet on desks, smoke-filled rooms and every third word being 'fuck' – Carol Curnock's PWU had a completely different vibe. There were many rules, but two of the most important were 'no smoking' and 'no swearing'. When Steph Whittle let fly a 'Sod it', Curnock told her that if she wanted to use language like that, she should join the CID. Another of Sergeant Curnock's rules was: 'You do the job once and you do it properly.'

Sometimes, in her early days, Michelle Tighe might return from an interview from a care case. After writing up the statement, she would pass it for Carol to read.

'What about the mother? Where was she? Are there extended members of the family who stay? What about an older brother or sister?' Curnock would enquire. And Michelle would be sent back to the house to ask the questions she should have asked first time around. The humiliation was enough that she made sure that all her future statements were comprehensive enough to pass the Carol Curnock test.

The comings and goings of the PWU were watched carefully by some – male – officers. They loved a new starter.

Weeks after she started, Michelle was sent to a suicide. The remains of a woman, who had been missing for more than 12 months, had been discovered in parkland. Her family was distraught. There had been a high-profile poster campaign in the city to try to get people to help find her, pictures of her had been placed throughout the neighbourhood.

The body was decomposed, skeletal limbs pecked and pulled by birds and other animals, and scenes-of-crime officers were examining what was left, alongside the bottle of pills lying nearby. Even though she had been dead for more than a year, she was still a woman, so Michelle was despatched. The new recruit hadn't worked with the scenes-of-crime officer before and she was slightly concerned by the twinkle in his eyes.

'I'll just need a hand in a second,' she heard him say as she stood under a tree, watching him peering into the bush under which the woman had been found. Moments later, she heard him shout and in the corner of her eye saw something flying through the air towards her. She instinctively held out her hands and caught a bag with something heavy in it.

'There you go, Michelle. Be a good girl, pop that in the van.'

Michelle looked in the bag and saw what was left of the dead woman's head.

He expects me to scream, she thought.

'Oh, her hair's grown a bit since she's died,' said Michelle, looking directly at the officer.

He grinned.

Michelle added, 'You'll need to do better than that, I have no problem sleeping at night.' She clutched the bag tightly and placed it carefully in the back of the scenes-of-crime van, resisting a deep urge to vomit.

Other times, Michelle, Steph and other PWU officers would run the gauntlet of CID. If they were working on a case which involved detectives, they would have to climb the attic stairs at Redland Police Station to the smoke-filled room where these self-proclaimed 'Gods' worked.

'Make us a cup of tea, sweetheart,' was the stock request shouted at the women before they could open their mouths to ask about whatever crime they had come to discuss.

This could be dealt with in different ways. Steph gave a stern look, which was enough to tell them how unlikely that hot drink would be. Michelle offered a flat 'fuck off', while others would be more polite. But sometimes the abuse went further than funny, and detectives – married ones – would offer straight invitations to take one of the girls out for the night.

If Sergeant Carol Curnock heard about any such invitation, she would head up to the Gods in the CID attic. Her verbal dismemberment of Chief Superintendent Malcolm Popperwell could be heard from as far away as reception.

Curnock was demanding, but she was also defensive. After all, she was Mother Hen.

Some of the detectives in the attic, however, were doing good work. Progress was being made in the hunt for the Clifton Rapist. House-to-house inquiries had led to hundreds of leads, the list of released sex attackers was longer than anyone expected, but the names were gradually being crossed off.

John O'Connor, the moustachioed detective constable who had wondered months earlier if the attacks were linked to the police, was tasked with making house-to-house inquiries along a Victorian terrace near the latest assault. He knocked at one house with a shabby wooden door. A woman answered. She said it had been converted to flats and that she owned the whole property and had bought it decades before after moving over from Greece. She lived in one of the ground-floor flats, but there were five other apartments in the house.

John went from one to another, speaking to each tenant. In the other garden flat was a young woman with her baby. No, she lived there alone, her parents paid her rent. No man there. On the first floor were two more flats. One was inhabited by an Indian family, clearly the wrong ethnic background to be the suspect. In the other one there was an old guy who could barely walk.

The second floor had two more flats. One was home to a pair of student girls. One had a boyfriend, but she showed John a picture and he looked nothing like the Clifton Rapist. There was one more door. John knocked. There was a shuffle and an 'Excuse me, wait a minute …' and the door slowly opened.

John found himself face to face with the artist's impression of the attacker: a tall man, a good few inches bigger than him, with a big mop of black hair and a handlebar moustache.

'Hello, I'm DC John O'Connor with Avon and Somerset Police …'

The man was nodding, looking over John's shoulder.

'We're investigating a couple of crimes in the area and we're keen to speak with people who were in the area on March 4th …'

John chatted gently as he watched the man stiffen. O'Connor was good at keeping things easy. He didn't want to terrify the man into saying nothing, he needed to start a flow of information from him. John smiled gently at the man, downplaying the question when he asked what he was doing on the date when a woman was attacked in her front garden.

Listen for the accent, listen for the accent … he told himself as the man opened his mouth to reply.

'Well, were that a Friday or a Saturday?' asked the man.

Definitely a northern accent.

John said it was the early hours of the Saturday.

'Well, I were travelling from Leicester to Bristol – I just got meself a job here, you know.'

'Oh, I see,' said John, his heart performing cartwheels. 'Were you with anyone?'

'Nah, I live by meself … Have a look around if yer like?'

Inside, the flat was a mess, with cardboard boxes of belongings and clothes strewn everywhere. There was a Led Zeppelin poster on the wall – the only attempt at decoration. John clocked that it had big windows overlooking a suburban street, but in the distance he could make out Whiteladies Road.

'So what crimes are you investigating?' asked the man.

John looked directly at him, keeping his face friendly, easy: 'A series of sex attacks.' He wasn't sure quite what changed in the man: his face drained of colour, he took half a gulp, pulled his gaze away from him. Just subtle things, nothing certain, but enough for John to feel a further prickle of excitement about this man.

'May I take your name, please?'

'Jeff.'

'And your surname?'

'Clancy.'

'Where did you live before Bristol, Jeff?'

'Well, I only moved here on the 4th of March. I were up in Leicester then for years, just moved here for work. I like it. Fucking expensive though.'

'Yes, it is,' said John, nodding and unsure of what to do next.

He asked to see Jeff's driving licence. Jeff went to another room and minutes later came back, unfolding a pink scrap of paper. It read 'Jeff Clancy, DoB 05/08/1948' and it also had an address in Leicester. This flummoxed John. He took Jeff's phone number, said goodbye and made a note of the flat number as he left.

John tried not to run down the stairs. Thoughts were flashing through his head: Jeff Clancy looked just like the photo-fits, he had been here on the 4th and he had a perfect view of Whiteladies Road from his flat. But it was his uneasiness about this guy which excited him so much.

Something was wrong, he just knew it. But what? He then saw the Greek landlady waiting for him at the bottom of the stairs.

'You get whatchya want?' she asked.

'Your tenants, have you got a list of their names?'

She beckoned him into her apartment and found a ledger. It dated back 20 years and the last five entries were the people John had just met in the block. Flat six had a name: Jeff Moore.

'This man here – is he the guy in the top flat?' asked John, pointing to the name.

'The man with the moustache just moved in a few weeks ago,' she said.

John looked at her, flummoxed. He asked to borrow her phone and called Redland CID.

'Can you run a quick check on two names? Both born on 5th of August 1958: Jeff with a "J" Clancy and the same first name but a surname of Moore.' He then gave the landlady's phone number and put the receiver back.

He waited with the landlady in her room, looking at the phone, silently pleading for it to ring. Had he done the right thing? What he had was flimsy, just a feeling really.

The phone started chiming and John grabbed it.

'Yes?'

'John, there's nothing on record for anyone of the date of birth and name of Moore, but Jeffery Clancy with that date of birth has a conviction for indecent assault. A spell inside too.'

It took less than five minutes for three patrol cars to screech to a stop outside the block. John had been waiting at the bottom of the stairs to ensure Clancy or Moore or whoever the hell he was didn't run away. Three pairs of detectives ran up the stairs and moments later, Clancy came down in cuffs, asking what was going on. He was shoved into the back of a car and John got in the seat next to him.

'I'm not the man you're after ...' Clancy proffered.

Four minutes later, the cars pulled up at Redland Police Station.

Christ, thought John, *all the Gods are here*.

Malcolm Popperwell, Brian Theobald, even the Chief Constable, Kenneth Steele, was there – he must have been on a visit. The top brass waited as Clancy was taken from the car and led inside.

'You, DC O'Connor?' asked Steele in his clipped, militaristic way. 'What makes you suspect this man?'

John said it wasn't just his looks, but the northern accent and the shifty way he'd answered questions, but the decider was the very obvious deceit of his landlady: that he had given the wrong name. Steele patted him on the shoulder and said, 'That's good enough for me. Good work.'

Detective Chief Superintendent Brian Theobald did the questioning as Kenneth Steele, Malcolm Popperwell and John O'Connor paced the corridor outside.

Half an hour passed.

A young detective appeared in the corridor, waving a scrap of paper.

'He's a wanted man,' said the detective, looking down at his notes. 'Leicestershire Police are after him for an attack. He must be down here in Bristol lying low. But he's not the Clifton Rapist – he was inside for the first two assaults.'

O'Connor didn't hear Kenneth Steele's groan, but he could see a twinkle fade from the Chief's eyes.

'Good work, DC O'Connor. Next time.'

Chris Gould had a rare Friday night off. He was at home, a police house in a Bristol suburb. He and his wife had eaten dinner and they were watching television. The documentary about policing in the US covered agent provocateur tactics: covert stings to catch repeat offenders. If there had been a string of thefts, they would set up an operation: have delivery vans with doors open, with goods waiting to be stolen, or a vagabond with an expensive watch sleeping in a doorway. Teams of undercover cops would be in place, waiting to see who struck. The moment someone made a grab for the box in the van, or reached down for the watch, the covert teams would leap in. The important thing was, the criminal had to commit the crime, had to try to take the box or the watch. Surely, this was too dangerous to try with a rapist? Surely, they couldn't do this with a man who had threatened to kill? But the whirrings in Chris Gould's mind had started.

CHAPTER TEN

Wendy Johnson had finished her shift at the Bristol Royal Infirmary and was walking in the dark through the Kingsdown district, about a half a mile away from Whiteladies Road. She couldn't afford a cab and wouldn't have taken one if she could. Used the walk to decompress. She was 21, tired of nursing, exhausted from her day and looking forward to bed. Her shift should have ended at eight o'clock but there had been problems in surgery and she had stayed on until nearer 11. No one had asked her, she just did it – it was the culture of her profession.

Wendy wondered again if she had made the right decision to be a nurse. Yes, it was nice to help people and work in a so-called caring profession but she would never earn decent money and how could she ever achieve her dreams of travelling the world?

She reached a junction in the road. The main street was well-lit but would take 10 minutes longer to get home. There was an alleyway to her right, a dark cut-through she knew well. Wendy quickly looked around and slipped into the dark alley. She was about halfway along when she heard fast footsteps behind her, tap-tapping on the flagstone floor. When she spun around, she saw the bright street lamp in the distance behind, creating a silhouette of the old lane: narrow walls and the figure of a man running towards her, getting closer.

Perhaps he's in a rush to get somewhere? she thought. *Maybe he's running for a bus?*

The man showed no sign of stopping and as he drew close, she barely noticed his arm reaching out.

He pulled Wendy into a side door, where he attacked her.

She noticed little about the man, except dark clothes and the smell of alcohol. Throughout the attack, she didn't see his face. Or if she did, through her trauma, she somehow wasn't able to recall what he looked like.

The report of the attack on Wendy Johnson came into C-Division a little after 2 a.m. As she was interviewed, examined and photographed, scenes-of-crime officers were sent to see if the perpetrator had left anything behind at the scene.

But it was clean.

Wendy hadn't shouted or resisted, her body had just seemed to go into neutral. And in the coming days, people living near the alley when questioned said that they had seen or heard nothing. Some detectives questioned whether it was the same offender. There was no throat-grip, he hadn't spoken so there was no accent to work with. Wendy had not been on the Whiteladies Road. Different modus operandi, different geography. Was the attacker changing his behaviour, or was this someone new? The poor description was also an issue for investigators – they couldn't produce an artist's impression.

Detective Chief Superintendent Brian Theobald decided to try something different.

Two days later, Wendy Johnson found herself in her front room with a man she had never have expected to meet. She hadn't really thought a hypnotist would help extract more information about her attacker than she could remember, but she had said that she was willing to give it a go.

The man, Kevin Darlow, wore a dark suit. He started counting to her slowly and before she knew it, she was in a trance. And now she was no longer in her front room, but an alleyway. There were cobbles and a silhouette of a man running towards her. It was the sound which sent shivers down her spine, the clip-clip-clip of his feet on the cobble-stones. And the silhouette drew closer.

She looked up at the man, at a faceless spectre. Then the smell of beer hit her. He was standing still, but echoing in her head was the clip-clip-clip of his feet on the cobbles.

The smell of beer. Clip-clip-clip …

She looked up … But could see nothing: there was no face.

When Wendy came to, the man in the dark suit had a puzzled expression. The sound of clipping had gone, as had the smell of beer and the cobbles – and the faceless attacker.

'Did that help you recall anything more?' asked the man.

'Yes, it really did,' Wendy replied, unconvincingly.

Hypnotherapy? Really? she found herself asking herself as she tried to stifle the terror of reliving the attack.

Even though the links to the Clifton Rapist were uncertain, news of another attack made front-page headlines on the *Bristol Evening Post*. 'Warning As Hunt Goes On for "Hate" Rapist', read the article. One of the lead detectives was quoted as saying: 'The offences go beyond rape. What he does is to degrade women to the lowest possible form. It is sexual abomination. I cannot imagine a man treating a woman like that if he had any respect at all for them.

'He could be against women because he is mentally ill, alcoholic or has been rejected,' the detective added. He said it was clear this attacker had been drinking and he wondered what impact alcohol had on his libido.

After reading about the attacks and the lack of police success, a group of campaigners in London decided to take matters into their own hands. The Women's Liberation Front set up a Rape Hotline in Bristol in March 1978, after the attack on Wendy Johnson. This had only ever been tried once before in the UK. Eleven amateur counsellors were hired and were on the end of the phone between 6 p.m. and 7 p.m. on Mondays and Wednesdays. If a woman had been attacked, she was encouraged to call. It may not have been at the hands of the Clifton Rapist; domestic assaults were far more likely than a stranger attack on the street, the WLF said. They estimated 10,000 assaults on women took place every year. The Women's Liberation Front would not pressure women to report their assaults to police, but they said it was important for them to have access to some form of support, however amateur and rudimentary. There was no other help out there for survivors of sexual assault. Councils did nothing, the Government, the NHS did nothing. It should be down to the police or the NHS to provide this hotline, they said. But they hadn't so the WLF would. Equally, the police were not doing enough to catch this attacker, they repeated.

A second group, Bristol Students Against Rape, was set up. BSAR featured as many men as it did women. The activists started patrolling Whiteladies Road themselves, wearing orange hi-vis tops to make them distinctive at night. They worked in pairs and in shifts. If a woman wanted a safe passage home, if she was without money, she just needed to wait in a public place until a pair of brightly clad students came past. She could trust them, ask for help and they would escort her home.

One night, Tony, the bouncer at Platform One, was ejecting a teenager who had pulled a knife on a couple of regulars. He managed to disarm the skinny, spotty boy, threw him to the pavement and looked up. There, in the darkness, was a pair of BSAR patrollers in orange, a man and a woman. From his brief glimpse, he was sure the woman was Joanna McGarry.

Rachel Doulton was 45 years old. She lived in a big, well-maintained flat in Clifton, the affluent, leafy part of Bristol. Doulton was aware of the rapist who was terrorising the streets. She had not known about the assaults from 1977, but as the newspapers printed more and more articles about the pair of attacks in March 1978, she began to feel a frisson of fear. Rachel rarely went out at night. She socialised on a Saturday, playing badminton in a club in Clifton Village. Her evenings were spent recovering from her job in the office as a travel agent.

On night in April 1978, Rachel was watching television at home when she heard something in her bathroom. Perhaps it was a cat? Or a fox? As she got up from her settee and padded across the lounge, she was surprised to see a man in the hallway. He reached for the light switch on the wall and turned the lamps off. He said just a few words to her, telling her not to say anything or he would hurt her. Then he tried to rape her.

Rachel pushed him away, kicked him. He made a grab for something on the table and ran from her flat's front door. It was only when she found herself in her hallway holding an umbrella mid-air that she realised how close she had come to an attack. Her mind started whirring about what could have happened and she started to cry.

Rachel was able to give police a better description: a man in his twenties or thirties with dark hair. She couldn't catch his accent, he said so little to her.

That's all the detectives had to go on.

So, few clues.

The following day, Steph Whittle was called to a briefing at Southmead Police Station. She squeezed into the smoke-filled inquiry room. *How many detectives were working here?* she wondered. *Thirty? And more at Redland.* And she had heard the force had parked a couple of mobile inquiry rooms in Clifton Village as a show to Bristol's most affluent community that the force was doing something.

Chief Superintendent Malcolm Popperwell stood at the front of the room by the wall, upon which was pinned a big map with more pins in abduction points. There were also artist's impressions of the Clifton Rapist.

'Catching this monster is the force's top priority,' he began. 'That's from the Chief. Seven attacks in under a year and it appears his behaviour is changing. If the last two attacks are the same man, then he is starting to operate in new locations.

'The last assault, the attempted rape in Clifton Village, is particularly worrying as he actually entered a home for the first time. He's moving on from street rape. He also stole this time – he took his victim's handbag. Inside was her cheque-book.

'There'll be news crews out today. People in Clifton are the kind to give us grief, so be polite, smile and show we are professional. You may get some flak.'

Steph was despatched to make house-to-house enquiries. The answers came with tedious predictability: 'No, I didn't hear anything last Thursday night,' 'No, I haven't seen a man hanging around, looking suspicious,' 'No, I didn't hear a scream or see anyone running around.' 'How long have these attacks been going on for? Ten months. *Ten months?* The police aren't doing a very good job of finding him, are they? How old are you? Nineteen? My god, police are getting younger these days! Women too? No wonder you can't catch this man, if the force is relying on teenage girls.'

Steph kept up her professional front while secretly want-ing to shout out loud.

She asked in shops if they had seen anything or if anyone had been trying to pass off stolen cheques.

Nothing.

Steph went back to her flat that evening feeling a strange mix of exhilaration, depression and futility. It had been nice to work on such a big, exciting inquiry, to feel part of something really important, but opening the door on that investigation showed just how little they knew about this man. And she wondered if they hadn't caught him by now, would they ever?

She turned on her TV set and was surprised to see herself on-screen. A reporter was talking about the latest attacks and the pressure on police. She was behind him, talking to a shop owner as part of her house-to-house enquiries. The report cut to a high-ranking detective she hadn't seen before, a man called Brian Theobald. He must have been one of the Gods. He spoke well, looked relaxed and easy on camera, but the content of his words was in stark contrast to his affable delivery: 'We can't describe the terror these women have gone through, the depths of depravity he has inflicted on them. For us, the biggest worry is this. So far, in the street attacks, all of his victims have been compliant. None of them has struggled or put up any kind of resistance. But we have no idea what he would do if one were to fight back. This is an extremely dangerous man.'

Steph felt a chill, but she realised it wasn't from her poorly insulated flat with the single-glazed century-old windows. It was a spring night, warm and colourful.

But still that chill …

CHAPTER ELEVEN

22 NOVEMBER 1963

By day, the scene looks so different. The Driver's car is slumped in a couple of inches of mud, but he can't quite understand how he came off the road and ended up here. It's a strange wilderness. On the outskirts of a town, but not quite in the countryside. The car cut deep skid marks in the mud when it came off the road the night before. They are drying, but the chances of getting the car out without help from a tow truck look remote. His hangover is long gone. He has changed, he sees his reflection in his car's window and notices that he looks respectable again – that makes him feel good.

The road is busy and cars whizz around the bend that he veered off last night. He gets his key, goes to his boot, unlocks it and opens it up.

The girl is still there. She seems pale. A blue tinge to her white skin. He slams the boot shut and sees a policeman walking towards him. The Driver's heart skips a beat.

'Hello there, sir.'

'Yes?'

The policeman has ginger hair and is young, maybe about the same age as him. He looks too small for his blue uniform.

His hat seems to fall down over his face. The officer looks directly into The Driver's eyes.

The Driver tries to think happy thoughts. Tries to stop a bead of sweat dribbling down his brow.

The officer opens his mouth.

What's he going to say?

'You stuck?'

Breathe, breathe, breathe …

'Yeah. Came off the road.'

'Thought so. Saw your car there this morning, was gonna try to find the owner. Was gonna wait till two to see if yer'd turn up.'

'Well, I'm here.'

'Yer alright? Yer look like yer've seen a ghost.'

'Yes, I'm fine. Just want to get my car out, late for work.'

'Jump in, I'll push yer.'

The man goes to the driver's door, opens it, jumps in and starts the ignition.

'Try it in second, mate,' shouts the officer. The policeman goes to the back of the car and puts his hands on the boot.

The Driver puts the car in second gear. The policeman tries pushing. The engine whines, the wheels spin, but the car goes nowhere.

The Driver realises that the policeman's hands are just a few inches away from a missing woman.

'No use, mate. Yer gonna need a truck.'

'I've called one.'

'Alright, matey.'

The policeman looks at him, studying The Driver, taking him in.

The Driver doesn't like it.

'Quite a storm last night, weren't it?' says the officer.

'Yeah, got fecking drenched.'

The policeman nods. Then he looks beyond The Driver's shoulder.

'Here yer are, matey.'

The Driver spins around and sees a rescue truck.

'Catch yer later, chap.'

The policeman winks and heads off to his car, waving farewell in the air as the rescue truck stops in front of The Driver's stranded vehicle. There is something merry about the police officer, The Driver thinks.

A merry stupidity.

He breathes out as the tow truck pulls up.

CHAPTER TWELVE

Opinion was divided among the younger police officers as to just how salubrious the Mandrake Club was. To some, it was a dive with a low ceiling, low morals and low prices. Because it was cheap, it was popular among many police probationers earning just over £3,000 a year (£19,000 in today's money). Some women felt safe there because there were so many young off-duty officers. And there were always lots of women. The bouncers adored the off-duty female officers. Nurses got in for free too.

The male clientele comprised largely single cops or married ones who would forget their wedding rings – and vows – on a Friday night. Under the dingy ceiling hung a thick layer of cigarette smoke through which clubbers could vaguely make out the friends they were with – or the people they were about to meet. The owners of the Mandrake liked the club to have that strong smell of fags – it hid the underlying odour of cheap booze, vomit and urine. There were a few stone arches through which were dark alcoves and the promise of a fumbled encounter. And a few chairs, though most of the main floor was dedicated to dancing.

Boney M. had been playing, but now 10cc's 'Dreadlock Holiday' was on the speakers. Steph Whittle, Sally Difazio and Michelle Tighe were at the bar, taking a break from the dancefloor. Michelle was in trousers, a blouse and pumps; Steph in jeans, boots and a stylish top. Both were admiring Sally's white-jeans-and-crop-top combo. As were a few men who had tried sidling over, but a simple glare was enough to keep them at bay.

'How are you finding the blokes at work?' Steph asked Michelle. 'Anyone trying it on?'

Michelle shrugged. 'I'm used to them – I worked in bars before, holiday camps. You see all sorts there, these are no different. I went up to CID the other day and one of them said to put the kettle on. I told him if he says that again, he'll have to extract the kettle from somewhere painful. I might even turn it on while it's up there.'

'Popperwell asked me to pick him up from home the other day,' said Steph. 'I don't understand why he couldn't drive himself in. I had to go all the way out to Patchway to be his bloody chauffeur. He ignored me the whole drive. Said nothing, no please, no thank you. He just had a bloody newspaper and pulled it up, read it all the way. Kept harrumphing every time I hit the brakes.'

Michelle and Sally nodded in frustration.

'Know what happened next?' continued Steph. 'We get to the police station, we pull up. He looks at me and says I was the worst driver he'd ever seen. Know what he did? He rolled up the paper, slapped my legs and said he was putting me on a driving course.'

A bassline hit the airwaves before a loud whoop and soon the whole club apart from the three police officers was gyrating to 'You're the One That I Want' by John Travolta and Olivia Newton-John.

'I had my first sudden death yesterday,' said Sally, her news entirely incongruous to the scene of drunken joy over her shoulder on the dancefloor.

'Who was it?' asked Steph.

'An old man. His neighbours hadn't seen him for a few days. One of them looked through the window, saw him in a chair and thought he was dozing. They banged, but he didn't answer. One of them broke in, found him.'

Steph nodded.

'I went with my tutor. I've never seen a dead person before. He was just sitting there, like he was asleep, but he wasn't. Had to look in all his drawers for pills and stuff. Christ, he had so many tablets, he would've rattled!

'I had to stay with him till the undertaker got there. The tutor left and it was just me and this man. He had a load of birthday cards on the shelf. He'd just turned 75. Read one from a granddaughter. I was in tears. I looked down at him. I just thought, *What are we doing? All this for three grand a year! What are we doing to ourselves?*'

'Could be worse, Sally,' joked Michelle. 'I saw a detective sergeant down there with his wedding ring off. You could be going home with him.'

'Give me a corpse any day.'

If there was one thing PC Robbie Jones loved more than the police, it was rugby. A fly-half for the force, he would often be found zipping past the Second XI, kicking goals from the tightest of angles or sipping beer in the bar afterwards.

Robbie had an easy charm and a cheeky face and was popular with women. Sometimes, his sergeant would deploy this athletic, charismatic rookie to deal with females as he had a way of 'getting them to talk' to him. As he sat at his desk in the mobile inquiry unit one morning, Robbie got a phone call to say that he was being sent to question a different type of interviewee.

'Rob?' It was a sergeant in Southmead Police Station.

'Yes?' he said, wondering who he would need to speak to. *Victim of sexual assault? Female students? Perhaps talk to women in the night-time economy?*

'I need you to interview a rapist.'

'Oh …'

'We've been working through a list of sex offenders who've been released from prison.' The sergeant went on to explain that Robbie would not believe the number of sex offenders who were out walking the streets and checking them all out was, frankly, a nightmare, so he needed help from someone in uniform.

'This guy, he's a boiler engineer. He's in the phone book as Stan the Boiler Man, so he's obviously going into people's homes.'

The three other detectives in the unit looked unsurprised.

'He spent two years inside for eight counts of rape,' continued the sergeant.

PC Robbie Jones sighed and took the address.

There had been no further arrests since John O'Connor had pulled in the rapist with a pseudonym who'd been wanted by Leicestershire Police. But Stan the Boiler Man looked good: the right age, originally from up north and a rape conviction to boot.

Robbie and a colleague went to a terraced street in the north Bristol suburb of Filton. Red-brick, working-class. The cars were all at least eight years old, he noticed. He knocked at number 28, a brown door with peeling paint.

A man answered. He was about the same size as Robbie, maybe 5'10". He had thick, sandy hair and a big moustache the same colour.

'Stan Freshman?'

'Yes.'

'Avon and Somerset Police,' Robbie smiled.

'I wondered why it's taken you so long to get here.'

Robbie felt a flash of excitement. 'Sorry?' was the most neutral answer he could give.

Don't lead the conversation, let him lead you there himself.

'The attacks … The Clifton Rapist. Come in.'

Freshman led Robbie and his colleague through a hallway with a red swirly carpet covered in toolboxes with spanners into a beige-brown lounge. There was a two-piece leather settee and a single faded grey armchair. Next to that was an ashtray on a pole. He sat down, lit up a fag and beckoned for Robbie and his colleague to make themselves comfortable on the settee.

'You know my record. Two years. I'm doing what I can, you know. When I did what I did, I was young. Didn't quite understand what "no" means. Get my drift? But I'm not your man. I've seen his photos in the papers, thought you'd have got here quicker. I've been keeping a diary.'

He reached down beside him and pulled out a black book with a gold '1978' written on the front.

'These are the dates of the attacks,' he said. 'You see, there was one two Thursdays ago. Whenever I've seen about an attack in the papers, I've made a note of where I was and who I was with. I knew you boys'd come knocking. That night, it was darts – I play darts down The Bear. There all night. And I've names and numbers here of blokes who saw me. I think the papers said that attack was about nine o'clock. I was in the pub, then.'

PC Robbie Jones was taken aback.

'We won, by the way. To the Robin Hood's Retreat. Gashead pub, nearly a riot.'

Robbie and his colleague returned to the police station, where Robbie successfully alibied Stan Freshman for each of the attacks. If only all convicted rapists kept diaries, his life would be so much easier. He was just about to explain this to Malcolm Popperwell when he noticed the inquiry room was abuzz.

Detective Chief Superintendent Brian Theobald was in, pointing to an experienced detective and Steph Whittle.

'We're not sure about this, Eddie …' said Theobald in his quiet, lilting West Country accent. 'But this last attack, on Rachel Doulton. In her flat. A theft. We think it's just the same as that murder two years ago …'

CHAPTER THIRTEEN

APRIL 1978

Detective Constable Eddie Chandler had never tried to climb the policing ladder. Instead, he saw himself as an 'on-the-street' man. He had passed his sergeant's exams 15 years earlier, but soon realised he'd be spending more time in the nick and less time on the road so he'd never bothered applying for the actual promotion. He liked dealing with people – and by that, he really meant criminals.

Chandler knew every thief in his neighbourhood. He knew how to catch them and how to obtain a confession. He could arrive in work on a Monday, see the list of week-end crimes and swiftly work out which local villain was responsible for what. If a couple of cars had been stolen, there was a good chance Big Phil had just got out. If Harry Gonzalez was back at home, he knew there would be a call from his wife. She never rang in when he hit her, but when their kids started getting bruises, that's when she would get in touch. And when Big Phil or Harry Gonzalez was inside, Eddie would do a whip-round in Redland Police Station. He would ask for old clothes or children's toys and deliver them to Harry's wife or Phil's family. This was community policing – and DC Eddie Chandler knew it like he knew women would never get their heads around the job.

Eddie didn't like women on the force. As far as he was concerned, birds were for the kitchen, the bedroom and for nights out. Not for policing. If they had to be forced upon him, he would protect the female officer. He would shield her from the worst aspects of the job. Women shouldn't have to see what he saw, it didn't suit their sensibilities.

Another thing Chandler knew about was the murder of Susan Donoghue. Like most of the detectives, he had put his life on hold for months, two summers ago. He knew the inquiry inside out and now he was having to explain it to a *woman*.

'You know, I didn't think of Susan with the street attacks, but the last one, in the flat in Clifton, same M.O. [modus operandi],' said Eddie. Chandler went off and reappeared five minutes later, clutching a brown A4 file titled 'Case Summary'. He pulled it open on Steph's desk.

The first thing she saw was a photo: a middle-aged woman sitting on a wall. The woman had brown shoulder-length hair, brushed back. She wore a brown-and-orange patterned dress with puffed sleeves, a three-chain necklace and was holding a smart light-brown handbag. Underneath the picture was a three-page report.

'Here we go,' said Eddie, reading aloud as Steph followed. 'Susan Donoghue was a 44-year-old divorced woman living in a bedsit in Downleaze, Sneyd Park. She lived with her fiancé. She had a 17-year-old son who lived in Ireland, where she was from.'

Eddie glanced at Steph. 'You know Downleaze? Go to the top of Whiteladies Road, just across the Downs. Big houses, posh?'

She nodded.

Eddie continued: 'She was a nurse and had worked nights at Brentry Hospital. Friends described her as cheerful but quiet. Colleagues said they knew little of her social life because night shifts were unconducive to work socials.

'On the night of August 4th 1976, Susan's fiancé had gone for a night out. She went to bed, wearing a night-dress. In the early hours of August 5th, Susan's fiancé returned home and called police.

'On attending the scene, officers found Susan Donoghue had been battered about the head and possibly sexually assaulted. There was a truncheon, similar to a policeman's truncheon, in the room.'

Eddie looked at Steph. 'The thing about the truncheon was always a worry, always wondered if there was a link to police, but we couldn't rule out that it could've been hers. There was also a pair of driving gloves, covered in blood. The gloves were old, grubby pigskin gloves, possible size eight.'

Steph said, 'The Clifton Rapist has never worn gloves.'

Eddie continued: 'A man's footprint was found on the inside of a windowsill of a room next to Susan's bedroom.' He looked up and added, 'A lot of it points to a burglar. An opportunist. You remember the summer of '76, the heat-wave? Her window was jammed open, it was under a street lamp – easy to see. If a bloke was out looking to steal, it was like an advert saying "Burglary, this way …"'

Steph considered the similarities to the attack on Rachel Doulton, the first sex attack in a woman's flat. Both in nice apartments on nice streets. A man had broken in on both occasions. The geography was compelling. Only a mile between the two. Between both properties was Whiteladies Road, off which nearly all the street attacks had taken place. But the truncheon? The Clifton Rapist had never been armed and the gloves were different.

'But there was another theory,' continued Eddie. 'She was a night sister at Brentry Hospital. You know, the madhouse. What if one of her patients or ex-patients had a fixation on her?' He glanced at Steph: 'Whoever did it would've been covered in blood, head to toe. We always thought it was more likely he was a career criminal than a nutter on the prowl. We'd better start looking. It was a big inquiry.'

'How big?'

'There's a summary here,' he said, turning to the back page. 'In the first year, police took 4,000 statements, interviewed 7,000 people and spent 45,000 hours on the case. I remember, I did about half of those hours. Never found the bastard.'

Steph swore – fortunately, Sergeant Carol Curnock wasn't within earshot.

Following the last attack in Clifton, Sergeant Kelvin Hattersley and his Task Force were sent out again at nights on a rota in shifts, alternating with others from the wider force area. High visibility to encourage confidence in law-abiding citizens that the police force was doing its job.

Springtime was turning into summer and the nights were getting lighter later. As they patrolled, Kelvin and his men made notes of number plates of cars driving down Whiteladies Road.

'Remember, lads, the only people out after midnight are police and villains,' he told his team again.

Kelvin would sit, scribbling away, and after returning to Redland Police Station, he would hand the list in to be analysed the following morning. He then went home.

Hattersley lived in a quiet suburb in the north of Bristol. He was unaware of the net curtain which was twitching in the house opposite when he pulled up and went through his front door. Upstairs, his wife and two young daughters were asleep. He sat and had a glass of whisky to decompress before bed. He'd been working double-shifts for weeks. So had his team. How on earth could they catch this man?

Number plates? Really?

The following day, he put on his uniform, got in his car and headed back to Redland Police Station. When Kelvin got into the station, he detected a buzz.

'What is it? What's going on?'

'One of your number plates last night. A yellow Ford Capri. Looks like a good lead. Bloke in Somerset, same age as the Clifton Rapist. We're sending a team down to interview him.'

WPC Sally Difazio was walking along a corridor in Redland Police Station when Chief Superintendent Malcolm Popperwell approached.

'You, WPC.'

CHAPTER THIRTEEN

'Yes, sir?'

'You're going to university.'

That afternoon, Sally Difazio found herself standing next to a chief superintendent on a stage in a large lecture theatre packed with maybe 200 students. She was surprised at just how many men were in the crowd.

Perhaps it's not just women who are scared about a sex attacker? Maybe their boyfriends are too, she wondered.

They were all Sally's age. Some were maybe a year or two older but they had come to listen to her because she was wearing a uniform and had half an idea what she was talking about.

The President of the Students' Union made a brief introduction. Then the Chief Superintendent said a few words, awkwardly. He must have been about 45 years old, but he looked ancient compared with the room of teenagers.

'But I have someone here who can explain more,' Sally heard him say. 'WPC Sally Difazio has been working on this inquiry. She has seen the scenes and read the files. She is your age and she understands just how dangerous this man is – and why you should take action now.'

He motioned Sally on, and as she walked forward to the lectern she was sure she could see a wave of relief pass over his face.

Sally looked across at the crowd and took a breath before saying, 'We are worried. *Really* worried. Rape is rare, stranger rape rarer. It is highly unusual for a monster like this to be in our midst, to be in our city. And for us to try and safeguard you, we are asking for you to do some unusual things. Some may seem extreme. But if you could understand what this man has done to his victims … well, we wouldn't wish this on anyone.

'He has attacked in the street, he has attacked in gardens, in doorways and alleyways and he may even have attacked a woman in her own home. None of these women will ever be the same again. He didn't know them – they were all in the wrong place at the wrong time.

'We know that your end-of-year exams are approaching and you will be going out and letting your hair down. That's great. But we're urging each of you to follow these rules:

'Do not go out alone at night. Go out in pairs, go out in groups. Just do not go out alone. We just can't guarantee your safety. We know you have organised groups of students to escort women home from clubs. This is an unofficial scheme, but it's safer than walking home alone.'

She paused.

'But we also have these …' Sally pulled out a black plastic box, about the same size as a perfume bottle. 'Put it in your handbag and if you do find yourself alone at night, put it in your hand. If you are attacked, hit this button.'

She pressed a small tab and an ear-splitting siren went off, before winces appeared on 200 students' faces.

'We're giving away free rape alarms. Take them, take two and pass one on. But if you take one other thing from hearing me, it is this piece of advice: as a police force, we have never had to issue this warning before but we must now. I can't say it loudly enough: do not go out alone at night. We don't know when or where he might strike again, but we think he will. And we have no idea what lengths he'll go to.'

* * *

PC Chris Nott was outside the Kings Head pub on Whiteladies Road. It was nearly closing time and he had a pile of leaflets in his hand. Every time a young woman came out, he would thrust one in her direction.

Some would look at it and shudder. Others would shrug. On the page were five different artist's impressions of the Clifton Rapist. In some he had a moustache, in others he was clean-shaven.

'Are you going home? Have you seen anyone like this man? If you do, please call this number immediately. Find a phone box in a public place and just call,' he would say.

Some of the women said they'd never seen anyone like the pictures. Others told him that the images looked like half the men in Bristol. After the leaflets were all gone, Chris Nott would stand back and watch all the men coming out of that pub.

And he couldn't agree more.

The pictures somehow looked like none of these men falling out of the Kings Head, but they also looked like half of them.

Detective Chief Superintendent Brian Theobald sat opposite a man with a thick head of dark hair, a Mexican moustache the same colour, and a suit which probably cost as much as the detective's monthly salary.

'Okay, Mr Simpson. Your car was spotted by our Task Force driving along Whiteladies Road in Bristol three times at night on May 25th. But you live in Yeovil. Can you give me a reason why you were 50 miles away in a strange city?'

The man might have been well-presented, but Theobald still didn't like the look of him.

'You're looking for this rapist chap?' said the man, smiling.

Why is he smiling? thought Theobald.

The detective nodded.

'Look, there's a very simple explanation.'

Theobald leaned back and waited, his face neutral. Over the last few months he had heard dozens of excuses why people were driving down Whiteladies Road when they had no obvious reason to be there: picking up girlfriends was a favourite and could be quickly alibied. But there was also 'Went for a drive to clear my head' or the very honest 'I went to pick up a bird.'

What would it be with this suspect?

The man continued: 'I am the President of the Unicorn Brethren, just took over from my dad. I was escorting Prince Philip around Bristol today. Look at the papers.'

Theobald nodded.

Now that was the first time he had heard that explanation given – it would also be the last. A quick glance at an old copy of the *Bristol Evening Post* proved that the Duke of Edinburgh had indeed been in the city that day, escorted by a young well-dressed man with big black hair and a handle-bar moustache.

After investigating Mr Simpson's whereabouts during the other attacks, Theobald confirmed he was in darkest Somerset for at least two of them.

The posh young man in the expensive suit was the head of a strange, secretive, well-connected charity.

He was not the Clifton Rapist.

CHAPTER FOURTEEN

22 NOVEMBER 1963

The Driver pulls up in his road. The houses are small post-war semis. Colliery workers live here, mostly. Perhaps it's his sixth sense, perhaps what he's done is sinking in, but there seems to be an eerie silence in the street.

He glances at his watch: 7.15 p.m.

Usually there are people about, but tonight there is no one.

He parks outside his house and walks up the pathway. The door opens as he's about to take out his keys and slide them in the lock. His wife is young and very pregnant but it's the look on her face which sends a chill down his spine. Her eyes are wide, her skin pale and she's looking at him with what he can only translate as disbelief.

Then she says the word: 'Murder.'

'What, love?' He notices his face reddening, feels a bead of sweat on his forehead.

She looks back at him, blankly. Her hands rest protectively on her huge bump.

'Murder,' she repeats.

Now his mother-in-law appears behind her. Her face is also white, shocked, eyes wide.

'He's been murdered,' she says. Then she continues: 'The President – you know, JFK. We were just watching *Take Yer Pick* on telly and there were a newsflash: he were shot dead. In Dallas.'

For a moment, The Driver forgets all about the girl in the boot of his car and goes into the front room. The TV is on, showing a man in a studio. He has a squashed-up face and a faint New Zealand accent. He's trying to get well-dressed members of the public to say 'yes' or 'no'. When they do so, they laugh and are led away.

The audience is in hysterics.

It seems so incongruous.

His mother-in-law switches to BBC and there's a revolving globe.

'I know you don't like the telly, but normally there's Cliff Michelmore on. Yer know, *Tonight*.'

There's an on-screen flash and a man The Driver doesn't recognise appears on the screen. He looks nervous, out of his depth.

'We regret to announce that President Kennedy is dead,' he announces.

'Fucking hell,' says The Driver.

'Language,' says his wife.

The newsflash continues with scant details before the picture returns to a spinning globe. All three of them stand there, staring blankly at the screen.

'Right,' says his mother-in-law. 'Well, I think we should go, we'll be late for bingo.'

They leave the house and start getting in the car. His mother-in-law takes the passenger seat, his wife's in the back.

'Right muddy in here,' she notes.

'Oh, I had some old clothes in back,' he says.

His wife's not paying attention to him. She looks outside the window, at the passing rows of terraces.

'How were that dance last night?' asks his mother-in-law.

'Yeah, alright. Late one. Some o' the lads were right pissed.'

'I hope you weren't drinking and driving?'

'Just a couple.'

'Did yer go to work after yer picked up the car?'

'Nah, it needed summat doing under the bonnet. Fuse blew or summat, not sure. Garage charged me a fortune.'

They reach the bingo club. His mother-in-law still calls it The Hippodrome because that's what it was in her youth. His wife still calls it Century because that's how she remembers it as a teenager. But for the last year it's been called the Granada Bingo Club.

'See yer later,' says his wife, struggling out of the car.

His mother-in-law says nothing. *Not even a thanks. Bitch.* He watches them go in through the club's door, puts the car in gear and drives away. At first, he heads out into the countryside. He drives through darkened fields, where the road closes in, trees hanging over the carriageway. Then they disappear and the night sky opens up as he crosses a colossal lake. There's a perfect mirror image of the moon and stars reflected in the still-black water

There are no other cars on the road, just him. He stops on the carriageway and flicks on his indicator. He gets out and walks to the edge of the bridge, where he looks down at the water, then at his car, eyes moving down it in the night and settling on the boot. After shaking his head, he gets into his car and drives ahead, off the bridge and into the country-side.

The Driver turns on the radio. He's used to the sound of The Beatles everywhere at the moment, but it's just a sullen announcer droning on about JFK: 'Eyewitnesses said the President was shot twice. The former Vice President, Lyndon B. Johnson, was sworn in …'

He pulls over in a layby, looks at his watch: Christ, he needs to pick up his wife and mother-in-law in Mansfield at 10.30.

Not long.

He has to decide.

'In local news, Nottinghamshire Police say they are worried about the disappearance of a 21-year-old shop worker. Kathleen Heathcote vanished after getting off a bus in the town just before 11 o'clock last night. Her family say it's completely out of character. They say they've checked local hospitals but there's been no sightings of her …'

The Driver spins his car around, back through the countryside. He feels his resolve returning as he nears the lake, then he pulls up in the same spot on the bridge he was at 20 minutes earlier. The Driver gets out of his car, takes another look at the moon reflected below in the barely rippling waters.

Not such a bad place, he tells himself. *At least here she'll have some dignity.*

He reaches in his pocket, pulls out his keys. He's about to open the boot when he hears a car approaching. He stops, waits for the headlights to appear then swing past and head off. Once the vehicle has rounded the corner, he turns the lock and opens the boot …

CHAPTER FIFTEEN

DECEMBER 1978

Summer had been and gone, the mood in Britain was darkening. The government seemed in a permanent state of crisis. Labour Prime Minister Jim Callaghan was relying on other parties to get business done. But the unions were angry, strikes were threatened.

In Bristol, the mood among detectives was just as bleak. There had been no more attacks on women over the sweltering months of July, August and September. When students returned to the University of Bristol for the 1978/79 academic year, they were handed notes about the Clifton Rapist and the threat he presented.

Outside the inquiry room, the leaves were turning. Inside, little progress had been made: few decent suspects, all alibied out. No new arrests. The Task Force made nightly patrols of Whiteladies Road. They made a few arrests for 'drunk and disorderly' – they did not find the man behind the photofits. Some in the force wondered whether stopping these patrols would cause the Clifton Rapist to reappear.

The mood in the inquiry room was sombre. It had been for weeks. Spirits didn't rise when one of the forensic scientists gave DC Eddie Chandler a disheartening phone call.

'Eddie?'

'Yes.'

'This is the lab. I've been looking at the scene marks of your murder from '76 and your Clifton Rapist.'

'Great.'

'Well, it's not. We were able to get the blood types from both scenes. The blood type left at the murder of Susan Donoghue is different to the blood type from the man in those stranger rapes.'

'What about the attack on Rachel Doulton, the women assaulted in her home?'

'Nothing matches.'

'So, Susan's murderer isn't the Clifton Rapist?'

'He's not the street rapist, no. But you don't know for sure if you have one rapist or two or three, do you?'

'No.'

'Good day.'

Eddie swore.

No forensic links with a murder. And in recent months, no sign of him. Some detectives wondered if he worked away from the city. Was he a long-distance lorry driver? Did he have a seasonal job, assaulting women wherever he went?

October came and went. November too.

In the early hours of 16 December, 20-year-old Anna Soltys was returning home from a night out. She'd been at Platform One nightclub with her new boyfriend. He had mentioned something about an attacker. He said he wanted to walk her to her door, but she lived a mile beyond Durdham Down and she didn't want the awkward conversation about whether he should stay the night.

He couldn't, the family wouldn't allow it.

Anna was an au pair. A few months earlier, she had been living at home in Poland when one of her best friends wrote from a year's study abroad.

Am in Bristol in England. Weather nice, people lovely. Expensive but good fun. Know a family who want an au pair. Want me to put you in touch? Come over.

Anna had been failing in her own degree. *What the hell?* she thought.

That had been four months ago.

When the family wrote back, they too said that Bristol's weather was beautiful, sunny most of the year. They added that their children were really well-behaved.

Anna had studied English at school and occasionally listened to the BBC World Service. She thought it gave her a better idea of what was happening on the planet than the nonsense from Poland's state-run radio stations.

When Anna had arrived in Bristol in mid-October it was raining. In fact, it seemed to always be raining. And the boy and girl she was caring for were actual monsters. The family home – beside a small woodland – was stunning, though.

She had met her boyfriend, Jake, through a friend of the family. And he seemed nice. Very pale. Quite reserved. Didn't talk much. But when he had a drink inside him he seemed to come alive. He drank these awful tankards of what he called 'ale', which seemed to change him.

At 25, he was a few years older than her and he was trying to grow a moustache. He had big, black hair like the guitarists in the rock bands he loved and he sounded different to the people in Bristol. The family said he was from 'up north'. They also said that if she thought the rain was bad in Bristol, she should try Manchester or Liverpool – it poured year-round up there.

She and Jake had been dancing with her Polish friend. Then her friend met some guy in the club and disappeared. Anna and Jake left the club and walked to the top of Whiteladies Road. They passed a small team of police in uniform, who seemed to be patrolling the main road.

Anna said she could carry on alone.

Jake had drunk four pints and asked if she was sure that he shouldn't take her home. Police had warned about this guy.

Anna said she'd be fine.

Jake kissed her on the cheek and turned back down Whiteladies Road. Anna started crossing the carriageway and walking on a wide pavement that skirted Durdham Down. A little over five minutes later, she heard a vehicle's engine behind her. As she turned, she noticed a yellow sports car following slowly. She didn't know much about cars, but she thought it was a Capri. Glancing up, she quickened her pace and saw the vehicle go ahead before making a U-turn at a roundabout. As the car headed towards her, it slowed again, then drove off.

A few moments later, she felt a pair of hands around her neck. She didn't understand his words, she was thinking hard and fast in Polish. He didn't shout, he just whispered, before pulling her away from the street and onto the dark expanse of Durdham Down. There, he attacked her.

Afterwards, she ran back onto the pavement. Like Hélène Baur the previous November, Anna had no idea how to contact the police in an emergency. What about those officers on Whiteladies Road?

As she fled towards the main street and the lamps, she saw a patrol car. She flagged it down and the driver pulled over. He was a young policeman. Her English wasn't great so she shouted loudly: '*Rzepak, rzepak …*'

He seemed to understand.

Anna Soltys was taken to a red-brick police station, where she gave an interview in broken English (officers said they didn't know anyone who spoke Polish and it might take a day or two to find a translator). She was then taken to a doctor and a photographer.

Five hours later, she found that a numbness from the attack had gone and she was starting to shake. And then came the beginnings of something she hadn't really felt before: shame. She couldn't tell anyone. Not Jake, not her friend and definitely not the family she was living with. They would judge her, she was sure.

Surprisingly, the police were able to find a Polish translator the following day who could take a statement. She was a middle-aged woman who had never worked for the police before, but they found her through a Polish church in the city.

Anna gave a full statement through this stranger. Her attacker was in his late twenties or early thirties with thick dark hair. He was white, English and smelt of alcohol, probably beer. She described what he had made her do and noticed the translator get increasingly angry with every sentence.

Through the translator, she helped an artist to get a like-ness of him. An image which the artist had seen so many times before.

Anna Soltys had been terrified. She vowed to book the quickest passage back to Poland possible. The family would think her unpredictable. They would not hire a Polish au pair again: Germans or Scandinavians were much more reli-able.

Anna did not tell the family of the terror she had endured. That kiss at the top of Whiteladies Road, moments before her attack, would be the last time she saw Jake.

Although it was a Saturday, Chief Superintendent Malcolm Popperwell came into the office. He had the new image of the offender in his hand and had placed pins in the map to show where Anna Soltys had walked and been assaulted.

'He's back,' he told the smoke-filled room of detectives. 'We've had nothing since April, nothing for eight months and the fucker's back.

'We're out tonight. Overt, covert. If your wives don't have plans, we can find a uniform that fits, shove 'em in it and throw 'em on the streets.

'You lot. You …' he pointed to the detectives. 'All of you, out on the roads. Pretend to be drinkers, clubbers. We'll come up with a plan how to divvy you up.'

Few of the drinkers in the pubs and clubs up and down the Whiteladies Road would have realised it, but there was barely a dancefloor or cosy snug that didn't have an under-cover cop in it on the night of Saturday, 16 December 1978.

'If you see a man in his late twenties or early thirties who resembles the Clifton Rapist, watch him, follow him. If you need to, arrest him.' Those were the orders barked by a red-faced Popperwell.

Chris Gould, by contrast, was in uniform. In fact, it was so cold, he had chosen to wear his police-issue cape for the first and – it would later transpire – only time. He was patrolling the lower end of Whiteladies Road, near a university venue called the Victoria Rooms.

'There been another attack?' asked a couple of young girls falling out of a nightclub.

He nodded.

'You look like a superhero in that,' they said.

Chris glanced at his cape and realised it gave him neither superhuman powers nor warmth against the December night. He was heading south, towards the nightclubs of The Triangle.

He felt it before he heard it.

Boom!

There was a shudder, a bang, then the sound of shattering glass.

Then the screams.

Chris saw people running towards him: young women dressed in short skirts or trouser suits, young men in their Saturday night best sprinting with a whitened look of terror.

'Bomb … a bomb. A fucking bomb …' he heard them shout.

He wondered what to do. Was it a bomb? Really? His initial thought was that if it was an IRA device, the first explosion was just that – one of several. There would be a second or third designed to injure or kill emergency service staff.

What choice did he have? Chris was used to dealing with suspicious packages and had even had some explosives training but he had never experienced a blast. He ran towards the explosion, people fleeing towards him. He turned the corner and saw the front of a department store had been blown out.

Chris looked around for casualties and saw a group of young men clutching their heads.

'You okay? Are you alright?'

Sirens were starting to get nearer in the background.

They looked foreign, Mediterranean. They nodded.

'We're just cut,' said one in a thick Italian accent.

'Has anyone been seriously injured? Was anyone in the store? A security guard, a cleaner? Anyone walking outside?'

They shrugged.

An ambulance turned up and the driver and crew leapt out.

'What is it?' one of them shouted. 'IRA? Animal rights?'

'I don't know,' said Chris and started trying to manage the crowds forming on the street.

As if the force wasn't stretched enough, Bristol had suffered a potentially fatal bomb attack. The force was being stretched like never before.

The Provisional IRA claimed responsibility for the attack. Bristol was not the group's only target. That night was part of a campaign which saw three devices explode in London, with more planted in Liverpool, Manchester, Coventry and

Southampton. No one was seriously injured, although the group of five Italian waiters in Bristol had a miraculous escape.

A second bomb was found in a car park in nearby Fairfax Street. The army's Bomb Disposal Unit was called in and defused the explosive successfully. There had been busier weekends for police in Bristol over the years, but only, probably, during the Blitz.

The following Tuesday, DC Eddie Chandler was tasked with making more house-to-house inquiries about the attack on Anna Soltys, but his mind was really on the bomb.

A man answered the door of the Victorian flat conversion. In his thirties, he was skinny with a pair of glasses and a yellow jumper. He had one of those huge Adam's apples that grab your attention and transfix you, Eddie noticed.

The DC said his spiel to the Adam's apple: had he seen or heard anything about an attack early Saturday?

'Saturday? The Saturday just gone? No.'

Eddie nodded.

'But Tilly did the week before.'

Eddie snapped back into the moment.

'Sorry?'

'Yeah, the Clifton Rapist? Yeah, Tilly in Flat Three – upstairs. He raped her.'

Eddie studied him.

'What are you saying? December 9th or 16th? Tilly? Who is Tilly?'

'Tilly? She's the girl upstairs. Lovely girl. He attacked her the Saturday before last, the 9th.'

'Did she report it?'

'Doubt it. She said the police hadn't caught him so far, so not much point in telling you.'

'Where's Tilly now?'

'She's on late shifts this week, so I'd have thought she'll be in. Shall I knock for her?'

'Yes, please,' said Chandler in as calm a voice as possible.

'One minute …' said the Adam's apple. And the door closed on Eddie Chandler's face.

Eddie saw a phone box nearby and half-sprinted to it. He found a coin, jammed it in and called Redland Police Station.

'It's Eddie. Send me a girlie WPC, quick.'

CHAPTER SIXTEEN

When the front door reopened, DC Eddie Chandler was greeted by a woman who seemed as dazed as she was dishevelled. She had a wild tangle of long blonde hair, pink pyjama bottoms and the look of someone who just wanted to not be awake.

'Yeah?' she said through sleep-slit eyes.

'Tilly, is it?'

'Yeah.'

'Can I come in to chat with you? I'm Eddie from the police.'

'If you have to.'

'I'm just waiting for a woman police officer to chaperone you.'

'What the fuck do I need a chaperone for?'

A marked police car screeched around the corner and pulled up on a yellow line. WPC Sally Difazio got out and waved hello. Tilly nodded, turned her body and with sagging shoulders, started pulling herself up the banister of the large staircase.

Eddie and Sally went through a door and into a flat which would have been beautiful had someone either cleaned or tidied it at any point in the last six months. Tilly led them through a hallway littered with coats, dresses, underwear and T-shirts. Eddie noticed a high-end kitchen covered in bowls, pans and breakfast cereal boxes. Tilly shuffled ahead of him into a large sitting room with two big settees, a large television set and more clothes. She slumped down on one of the settees, pulled a packet of cigarettes from somewhere, flicked one out and lit it with a match. She beckoned Eddie and Sally to sit on the other settee, which they did after moving a large red duffle coat and a copy of *Vogue*.

Tilly blew out smoke. 'What do you want?'

'I called at your door, I'm making inquiries about an attack by the Clifton Rapist on the Saturday just gone. Your neighbour said you were assaulted the previous Saturday. Is that right?'

Eddie held his breath, Sally too. Tilly blew out more smoke.

'Yeah.'

'Look, I know all of these attacks have been deeply traumatising for the victims. We've got to get you help. But we need to know what he's doing, so we can catch him.'

'Why? You haven't caught him yet. I didn't see him, it was dark. Not sure what I'm gonna bring to the party.'

'Can you tell me what happened?'

'Yeah. I'd been at Platform One. I walked back with mates, they went their way at the end of the street. I turned into my garden. The front light's broken. I was putting my key in the lock when I felt someone's hands round my neck.

'He said, "Don't scream or I'll kill you" or something like that. Pulled me in the bushes. But it was dark, I didn't see him.'

'Was there anything distinctive about him?'

'He smelt of booze. Beer, I'd say.'

'Anything else? Was he high-pitched or did he have a deep voice?'

'Oh yeah,' Tilly said, taking another puff of her cigarette. Then she turned to Eddie and he noticed for the first time that morning that her eyes were sparkling: 'He had a northern accent.'

It was the call that Chief Superintendent Malcolm Popperwell had been waiting for but wasn't sure he would ever get. One of his detective constables in the inquiry room took it. Popperwell noticed the DC go quiet and serious. A few minutes later, the DC put down the phone and sidled up.

'Guv?'

'Yes?'

'A call from Nottinghamshire Police. They've just arrested a guy up there for raping women in Worksop. Said he looks like the Clifton Rapist. He's cagey about where he's been for the last few years. They say his name is Daniel Wilson. They wonder if we want to look at him.'

John O'Connor and Michelle Tighe peered through the doorway to see Daniel Wilson among the line of six men standing next to a wall in the police inquiry room. The prisoner brought down from Nottingham was third along in the line-up and the tallest, with big, brown curly hair and a handlebar moustache. He sneered as he looked either side of him.

'Who are the others?' he asked Michelle Tighe.

'Well, you know Richard …' First in line, Richard was the owner of the Mandrake Club. He was red-faced and sweating in a blue tracksuit. 'Not sure where they dragged the others in from.'

They had been unable to get hold of most of the surv-ivors: Alice Matthews had returned to her husband in the West Midlands, Patsy Delaney had gone travelling, Denise Turner was performing with her band up north, Hélène Baur and Anna Soltys had returned to Austria and Poland. Detectives were still unconvinced that the attacks on Wendy Johnson and Rachel Doulton were the same man. That left Tilly Sanderson, the victim who hadn't made a complaint, and Joanna McGarry, who had been driving home after finishing work at a nightclub, followed by the yellow Ford Capri as she went.

Both Tilly and Joanna had been attacked in their own front gardens. They were sitting next to each other in recep-tion when Michelle and John walked in.

John had been tasked with guiding Tilly through the identity parade, Michelle with Joanna. John heard Tilly say, 'You here for the line-up as well?' before he was able to interrupt as politely as possible: 'Please, you're not meant to have any contact with each other.'

Tilly looked up at him and shrugged. Michelle took Joanna into an interview room and asked if she wanted a cup of tea.

John slowly led Tilly through the office towards the room in which the line-up was assembled.

'Right, you're going to see six men. We know you said his voice was distinctive, so we're going to get them all to say something to you as well, to help with identification. If you see or hear the man, you have to touch him on the shoulder. I know it sounds strange, but that's the system. That's part of the process, but you have to do that. You ready?'

Tilly nodded, then just as John started to walk through the door, she pulled his jacket: 'Just one thing. It was dark, I really didn't see him. I'm gonna close my eyes, you're gonna have to guide me through it.'

John raised his eyebrows then said, 'Okay.'

Tilly shut her eyes, John moved behind her and gently guided her, saying, 'Forward a few steps, please. Just to your left … Great, no, left a bit, forward a bit. Okay?'

John looked to his right and saw Detective Inspector Tom Evans standing there, eyes wide, seemingly popping out of his head, his brows furrowed in a question mark.

John just nodded at him.

'Man One,' said Tom.

Tilly stood, eyes closed, in front of Richard, owner of the Mandrake Club. He looked down at a piece of card. In a thick, slow Bristolian accent he read, 'Don't scream or I'll kill you.'

Tilly shook her head. John moved her two steps to the right. Man Two went through the same process.

John moved her to the right, facing Daniel Wilson. He looked down at his card and looked up, snarling: 'Don't scream or I'll kill you.' John noticed Tilly recoiling. He wasn't sure if it was because Wilson's voice was so big, proud and angry, or if it had unleashed some supressed recollection in her. She took a breath, he saw, then he pushed her on to the three other men.

'Man Three,' she said to John.

John allowed himself to feel a quick moment of victory: she had chosen the right suspect.

'You've got to touch him on the shoulder,' he urged.

'I can't see.'

He moved her to the left and she put out her hand and touched Wilson's chest.

Tilly, with her eyes closed, was unable to see his silent glare.

John spun her gently round and moved her out of the room. Afterwards, in the office, he noticed her taking deep breaths. She seemed so different to the nonchalant, bedraggled, pyjamaed girl described to him by Eddie Chandler.

John saw Michelle Tighe walk Joanna McGarry through to the line-up. He watched as Joanna caught a glimpse of Tilly taking deep breaths, her face turning pale as she passed through the door. The moment he saw Michelle, he got that deep-seated feeling of disappointment. He had just let Tilly go and was re-entering the office as she came through another door with Joanna after her line-up.

Michelle was shaking her head. She went out to take Joanna to the front desk. When she returned, she said: 'She chose Richard, the club owner. In fact, she didn't think it was even him. Said that was just a guess. We can't proceed purely on the sound of Daniel's voice, there's not enough on him. Are we ever going to get this man?'

Chris Gould had heard about the new victim, found days after the IRA bomb. He heard about the arrests and the line-ups.

How much more desperate can we get?

But he had been playing around with some ideas: the success of his covert methods in the Magic Fingers operation, but more than anything, the documentary he had watched at home about agent provocateur tactics. So far, they had tried overt tactics, public announcements and even some fledgling attempts at undercover work, sending plain-clothes detectives out to walk the streets on the off chance they would see someone looking like the Clifton Rapist.

What if they were to try something new? Bigger?

What about a full-scale covert operation to catch the Clifton Rapist?

He mentioned the idea to his sergeant. And that, thought Chris, was that. But soon the idea was passing up the ranks. From Chris to his sergeant, to an inspector, to Chief Superintendent Malcolm Popperwell.

Then it reached the Chief Constable. And Kenneth Steele was fast running out of time and patience. Chris knew nothing about Steele's plans for retirement – he didn't want to leave the force with unfinished business. And one of the country's most dangerous men at liberty *was* unfinished business. A stain on a near-impeccable career.

Under normal circumstances, perhaps no chief constable would have approved such a large, expensive operation for anyone less than a murderer. Perhaps not even then. But the idea had one big thing in its favour: Steele's ego. The pride of a man with a reputation to preserve and limited time could go a long way.

CHAPTER SEVENTEEN

JANUARY 1979

'Okay, ladies, we've got a little operation planned …'

WPC Sally Difazio was a recent transfer to the Police Women's Unit. She sat with Steph Whittle and Michelle Tighe when Sergeant Carol Curnock said the words which would change their lives: 'There's a briefing in ten minutes. I'd like you to be open-minded but I don't want you to feel any pressure. If it's not for you, that's fine.'

They were led to the inquiry room in Southmead. Chief Superintendent Malcolm Popperwell stood at the front, red-faced under his pork-pie hat. It was a cold January day, but he had removed his trench coat for the occasion: this must be important.

The whole of the Women's Unit was there: Denise Pollard, Gillian Skinner, Diana Day, Kathy Ryan, as well as Michelle's flatmates Jean Castle and Jackie Clair. Another WPC from the division was also there: Cathy Holbrook. The room was full to bursting. Chris Gould, John O'Connor, as well as other officers including a former cadet they all knew called Andy Kerslake; also older PCs: Robbie Jones, Chris Nott and Stu Sexton.

'We are trying something new in our attempt to catch the

Clifton Rapist,' said Popperwell. 'He's been attacking women now for 18 months. We know of seven confirmed cases, two possible others and who knows how many other women have not reported an assault. He's an animal. And he's free.'

There was a slow murmuring in the room.

'The Chief Constable has approved a new operation, a covert op. We've never done anything like this before – we don't think any other force has done this before. It'll be big – and it'll operate until we catch him.'

He pointed to the photo-fits of the man, which were pinned to the wall.

'There is no pattern to when he strikes. He's attacked at all times of year but there are enough similarities that we can make an educated guess about what time of day, how and where he might appear next.'

He then pointed to a map of north Bristol on the wall.

'Apart from two attacks, all of his victims have been walking home late at night or early in the morning along Whiteladies Road. But he hasn't assaulted them there, so we reason that he's seen them there and followed them when they've turned off into the side streets, where the lighting isn't as good. If you see the attack points, they're in different places, but all of the women have walked along the same few hundred yards beforehand.

'We think he's been watching and waiting there.'

There were nods from the audience – most of them knew this.

'Our new operation will involve a team of undercover female officers dressed as students walking along that stretch of Whiteladies Road.'

Popperwell looked over at the Women's Unit.

'That's the bait. But like any honeytrap, it can't look obvious. We know he won't attack the women on the main road so we will have a series of predetermined routes which will involve the women turning off. There, a team of observation officers will be waiting.

'Our intention is that he sees the girl, is lured into the dark, pounces and is caught.'

Popperwell slammed the map with the palm of his hand.

'This is a dangerous man,' said Sergeant Carol Curnock. 'He's subjected women to the most depraved assaults. Before we ask for volunteers, we ask for you all to realise that you are putting yourselves in the line of fire. And more than that, we need grounds to arrest him – we can't arrest him just for following you into the dark, that's not enough. This man, the Clifton Rapist … well, he has to touch you, he has to assault you. And you need to know that.'

Popperwell picked up again: 'The observation officers will be both fixed-point and mobile. The girls will be watched every inch, every second of the way. We'll need teams, not just of decoy officers, but also people to watch the decoy officers.

'With that in mind, the Chief has decided it's going to be called Operation Argus – apparently, that was a mythical beast with a hundred eyes. I think the Chief went to a different type of school to me.'

Sally Difazio hadn't known Malcolm Popperwell make a joke before.

'But there is one more proviso: the operation will be big, but it must also be secret. Even within the force. You have a role to play, but you tell no one else about it, unless they're part of it.'

Sally felt a frisson of excitement. An operation so secret, it was being concealed from most police officers?

Carol Curnock spoke up: 'We need to be clear what we're asking of you: you are a decoy. But there's a fine line with this: you can't lead him on. That won't stand up in court. We're not asking you to initiate anything or provoke this man. Your job is to be just a normal woman walking down the street. You do nothing more than that.

'You must attract not seduce, entice not entrap.'

'Most of the attacks have happened later on the week, so the operation will run between Wednesdays and Saturdays,' Popperwell continued. 'Think about it and tell Carol or me if you want to take part.'

Sally looked around and realised she had never known this team of outgoing young officers to be so silent.

'I'm going to do it,' said Steph. 'Wouldn't it be great to say you were the officer who caught the Clifton Rapist?'

The Police Women's Unit was buzzing.

'They're treating us just like bait,' said one officer.

'What's wrong with that? He attacks young women. Better he goes for us with blokes watching us than a lone woman who's got no one. Put my name down ...' said Steph.

'What do you think he'd do in the attack? He's put his hands around all the women's throats. He could break your neck,' added another officer, who was clearly wavering.

'We'll give you some self-defence training,' offered Sergeant Carol Curnock.

'I feel more sorry for the blokes lying in people's gardens – it's freezing. At least we'll be walking,' said Sally.

She pictured herself heading down a darkened street and a man with a face like the photo-fits leaping out. She was sporty, she told herself. She was a champion runner, she would be ready and waiting for an attack … Surely she could just sprint out of his grasp?

This is my job, she told herself. *I get paid to protect people and property. And it might be a thrill.*

'I'll do it,' she said firmly, noticing how enthusiastic she sounded.

'So, what you're saying, Carol …' Michelle Tighe continued, 'is that we've got a monster out there. You know, a proper nailed-on monster. As a police force we've tried every trick in the book but he just keeps popping up – attacking women, attacking women, attacking women, then vanishing. We don't know when he'll strike next, we can't guess for sure where, and he could pick on any poor young girl who's in the wrong place at the wrong time. And the only thing now that stands between this girl-attacking monster and a city in fear is us? Look at us: I'm 23, Sally's 19. We're no age. Some of us were in school a few months ago.'

'I know,' said Carol. 'I said this to Malcolm, I said it to the Chief.'

'So, what you're saying is that yes, we'll have backup and yes, we'll have radio earpieces and we'll have observation guys. But for a moment, no one knows how long that moment'll be. We'll be by ourselves with this girl-attacking monster? The only thing between this man and this city in fear is us, a bunch of teenage twenty-something girls?'

'Yes, Michelle,' said Carol.

'I'm in,' said Tighe, her eyes glinting.

CHAPTER EIGHTEEN

Chris Gould had always described himself as 'auburn' or 'strawberry blond' but no one on C-Division had ever used his more poetic definitions. Combining his red hair with giving the decoys self-defence classes, the nickname was cruel and obvious.

'The Ginger Ninja? He's teaching us?'

No one could quite work out who said it.

He stood in the canteen at Redland Police Station. The tables and chairs had been moved to one side and six WPCs were lined up in front of him. A further six women police officers had volunteered, but he would train them another time.

'Okay, we know a few things about the attacker's technique. He strikes from the rear, he uses two hands around the throat, he then pulls his victims back in a dragging motion.' Chris was gesticulating the movement with his hands. 'It's really worrying. This delivery means two things happen. Firstly, he shocks his victims, but secondly, that physical movement means it reduces his victim's ability to scream, or make any kind of noise.'

He noticed a couple of the officers had started to pale.

'But because we know what he does, it allows us to take

preventative measures and to plan how to react in the event of an attack.'

He took in all the trainee decoys.

'Firstly, your clothes. What you wear can make a big difference. If you have a scarf or even a collar up, that means his grip will be less secure than around a bare neck. It'll create a gap or at the very least some friction between his hands and your throat. And that might buy you a few seconds. Remember, your priority to is keep your airway clear at all times.

'Sally, can you come here?'

WPC Difazio walked forward and he beckoned her to turn, facing the other five. Chris stood in front of her.

'Okay, Sally, you're the attacker. Two hands, from behind, round my neck.'

She reached round and placed her fingers around Chris's throat.

'Right. That's it, they might be just on your windpipe like this … Okay, Sally, loosen it a bit – this is just a demonstration.'

Then Chris put his hands up and tried to thread his two index fingers under her grip.

'The worst-case scenario is that this happens: his hands are around your neck. Your priority is to get a finger between your throat and his grip.'

Chris showed how he could extend a digit under Sally's hands and was, eventually, able to pull himself free. He then walked around each of the officers, grabbing them from behind, showing them how to reach up, slide a finger under the hands and try to pull themselves clear. Then he moved on to other techniques: using an offender's weight against him to throw him over. Reaching up to the attacker's arms and pushing them together to prise apart his hands from the neck, like a lever.

Chris showed the officers finger-locks, then hitting the offender in the face, punching him in the eyes, using elbows in different ways to defend themselves. Then he moved on to ground techniques using legs as shields and survival procedures if the attacker was trying to choke his victim out.

Afterwards, the trainees nodded, thanked him and left the room wondering how long it would take for the red marks to pale from their throats.

Sally Difazio was waiting in one of the rooms in Redland Police Station. She could hear voices in the distance, down the corridor and a clip-clipping of shoes. And she was sure that she could hear a man's voice saying, 'Yes, I'm teaching the tarts how to use radios.' Then the duty sergeant appeared at the doorway. He was holding a bag and looking at a clip-board.

'So, you are Sally Difazz … How do you say your surname?'

'Difazio.'

'Have you used a radio before?'

'Yes.'

'Good – well, these are new ones. Tell you what, it's a good thing it's winter. No idea how we'd get these on you in a summer dress.'

He reached into the bag and pulled out a hand-sized block of light-blue metal.

'I call it a Burndept UHF Handportable Radio-Telephone BE471, you'll call it a brick. They're new – the latest in covert communications. Each kit costs the force about a grand to buy. What's your salary?'

'Three and a half thousand a year.'

'Good, so this is worth a third of what you are. It's expensive and it's good. Don't break it, don't lose it, don't put it in your handbag and dance around it in the Mandrake Club.'

'Why would I do that?'

He chose to ignore her reply.

'They're good, really reliable, although we do have a few black spots in hilly areas.'

Sally thought immediately of all the hills in Bristol – in particular on Whiteladies Road, which was one big incline.

'Most of the time you'll wear it around your neck but if that doesn't conceal it, you can put it in your handbag. We have two cables. One'll be connected to an earpiece so you can receive instructions so when you're dressing up, you'll need to have hair over your ears and probably a scarf to hide all the gubbins.'

The duty sergeant got a long electric cable which connected to a clear see-through tube, which led to a small bug-shaped piece of pink plastic. He plugged it in her ear then picked up another unit and twisted a knob. There was a hash of static which made her recoil.

'Can you hear me, Sally Defazz …? What's your surname?' he said in a deep voice into his unit's microphone.

'Can … me … Fazz … surname?' crackled in her ear.

'Not really,' she replied.

He shrugged in the way techies do when they have no way of improving the equipment they are working with.

'The second cable is your throat mic. Keep your hand in your bag as you walk, keep your finger on the microphone button. If you want to speak, or are in distress, hit the button, then the microphone's activated and we can hear what you're saying. Comprendez, Sally?'

'I think so.'

She was pushing the button and playing with the microphone. Then she looked up at him: 'How reliable is this? What if the attacker strikes and the kit's failed? What if I haven't heard a warning?'

'Well, it's called a brick for a reason – you hit him over the head with it.'

They were back in the big briefing room in Southmead Police Station – all of them. The women, the men, the top brass … Under his pork-pie hat Chief Superintendent Malcolm Popperwell's face was a darker shade of puce than usual, possibly owing to the presence of Chief Constable Kenneth Steele, who stood silently in the corner, back erect, surveying the team of 50 officers.

'Okay, Operation Argus goes live for its first covert night tonight,' announced Popperwell. 'You know the score: the Task Force will be in plain clothes. Okay, Sergeant Hattersley?'

Kelvin nodded.

Popperwell continued: 'Over the course of the operation, we'll release the decoys through both cars and from two safe houses. Tonight, we're going to start with a fully mobile, vehicular release of the decoy. That will be your covert car, Sergeant Hattersley.

'Tomorrow night, we'll leave from WPC Whittle's flat.

'The first two decoys are ...' Popperwell glanced at a piece of paper, then continued: 'Sally Difazio and Sergeant Curnock.'

Carol Curnock? Mother Hen? It had never occurred to any of the younger women that she would be a decoy. Weren't they were meant to look like students? She must be nudging 40?

'Tonight, the decoys will be released on St Paul's Road, by the crossing with Whiteladies Road. The decoy will then proceed north up Whiteladies Road on the western pavement. We will have fixed observation teams in these points here on the other side of the road, the eastern pavement.' Here, he pointed to five pins along Whiteladies Road.

'We will also have four mobile observation officers walking in the other direction from the eastern pavement. I have discussed the tactics with our mobile officers. We will need to develop our undercover techniques further in the dynamic situation.

'Hunting the Clifton Rapist will be like hunting for a predator in the wild.

'The decoy will be bait. She'll continue north until she reaches Chantry Road. By that point, we hope that the rapist will have noticed the decoy and be on her track.'

Steph glanced round and noticed a stillness in the room, a collective holding of breath.

'He won't attack on Whiteladies Road, but the plan is for

the decoy to turn into Chantry Road, which has hardly any street lighting.'

Popperwell turned and looked to the Women's Police Unit, then said: 'It's *exceptionally* dark, but we'll have eyes on you. Five more fixed observation posts in gardens and bushes will be watching. By this time, too, Sergeant Hattersley will have driven up the back roads to Hurle Crescent as the decoy reaches here too.

'If the Clifton Rapist were to strike, this is where we believe it will happen. Depending where on Hurle Crescent he strikes, the decoy will have a maximum of a few seconds on her own with him but the observation officers will react, as will Sergeant Hattersley and his covert Task Force, who are in their second position. If he doesn't strike, the decoy gets in Sergeant Hattersley's van, we swap decoys and the second female officer is deployed. Then we do it again. Depending on what happens, twice a night each, maybe more.

'Does everyone understand?'

There was silence.

Chief Constable Kenneth Steele walked forward. 'I just want to congratulate you, Chief Superintendent, for putting together such an incredible plan and team. Looking at you here, I can see in your eyes a determination to get this man. In more than 40 years of policing, I have seen many things, but I have never come across a man as cold, as brutal and as menacing as this monster. It would mean so much to women in Bristol, to the force and to me personally if you are able to catch him.

'I thought I'd seen everything there was to see in policing, but even towards the end of my career it's inspiring to see something truly innovative. I've never heard of any police operation quite like this. I've never heard of an undercover operation this size either. Not in England, not anywhere. And you decoys, he is targeting young women so we're having to use our youngest, least experienced officers. We're asking a lot of you. You're putting your lives on hold to work extra shifts, putting your lives on the line. And I want to thank you personally. Chief Superintendent Popperwell just described this as akin to hunting a beast – I just want to wish you happy hunting.'

There was a glint in his eye which Steph Whittle tried to read: was it emotion? Hope? Or maybe something else? As she left the room with the other members of the Women's Police Unit, she heard a man's voice say, 'Hope the birds don't fuck it up.'

Steph fumed silently.

CHAPTER NINETEEN

MONDAY, 25 NOVEMBER 1963

Torture, just torture, The Driver thinks.

It's lunchtime in the colliery canteen and all anyone's banging on about is death.

A dead president and this dead girl.

The Driver has decided that his workmates are so stupid, they care more about her than they do the leader of the free world. When Kennedy was shot, it was an international tragedy. A whole country needed a new president, the world was shocked. For the rest of their lives, people will remember where they were when they heard about the assassination. But as he sits there with four mates, eating his ham sandwich, they keep bringing the conversation back to *her*.

It's not as if they knew her. This girl was just a shop worker from Mansfield, he says to himself. He knew her family would miss her – that's only natural. But why does everyone in the pit keep talking about her? It's not as though she was particularly important.

'You know, she worked in the Co-op, the one in Mansfield centre,' says one of the guys.

'I thought she had two jobs. She were saving to get married. I'm sure I saw her in a shoe shop, serving,' another says.

He says to himself that none of them know that this was *her* fault. *She* screamed. He warned her. *She* didn't listen. The newspapers keep going on about her as well.

One of the guys unfolds his copy of the *Daily Mirror*.

'Christ, they're on about Kathleen in the national papers,' he says. He turns the front page around and there's the headline: '100 Policemen Search Tip for Girl's Body'. He reads details out: 'They found her pants on that waste ground near Prince's Street. Her hat, umbrella and glasses.'

The Driver notices a bead of sweat on his brow. One hundred officers? That's a lot of officers, they could do a lot of searching. He thinks about that ginger cop who gave his car a push.

The *Mirror* reader passes it on to one of the others. He starts going through the article: 'They've brought in bulldozers too, they're clearing the area.'

That makes The Driver feel better – they can search the wasteland as long as they like.

'They've found a knife, here, it says it's a cork-handled steak knife.'

The Driver sighs silently: he has no knife, never goes out armed.

'But they're treating it as a murder inquiry with no body. Look, they've brought frogmen in.'

Now, The Driver starts to panic. He remembers the perfect reflection of the moon in the lake's surface before it was broken.

'Ah, here, yer see … That's an obvious place. They're going down in the River Maun. Bloody papers, they call it the River Maum. Bet those journalists are from London.

'Here, they've spoken to her mum. It says, "Mrs Edith Heathcote said: 'My daughter was waiting until George was 21 before they got married. They were very happy.'"'

His mate actually wipes away a tear.

Is this bloke a man?

One of the other guys hasn't fully started crying, but it looks as though he's close to tears: 'Do you know her bloke? George? George Whalley? An apprentice. Just 19. Imagine him with this for the rest of his life. Good thing he were at work, they might have thought he did it.'

'They questioned him.'

'Did they? Bet they did. He 'ad an alibi, though.'

'No, he didn't do it. There's some sick fuckers out there.'

'What d'you think of it?'

They're looking at The Driver. He shrugs and says something about it being sad.

'Sad? It's more than sad. I know they're banging on in London about getting rid o' hanging, but whoever did this should be swinging, I'd say,' says one.

The driver hadn't thought of this. An image of a gallows appears in his mind.

'Ey up, look at this. Paper says they found tyre marks next to her stuff on the wasteland.'

Something happens to The Driver: the room starts looking fuzzy, he can't concentrate. The three men become blurred images. He gets up and stumbles from the table, walking quickly towards the toilets. The Driver bangs through a door, finds a cubicle, throws down the seat and sits, panting heavily. He swears under his breath, again and again.

CHAPTER NINETEEN

There's a knock at the door: 'Y'alright, pal?'

'Yeah, yeah.'

Images of tyre marks in mud and a moonlight lake flash before him.

'Not feelin' well. Keep thinkin' about becomin' a dad,' he murmurs.

He carries on breathing deeply and he hears the door slam as his friend leaves the toilet block. If he can get through the next few weeks, he'll be all right, he tells himself.

CHAPTER TWENTY

WPC Sally Difazio and Sergeant Carol Curnock sat in the back of the unmarked Task Force van as it juddered, left and right, through the streets of Bristol. There was little light, but occasionally Sally would see Carol's calm face looking ahead at the streets.

'When was the last time you went out on something like this?' asked Sally.

'Undercover? Years ago. A decade?'

The van turned a corner and they slid along the seats.

Carol stayed quiet, thinking. Then she said: 'It was a back-street abortionist. In Bedminster, Nailsea Close. A Brian Theobald job, he ran the inquiry. A pair of women were doing private operations before the law changed. I had to pretend to be a pregnant woman. Had to go in for my consultation. They went through all the reasons I needed the abortion. They didn't really care, they weren't doing the operations for any moral reasons – they just wanted the money. We had a load of guys outside, ready to dive in.'

She looked ahead, the red glow of a traffic light on her face: 'I wasn't pregnant, I had padding up my top. Got as far as them asking me to lie on a bed to perform the operation then I had to leap out and tell them who I was.

'Maud Tanner. Never forgot her. She must have been over 60 back then and she had a friend who wasn't far behind. I remember being scared but I trusted the guys and I didn't get hit or anything.'

Sally had never heard that story. In fact, she realised how little she knew of Carol Curnock – she really must ask more questions.

The van came to another halt and Sergeant Kelvin Hattersley said from the driver's seat: 'Okay, Carol, you ready?'

'Yes, Kelvin.'

'Actually, could I do it, Carol?' Sally didn't know where that came from.

'I wouldn't ask you to do anything that I wouldn't do myself – I should go,' her sergeant insisted.

'Well, you will. You can do the second one, I'd like to do the first.'

Carol looked back at her, lips closed, but her eyes smiling: 'Okay.'

'Testing comms, Sally,' she heard the words in her ear.

Sally reached into her pocket and found the button for her microphone.

'Yes, I can hear you. Can you hear me?'

'Yes,' said Kelvin. 'Control, do you copy?'

There was an electric crackle in Sally's ear and then she heard: 'Okay, Sally. You receiving?'

'Receiving.'

'Okay, let's get the Clifton Rapist. Are you sure you'll be warm enough, Sally?'

The WPC nodded, pulled open the door of the unmarked police van and got out onto St Paul's Road. It was like walking into a wall of cold. The temperature had only reached as high as -2 all day but now it had sunk to something nearer -5. Difazio wore a heavy jacket, jeans, boots, a scarf and a hat, but her cheeks were already being bitten by the cold. She thought of the 15 or so men who had been lying in gardens for the last 20 minutes, waiting for this moment. Glancing either side quickly, she then headed straight towards Whiteladies Road.

Sally could see her breath.

She passed a pub, noticing how cosy it looked with its fire, laughter and yellow light from the side lamps.

'Alpha One, subject's in view,' Sally heard in her ear.

She saw two women, arm in arm, cackling past her down the hill as she walked up. On the other side of the road a man was walking in the other direction. Was that one of the mobile observation guys, or someone else? He was holding an umbrella. Why would he be doing that? No rain was forecast.

'This is Alpha Two, subject's in view.'

Sally looked ahead now. She heard feet on the pavement and saw the outline of a woman. As she drew closer, she saw the woman wearing a red swirly minidress with billowing sleeves and long boots – and no tights.

No tights? How on earth is that woman not freezing? she thought to herself. *But a great outfit … for a summer's night.*

The woman stumbled and as the two of them passed, Sally caught the scent of ale in the air.

That's why she's not cold. Taking risks, though, isn't she?

She pushed her microphone button and said: 'Woman by herself, walking south, please keep eyes on her. I think she's drunk. Miniskirt, tall, pretty.'

'Alpha One. Don't worry, I'll keep eyes on,' said a voice in her ear, half-leering.

'Subject in view. Alpha Three,' Sally heard.

She was passing Whiteladies Gate now. Platform One was buzzing, she could hear Rod Stewart's 'Da Ya Think I'm Sexy?' blaring out. A couple of bouncers were pulling a man in big jeans out of the club. She looked over: one of the bouncers had a handlebar moustache and dark hair, but was he too young to be the Clifton Rapist?

'Oi, fuck you! And fuck yer mum!' she heard the man say to the bouncer.

The bouncer looked straight ahead at the man, impassive. Then he glanced and saw Sally and nodded. She passed the scene. Then she heard a thwack, followed by a scream – the man's, she guessed.

'And fuck yer dad too!'

Sally pushed the microphone button: 'Check the bouncer at Platform One. Man with black hair and moustache, resembling attacker. Not sure though. He's young. Keep a watch.'

As Sally Difazio was walking by the nightclub bouncer who had a passing resemblance to the Clifton Rapist's photo-fits, a short distance away, PC Andy Kerslake lay freezing under a bush. Andy was a country boy, Somerset-born with a lilt-ing accent and an easy-going, affable manner which belied a gently hidden shrewdness. Two years earlier, he had joined the force. He had no particular ambition to be a cop, in fact he'd applied for the army at the same time. Avon and Somerset Police said yes first, so that's what he did. Now he had moved from the drunk-and-disorderlies, thefts from farms and petty shoplifting of the rural teams to be an observation officer in the force's biggest-ever operation. And he could barely feel his feet, let alone speak without chattering.

The older officers, those with even just a few years under their belts, were on mobile observation watches. They could walk to keep warm.

Andy peered through the bush of a family's garden and watched as youths left nightclubs, drunks fought and taxis whizzed up and down Whiteladies Road.

He shivered again.

Andy had heard in his earpiece the radio traffic as Sally Difazio passed from Alpha One to Two to Three. Now he looked to his left, where he could see the outline of a person heading towards him – was that Sally?

A cyclist clinked past down the hill.

Yes, that was Sally, he was sure. What should he say again?

He was just about to push his microphone button when two pairs of legs appeared in front of his eyes. He couldn't see Sally any more. And he couldn't say anything into the microphone. He felt helpless.

What am I going to do? he thought.

There was a crackle in his ear: 'Alpha Four, do you have eyes on?'

'Did you hear something?' It was a man's voice, the owner of one of the pairs of legs.

'What? No? This is a nice spot. Tell me, how long have you been thinking about me in that way …?'

It was a woman. She was slurring her words. The legs were more distinct now. A pair of bigger legs in blue jeans, and a long coat that seemed to be covering a dress. And her legs had turned to face his. She raised herself on tiptoes.

'Later, tiger, later,' he heard the man say.

'Alpha Four, do you have eyes on?'

He heard two lips meeting and a sucking, kissing sound.

Couldn't they just canoodle a few metres away so that he could see Sally and talk to Control?

'Do you love me?' she asked.

'Let's take this upstairs,' he said.

Yes, please and then we'll all be happy, thought Andy.

They moved away. Andy heard a metallic grate and realised they were heading into the front garden he was lying in. He looked around and noticed his left leg was visible, illuminated by a shaft of light beaming from the front room.

If they look to their left, they'll see me, he thought.

Andy wondered whether to move his leg slowly and quietly or quickly. He decided on speed. There was a rustle as his leg spun on the ground, but by moving it just a few inches, he managed to get it in the shadows. He heard two pairs of feet climb the three stone steps and a key wriggle into a lock. The door opened, there were more steps and then it closed.

Andy could still see Sally. He hit the microphone button: 'Alpha Four, subject in view.'

'Roger.'

Sally Difazio disappeared from view and Andy heard through the radio that she had been picked up by Alpha Five.

Andy Kerslake suddenly realised that despite having spent the last half hour lying on the ground in -5 degrees, he was no longer cold.

Sally Difazio had not noticed the canoodling couple on the east side of Whiteladies Road, but she had just seen two men jostling past her. Neither of them looked like the artist's impressions. She had heard Alpha Five pick her up and a mobile observation officer – Delta One. Now she only had another 50 yards to go until she turned from the main street into the side road.

She took a breath.

If he's following me, he'll attack me in a moment, she thought.

Sally looked at her watch: 10.30 p.m. Turning the corner into Chantry Road, she realised just how dark the street really was. She glanced quickly again at Whiteladies Road. It seemed golden almost, with the sodium street lamps, warm pub lights and neon signs. But this was like heading into an abyss: just black.

In the distance was a single street lamp, maybe a hundred yards away. But no one seemed to be awake in the houses, not a single light was on. Sally found herself quickening her step.

'Delta Three: subject in view,' she heard in her earpiece.

Who was that? Where is he? she thought. *They're good, I can't see him at all.*

'Slow down, Sally,' she heard in her earpiece.

Difazio checked herself and noticed she was cantering along so she slackened her pace. The street lamp was emerging ahead. She needed to turn right into Hurle Crescent, where it was much brighter.

She saw the Task Force van ahead. A front door light flashed on from one of the houses to her right. Sally gasped silently but then she realised that she had reached the van. She opened the door and slid inside, welcoming the warmth – she had forgotten how cold she was.

'Okay, Sally?' asked Carol. 'Any problems?'

'No, no problems at all. It was fine.'

'Good,' said Carol. 'My turn.'

CHAPTER TWENTY-ONE

10 JANUARY 1979

Steph Whittle looked out of the single-glazed Victorian sash window. Some of the condensation had started to freeze over, but tonight must actually be warmer than Sally and Carol's first run, she thought. Leaning closer to her storage heater, she wondered what the team would think of her little flat.

She could see her reflection in the frozen glass: tall, dark-haired and young. *I look really young*, she thought. She was wearing blue jeans, a white blouse and a heavy black cardigan with a hood. Sometimes she wondered if she thought differently when she was in uniform or not. Dress the part to be the part. Did she suddenly become professional when she wore her police skirt, or more playful when in scruffs?

The radio was playing. News headlines about how this was already being called the Winter of Discontent, as well as being one of the coldest on record. Everyone seemed to be going on strike: lorry drivers, bin men, even gravediggers.

There was a knock at the door. Michelle Tighe stood there, shivering.

'Come on in, it's not much warmer in here, I'm afraid,' she told her.

Michelle opened her bag on the kitchen table. Cables, earpieces and other bits of radio kit spilled out on the yellow Formica top.

'There's a little knack to getting these to clip in,' she said. So, they sat and assembled the equipment, hanging the microphone from a neck-strap and plugging the earpiece in – they turned everything on.

'Control, this is Steph,' said Steph.

'Receiving, over,' crackled a reply. 'Michelle?'

'Yes, hello, receiving. Do you copy?'

'Receiving, over. Just waiting for Alpha team to get in position, then we're ready. Please wait.'

'What do you think? What are our chances?' asked Steph.

'Of catching the Clifton Rapist? What's the point in doing this if we don't think we can get him?' said Michelle firmly. 'We've got to be positive.'

There was a crackle of static and then they both heard: 'Okay, Steph and Michelle, we're ready. Do you have any questions?'

'Yes,' said Michelle. 'Why are all you blokes earning overtime and we're not getting a penny extra?'

Steph and Michelle looked at each other. The fact that they, the women, were unable to claim extra was already a sore point.

'Steph, are you ready? Please deploy,' came the flat reply through the earpiece.

Steph Whittle put on a scarf and her coat and checked herself in the mirror. She could see neither her microphone nor her earpiece. Out of her uniform, she looked so young, she thought to herself again. She said goodbye to Michelle and slipped out of the front door.

On the night of 10 January 1979, the mercury in the thermometer surfed just above freezing. Steph turned right onto Whiteladies Road, crossed the carriageway, hearing in her ear that she was being passed between Alpha One, Two and Three. There was also Delta One, the mobile observation man, who had seen her.

It was quiet, really quiet.

Wouldn't it be amazing if I'm the one who catches him? she thought, as she walked past a dark alleyway. But another part of her mind seemed to be whispering at her to face the stark reality of what she was doing.

Look at me – I know there are guys out here to watch, but I'm the target. It's me. I've got no protection, I'm just wearing a heavy jumper. What good's that against a monster? What if he has a knife?

Pub closing was a good half-hour away and the few people she saw were just silhouettes behind the condensation of pub windows. About halfway up Whiteladies Road, Steph noticed a yellow Ford Capri heading north, away from the city centre. She couldn't see its number plate. She concentrated on the pavement, at a pair of men heading her way.

'Alpha Four, subject in view,' she heard.

They passed her and neither looked like the artist impressions. But one of the guys, who must have been in his early twenties, offered an 'Alright, love?'

Steph ignored him and ploughed on up the hill. Now for Chantry Road … She took a breath. A few lamps were on in front rooms, which threw the occasional shaft of light onto the gardens.

Christ, these are big houses, she thought to herself. *You could hide away beautifully in the basement steps or behind nooks or crannies or hedges.*

'Steph, someone's turned into Chantry Road, he's behind you.'

Steph gulped. She decided to not look back, but carried on ahead towards a single street lamp.

'Alpha Seven. Subject in view, he's getting closer …'

Steph could hear his steps now, they were getting louder. She walked towards the lamp then heard the sound of an engine. A car headed towards her, headlights on full.

What can I do? she thought. *Just carry on? You have to trust the plan.*

The car sped towards her before screeching to a stop. She heard steps running behind her. Steph couldn't help it, she looked round. She felt trapped: a car in front of her, someone on the street behind her. She saw the outline of a man, running towards the car. He was now shadowed by the headlamps. He pulled the passenger door and Steph heard a shout: 'There you are, Mum. I was waiting outside the pub for ages.'

'I got the wrong King's Head …' she heard a woman say.

The door slammed shut and the car drove off.

Steph stopped and breathed out. The road had returned to silence, all she could hear now was the sound of her breath; she felt blood pumping through her brain.

A lamp from a house's front room switched off and the road fell into darkness. Steph heard a crash and spun around.

What was that? Metal, glass? Who was there?

'Sorry, that was me.' A sheepish-looking observation officer peered through a hedge. 'I knocked the bloody milk bottles over.'

Realising she had put her arms up in a judo attack position, Steph let them fall to her sides and told him to put the milk bottles back.

What on earth am I doing? Steph thought to herself and started to laugh.

It was the coldest winter any of the officers could remember and the decoy runs continued every Wednesday, Thursday, Friday and Saturday for weeks in appalling conditions. The women felt they were at risk from a monster, both sexes felt that they were at risk from the meteorological forecast.

By Wednesday, 24 January, there was a small blizzard but Operation Argus continued with the women walking through inches of snow, the men lying in it, hidden away in gardens. One observation officer needed hospital treatment for frostbite. Another had to be put in a car, the heating whacked on full while he shuddered the contents of a flask of coffee all over himself.

As the snow settled around him, Sergeant Kelvin Hattersley watched the figure of a man move slowly towards the unmarked Task Force car. He was trying the handles of each car. Eventually, he tried to open the vehicle next to Kelvin's.

Kelvin jumped out: 'Okay, matey, you're nicked.'

'What for?' said the startled man.

'Attempted theft of a motor vehicle.'

CHAPTER TWENTY-ONE

'You can't prove nothing.'

'Look at your trail in the snow.'

Down the street was a track cut in white, going from car door to car door. The man was arrested and duly charged.

The observation officers were finessing techniques. There were no formal reviews, but in downtime they'd swap stories and ideas for improvements. After nearly being caught by the courting couple, Andy Kerslake taught himself how to use the topography and shadows to completely secrete himself away: all he needed was a garden, a shadow or a car and then he could vanish in a flash – a self-taught master of disappearance.

Chris Gould made both fixed point and mobile observations. There was only so long he could spend looking in estate agent windows as cover, so he needed to change his tack. He found bus shelters a particularly useful tool. Waiting for a bus, reading a timetable, looking at an advert, even pretending to be annoyed at yobs who might have graffitied the shelter or smashed a window. He would have a reason to be there, on the eastern side of Whiteladies Road, with one eye on the female form walking on the western pavement.

John O'Connor also performed undercover work. He was one of the few who already had several years of covert experience under his belt. Between walks, he would regale other observation officers with stories of when he had been a street-theft decoy in St Paul's and had been held up at knifepoint. They'd seen his microphone under his coat, realised he was a cop and fled. O'Connor chased the offenders to a Greek Orthodox church, where the minister pointed out two scared teenagers hiding under a bush.

'At the trial, I came face-to-face with a man, a six-foot-six black guy, who utterly terrified me,' O'Connor would recall to younger observation officers. 'He asked if I was the one who'd arrested his son. I said "Yes" and he shook me by the hand, said his son was out of control and needed locking up.'

John's favourite technique as a mobile observation man was to use an umbrella. Great in winter, even useful in British summertime, all you needed was to tilt it one way to keep eyes on the subject, tilt it just a fraction the other to hide your face. Just a subtle lean one way or another was enough to watch and remain hidden.

The weeks were passing, January slipping into February. Although techniques were being honed, the decoy walks being run, there was no sign of the Clifton Rapist. Time was not on Operation Argus's side. A total of 12 women were going out as decoys. Two a night, with backup teams on the streets, in vans and in offices. PCs and detectives were drawn in from other divisions to help man phones or observation points. More than 200 officers were involved in the case, one way or another. The cost was exorbitant, the results negligible, and with every week that passed, Chief Constable Kenneth Steele was closer to his retirement with this monster at liberty.

No one can recall who came up with the operation's craziest idea, but after a few short weeks a new strand of Argus was suggested and approved. It would take the hunt for the Clifton Rapist into a whole new level of covert creativity.

CHAPTER TWENTY-TWO

Chris Gould noticed a strange vibe from the top brass as he sat down in the small briefing room. Nothing he could put his finger on, but Malcolm Popperwell was exuding a strange edginess. He looked around as the dozen or so seats started to be filled by a few PCs: all men, all young, Chris realised.

'There's no other way of saying this, gents, but we're running out of time with Op Argus. Also, the Chief is terrified that one of the girls is going to get hurt. They're bait, they're in the line of fire. All of the attacks have been on the side streets and most of the walk is on Whiteladies Road. We now think the chances of him attacking there are so slight that we want to start a second strand to the operation. We need to trap this man in *his* world, in the dark corners where he operates.'

'Are you suggesting we move the girls to the side streets?' asked Robbie Jones.

'No, no ... that's far too risky.'

'So, you're going to put men there?'

'Yes.'

'But he doesn't attack men.'

'That's right. But these men, these decoys won't ...' – there was a pause before Popperwell said it – 'look like men.'

'You want men to dress up as women?' snorted someone.

'Yes. And we're asking for volunteers.'

'No way,' said one of the PCs. A couple of the other officers said that there might be snow on the ground but hell, as well as Bristol, would have to freeze over before they wore drag to catch a rapist.

Chris looked around. Robbie Jones seemed unpersuaded, but more positive than the others, who appeared dead against the plan.

'I'll do it,' said Chris, as he felt the eyes of his colleagues turn towards him.

Chris Gould looked in the mirror and started applying a pale cream onto his just-shaven cheeks. He was sitting at his wife's make-up table. She had given him some basic tips. And her green skirt and roll-neck jumper were laid out on their bed behind him. He didn't question why he was doing this. As he rubbed in the foundation, there was no doubt in his mind, this was something he *had* to do.

Robbie Jones had also volunteered. And somehow the top brass had persuaded eight other extremely reluctant men to wear women's clothes to be decoys.

Chris thought about what he would face in the hours ahead: a freezing-cold night, a dusting of snow and walking in his wife's wedge heels. He had spent a few hours practising in them at home. It had been tricky at first – the heels weren't high, just a couple of inches, but enough to feel like a completely different way of walking. But after a little while he had got used to the technique.

Next came the powder. Then eye shadow, eye-liner, mascara and lipstick. He felt different, but he didn't feel transformed. Underneath the make-up he was still PC Chris Gould.

He turned to the bed, pulled on a pair of tights and his wife's skirt, which reached to the top of his shins, then strapped on a bra padded with odd socks. Now for the jumper. Chris had chosen a roll-neck as protection against the attacker's throat-grip and as a means of concealing the cable which led to his earpiece.

He slipped on a second jumper, a V-neck, just to keep him warm. After this, he looped the transmitter from the radio in his wife's handbag. He tapped the brooch on the coat, which was his microphone. Then he put on his wig. It was a blonde hairpiece, shoulder-length and flicked at the front. As he looked back at his reflection in the mirror, he didn't know quite what to think, but it didn't matter: he was doing this for a reason. He reached down, flipped open a container of rouge and dusted some on his cheeks.

Chris then slipped on his wife's size-eight sling-back shoes. By chance, his feet were just a single size larger and the straps offered enough give for him to wear them. He walked out of the bedroom. As he went down the stairs, he noticed how different his steps sounded in women's foot-wear.

His wife was walking out of the kitchen and did a double-take: 'Oh, Chris, no! Get out. Go. This is so creepy.'

He opened the door and left the house.

Chris's home was one of a string of police houses built soon after the Second World War. He walked up the path to his car and bumped into a neighbour, who had retired from the force five years earlier.

'Alright, my love?' said the neighbour.

Chris nodded in relief. Perhaps his disguise was believable. He waved, got in his car and drove off for his first shift as a decoy in drag.

The bar in Redland Police Station was always busy on a Friday night. The day shift had finished, and detectives and uniformed officers sat around tables supping pints of beer while ashtrays gradually filled with stubbed-out butts. The conversation flitted from office politics, crazy arrest stories, gossip about new starters in the Police Women's Unit to rueful nods about ex-colleagues who had recently died.

'Heart of Glass' was on the speakers. Even the older detectives had an opinion about what they would like to do with Debbie Harry. Then on came the current number one: Ian Dury and The Blockheads' 'Hit Me With Your Rhythm Stick' – the title had already been adapted by some officers who were readier to use their truncheon than others. Then in came Robbie Jones: Police Constable, fly-half for the force rugby team. But tonight he was in full drag as a decoy operative on Operation Argus. He wore a woollen hat, a long wig, a tight green jumper and a patterned ankle-length skirt.

The conversation stopped, as did the clinking of glasses. Jaws dropped. The only sound came from the speaker, Ian Dury's London talk-singing: 'hit me, hit me, hit me …'

'Pint of Courage, Dave,' said Robbie in his deep Bristolian accent.

CHAPTER TWENTY-TWO

'You need more of a *pint* of Courage, Rob,' came the reply.

Then it started: 'You want coconut round the rim of that pint, Robbie?'

'Are you Robbie or Roberta?'

'Shouldn't that be a Babycham, Rob?'

Robbie rarely drank before a night shift but no sergeant was going to tell him off for a cheeky pint before going out in drag. The comments kept coming as Robbie sipped his beer. After he had drained the glass, he bowed to the Redland Police bar and made an exit, stumbling slightly in his heels.

'He's a lucky fella, your man, Rob,' came a shout as Jones raised a finger to the closing door.

Now Operation Argus boasted two strands. Every Wednesday, Thursday, Friday and Saturday night, female decoys were deployed, either from Steph Whittle's flat near Whiteladies Road or from a Task Force van. At the same time, a male decoy in drag started a long route through the back streets and alleyways. Some nights they walked more than six miles in heels.

Chris watched the other men dressed as women before they left for their run. Robbie Jones could just about get away with it, he thought. But the others were hopeless. None of them wanted to be dressed in drag and this added to their discomfort as their big frames squeezed into tight skirts and they tottered out in shoes which really didn't fit.

The wigs were hysterical.

They would return with stories of how their feet hurt because of 'those bloody shoes' or how they'd been approached by a guy who'd asked if they were a bloke.

In these less enlightened times 'Fucking tranny!' was shouted at more than one of the male decoys.

Quickly, the men started to give up: the humiliation was too much, they hated the idea of being exposed in public and just couldn't get over their colleagues joking about it all the time. And the officers couldn't compel anyone to do this kind of job. Chris, meanwhile, seemed able to make it work. He had invested so much time, effort and energy in getting the right clothes and walking the correct way that he seemed impervious to the failure other decoys had suffered. He could even manage a few words in a higher register to try and get him out of trouble if approached.

Within a week, the number of male decoys had been whittled down from ten to two: rugby player Robbie Jones and judo champion Chris Gould. They had staying power, perseverance and an ability to ignore the hounding they received from colleagues on a daily basis. In truth, Malcolm Popperwell was surprised that as many as two men carried on.

One night before a decoy run, Chris went into the bar at Redland Police Station, dressed as a woman. He approached a colleague who had been particularly tough on him, watching as the PC's face lit up at the unexpected and unprovoked female attention.

Chris said hello in a high-pitched voice, held the man's hand for a moment, pecked him on the cheek and left. It was only when the bar-room exploded in fits of laughter that the PC realised who the mystery woman had been.

Both Chris Gould and Robbie Jones had joined the police seeking a life less ordinary: excitement, adventure and variety but surely when they had filled out their application forms, neither of them quite had *this* in mind.

Michelle Tighe was alone in her flat in the north Bristol suburb of Westbury-on-Trym. She had finished a day on the Police Women's Unit, which had involved a care case and the processing of a woman shoplifter. She had also rejected the advances of two married detectives.

'These birds are getting harder to pull, Geoff,' she heard one say to another as she left the CID room in Redland Police Station.

She shared the large flat with two other members of the Police Women's Unit: Jean Castle and Jackie Clair. Three women in their early twenties in a flat within five minutes' walking distance of eight pubs. It was known within C-Division as a party flat. Often people would drop in unannounced but tonight was a rare Friday night for Michelle to be alone. Both Jean and Jackie were making decoy runs for Operation Argus.

She had eaten her tea, pulled out the ironing board and went to find her just-laundered uniform blouses. Coming back into the room, she switched on the TV, a recent acquisition from Radio Rentals. There was a musical sting and a blue graphic with white writing, which said 'HTV News'. A man and a woman appeared behind a large desk.

The first news report was about the strike negotiations. Bristol's gravediggers were considering whether to go out on strike like their compatriots in Liverpool. The authorities up north were talking about families of the dead being allowed to dig graves, or perhaps even burials at sea. Then the weather man popped up, earlier than usual in the show, talking about how there was little chance of the cold spell ending soon.

'And now …' continued the newsreader in his posh voice, 'campaigners ask what are Avon and Somerset Police doing to catch the Clifton Rapist?'

The woman newsreader spoke next: 'The Bristol suburb has seen at least nine attacks attributed to the man over the last 18 months.'

Michelle started ironing the sleeves of her blouse.

The male presenter picked up: 'Police say they are doing everything they can. Well, now a national campaign group, Women Against Rape, has come to the city to highlight what it says is the force's failure to catch one of Britain's most wanted men. Here's our reporter, Ken Rees.'

The footage cut to pictures of women dancing in night-clubs in short skirts and platform heels. The commentator mentioned how popular the city of Bristol was for its night-life.

A man with a brown moustache and beard combo appeared on screen.

'But for the last 18 months, a man has been preying on women as they've walked through the darkened streets by Whiteladies Road. There seems to be no pattern to when he attacks – sometimes they happen in clusters, other times he goes quiet for months. But he is, campaigners say, one step ahead of police.'

The reporter began talking to a woman with red, curly

The disappearance of Kathleen Heathcote was front-page news in November 1963. The *Daily Mirror* reported on the search for her body in Ladybower Reservoir.

Kathleen Heathcote vanished on the night of 21 November 1963. She was last seen getting off a bus near her home in Mansfield, Nottinghamshire, after seeing her boyfriend.

Kathleen with her parents, Harry and Edith, and her nephew Tim. Edith normally picked Kathleen up from the bus stop but was prevented from doing so that night by a storm.

The murder trial in 1964 made headlines across the country. This was the first time the defendant had given his version of events of the night he killed Kathleen. The jury didn't believe him.

By the time of the attack on Joanna McGarry in March 1978, the assaults on women were front-page news in Bristol and beyond.

December 1978: anti-rape groups across Britain focus on Bristol and the police's inability to catch the attacker.

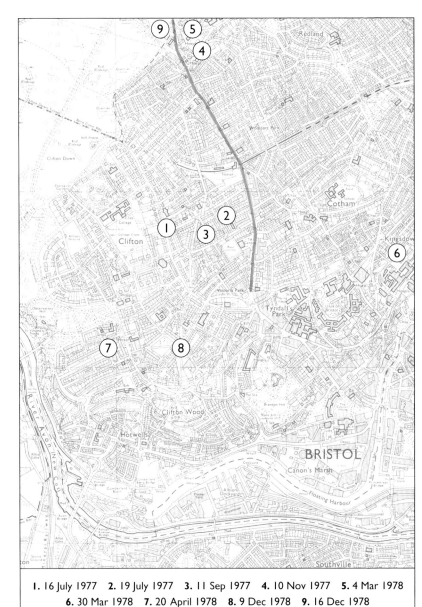

1. 16 July 1977   2. 19 July 1977   3. 11 Sep 1977   4. 10 Nov 1977   5. 4 Mar 1978
6. 30 Mar 1978   7. 20 April 1978   8. 9 Dec 1978   9. 16 Dec 1978

None of the attacks happened on Whiteladies Road, but all of the victims
had walked along the main street in the moments beforehand. All the
attacks took place late at night or early in the morning, but there
was no pattern to when in the calendar they occurred.

WPC Michelle Tighe was 23 years old in 1979, making her one of the older decoys. She had joined the force the previous year and had gained a reputation as a 'go-getter'.

WPC Stephanie Whittle joined the force after winning two awards as a cadet in 1976. She lived just to the east of Whiteladies Road and her flat was one of the bases for Operation Argus sorties. She was 20 when Operation Argus began in January 1979.

PC Chris Gould (left), 20, suggested the plan for Operation Argus to his sergeant, but he had no idea that months later he would be asked to dress in drag. He arrested 36 men while dressed as a decoy. Rugby player PC Robbie Jones (right) was the only other male officer who stayed the course on Operation Argus.

Steph Whittle making door-to-door enquiries after the attack on Rachel Doulton in Clifton Village, April 1978.

'We didn't think twice when we were asked to volunteer,' said WPC Sally Difazio, who had joined Avon and Somerset Police a year before Operation Argus was launched. 'It was our job to protect life and property. We thought it would be exciting.'

The face from the headlines and the face of a killer. The photo-fit images bore a striking resemblance to the man who was caught in March 1979, a murderer released on life licence.

Kenneth Steele with the female Operation Argus decoys. He had
won a King's Police Medal for pulling a woman from a burning house
in the 1930s and by January 1979 was the country's longest-serving
chief constable. Here he presents Michelle with an award,
with Steph, Sally and the other decoys standing behind.

In the words of a judge at
the Old Bailey: 'Still a danger
to women.' Britain's longest-
serving prisoner was returned
to jail again at the age of 82
in November 2023 after
being convicted of another
sexual assault. The Met
Police couldn't find him
on the Police National
Computer and he was only
arrested after his victim
saw my documentary
on television.

hair from the group Women Against Rape: 'What is happening in Bristol is a disgrace,' she said. 'Nine women's lives have been changed forever by one man. But what are police doing? They say they've made an arrest or two. They've put a few officers in uniform out on the streets but still the attacks are happening.'

The film cut to a shot of Durdham Down, which the reporter flagged as the scene of the latest attack, six weeks ago. Michelle knew he was talking about Anna Soltys. She carried on pressing away at her blouse.

Artist-impression images of the Clifton Rapist appeared, some with the handlebar moustache, others without, before Chief Constable Kenneth Steele came on screen, in uniform, in his office.

'Well, catching this man is one of the force's top priorities,' he said in his clipped militaristic tones to the reporter. 'We have teams working round the clock following hundreds of leads. And we are also asking women to take preventative action, to not go out by themselves, just until we have apprehended him.'

The report cut back to the campaigner: 'Women have a right to walk where they want, when they want, without fear of danger or molestation. I just think the police don't have the determination, the wit or the innovation to think how this kind of monster thinks. They may have the resources, but I don't think shoving a few uniformed officers out on Whiteladies Road is the answer. This is a failure of catastrophic proportions by Avon and Somerset Police.'

Michelle finished pressing her blouse. She hung it in her wardrobe, next to the outfit she planned to wear on her decoy run the following night. But from the lounge she could still hear the reporter's voice: 'Already the city's night-clubs are reporting a drop in business because women are not coming out at night. But what about those who do? And those who walk alone at night? Despite warnings from police, women continue to go out by themselves, they continue to take risks. And leading detectives tell me it's a question of if, not when, he will strike again. And they genuinely fear he might develop from assaulting women to killing them.'

CHAPTER TWENTY-THREE

WEDNESDAY, 27 NOVEMBER 1963

There's a click and a clunk and The Driver springs around. He's jumpy these days. *Very* jumpy. He notices a bead of sweat on his back and feels a reddening in his cheeks. He looks at his toaster, which has just popped up a couple of slices of bread. He breathes out – his wife must have put them in.

The radio's started playing music again. For the last few days it's been wall-to-wall news about dead presidents but now the station controllers must have started allowing music again. For once this year, The Beatles are not at number one, but another Scouser has claimed the top spot. The little transistor radio in the kitchen blares out 'You'll Never Walk Alone' by Gerry and the Pacemakers.

But he *is* alone.

His wife may be fussing around, getting the bedroom ready for the baby. His mother-in-law may be a near-permanent fixture, fussing over his wife fussing around getting the bedroom ready for the baby.

But he is alone.

He can't tell anyone what he's done.

Anyone.

He tries to hide from the mental images but they flash back. He'll be doing something normal and an image of that girl either on the waste ground or in the boot of the car, or just before he ... Well, he can't think too much about *that*.

His wife comes into the kitchen and asks if he can butter the toast and pop some jam on too. 'Thanks, love,' she adds, heading back to the settee.

He hears a rustling of newspapers and her mother starts off: 'They still haven't found that girl yet, have they? Heard they were diving in some reservoir over Newark way.'

The Driver starts buttering the toast and turns up Gerry Marsden.

'Who would do summat like that? She were gonna get married next year, poor girl,' says his wife.

He brings the toast into the front room and hands the plate to his wife but he doesn't offer his mother-in-law anything.

There's a knock at the door.

The Driver spins around. Through the frosted glass he can see the outline of a man in dark blue. He looks through to the kitchen: there's a back door there. He can be out of the house, down the alley and away in seconds. But if they've got 100 police on this murder, surely they'd have backup? Cops surrounding the house?

'You going to get it?' asks his wife, frowning.

The Driver turns to her in her floral maternity dress, biting a jam-covered crust. Then he looks at his mother-in-law.

'Might be easier if you get it?' she says, a questioning look in her eye.

The Driver looks at the door: the dark blue figure is just waiting. He looks again at his wife and heads to the door. He closes his eyes, takes a deep breath and opens the door.

'It's an awkward one,' grins the postman, holding up a large package. Looks like there's a magazine inside. 'Think it's about babies. Won't be long now? A month?' He passes The Driver the package. 'Think you need to get a bigger letterbox,' he grins, pointing to the small brass flap in the front door.

'Well, bet you've got other things on your mind.' He grins again.

Christ, this man is a gurning fool, thinks The Driver.

The postman says goodbye, turns around and starts up the garden path.

The Driver looks down at the package.

'Oh hiya,' he hears the postman say. He looks up and sees two policemen walking towards him.

'Alright, pal?' says one.

The older one must be in his early forties. He wears a suit, tie and trench coat. The other one is young, is in uniform and has ginger hair.

The Driver recognises him immediately.

CHAPTER TWENTY-FOUR

Chris Gould's feet were killing him. He was reaching the end of his second run of the night and he must have done nearly eight miles in heels. He had just emerged from the dark network of side streets which led from Clifton Village and was on Apsley Road. Up ahead, he could see the bright lights of Whiteladies Road.

An observation officer was two corners away, he knew, but he was on his own for now. *How do women wear these shoes all the time?* he asked himself for what must have been about the hundredth time that night. On the opposite side of the road, a street lamp beamed down a yellow-orange glow onto a line of five or six cars parked by a terrace of houses.

Ten more minutes till a cup of tea, thought Chris.

By now, he had become accustomed to the sounds of the night, the nocturnal orchestra: the normal patter of people's feet on pavements, the passing of cars, the hubbub from inside pubs, the flushing of toilets from inside homes, even. He also knew how to recognise the sounds that were not part of the normal symphony. When he heard these, his spider-sensors started to prickle. And he was sure he could hear something that wasn't quite right.

Chris took a breath and slowed his pace. He tried to look subtly ahead without appearing to search out the noise.

What was that sound? A whisper?

He glanced over again and saw a figure behind a car ahead, in the road. His heart started racing. He slowed his pace along the pavement. Ahead, in the light, he could see the bump of someone's head. Now he could distinctly hear a whisper.

And then a second head popped up.

Two pairs of eyes looked at Chris. He glanced quickly at them, trying to get a clear view of their faces, before looking ahead as a woman on her own at night would do.

Two men. Both in their twenties. One had a round face, blond or fair hair and a beard. The second was darker. He had a moustache but couldn't quite work out if it was a handlebar moustache.

Chris carried on further. Suddenly the tiredness in his legs had vanished. He heard a scraping, a rattling, metal-on-metal. As he drew level with the car, he took one more glance. He clocked that it was a brown Morris Marina: the men had sunk back down behind the car.

Chris strained his ears. Then he heard: 'Don't worry, it's just some bird.' But then he heard another metallic rattle, rattle, rattle. He wondered what to do – he couldn't take them on by himself, but also, he couldn't let them get away with stealing someone's car.

He carried on click-clicking along the pavement.

When he was far enough away from the car, he pushed the button on his microphone kit: 'Two males attempting to steal a brown Morris Marina halfway down Apsley Road, on the south side. By Number 32. Request Task Force backup.'

Chris click-clicked up to a large pillar which marked the entrance to one of the grand houses and waited behind it. The Task Force must have been just a few streets away – he saw the unmarked van fly down Apsley Road and heard the thumps as doors opened. There were shouts – Chris wasn't sure whose shouts they were – and he started to jog as quickly as he could towards the van.

Two men ran towards him, one heading to his right, the other in his direction before suddenly darting left down a side street. The Task Force guys were chasing the man heading towards Whiteladies Road.

Chris kicked off his heels and started sprinting in his stockinged feet after the man to his left. The man was about 50 yards ahead of him, running flat out. Chris could make out the condensation from the man's breath pumping from his lungs in the cold night. He was thankful the road wasn't cobbled and was starting to catch the man up.

Was this the blond man? Or the one with the moustache?

Chris kept up the pace, he could feel his legs flying underneath. He was 40 yards behind now.

The man spun back. *Was that a look of fear on his face?*

Chris kept up the pace, kept gaining ground.

The man glanced back again. Chris noticed the look on the man's face had changed. The fear seemed to have gone, but what was that expression?

Bewilderment?

Chris looked back too and saw two Task Force officers were following him after the man.

About 20 yards behind now.

Ahead was an alleyway that Chris knew well – he had walked it in heels on the last three nights. Now he was sprinting towards it in hot pursuit of a man who was guilty of who-knew-what. Attempted car theft definitely. But rapists tend to have convictions for other crimes, he knew.

Who was this man?

Ten yards.

The man was slowing.

Five yards.

The man looked back, his face an odd mixture of white fear and crazed bafflement.

Chris was an arm's length away – he had to do it now. He leapt and rugby-tackled the man, bringing him down to the ground with a thud.

'Get off me, you crazy fucking bitch!' the man yelled.

The two Task Force officers caught up and silently cuffed the guy. As they led him away, one of them was reading him his caution.

Chris stood under the street lamp in his stockinged feet, watching as the man was led away, occasionally looking back at him. After checking his wig hadn't slipped, the fiction hadn't been revealed, he started back up the hill.

PC Joe Harford was 19 years old. He had just passed his probation, to the surprise of everyone including himself. Originally from the quiet farming town of Yeovil, he had been posted to Bristol and struggled with city life. He was awkward and had an appalling knack of getting things wrong. These features, combined with a strong Somerset accent, gave his city-sharp colleagues all the ammunition they needed for his nickname:

'Oi, Slow-Joe! Watch out for that big thing on the street. It's called a bus – we 'ave 'em in cities.'

'Oi, Slow-Joe! I've never seen a bumpkin on the beat.'

At first, 'Slow-Joe' Harford wasn't trusted with observation work but as the weeks dragged on, the need for PCs to sit in the cold grew and so this accident-prone, bumbling, forgetful rookie was asked to take part. But Joe had somehow managed to last three weeks on Operation Argus without blowing the whole thing. Again, this achievement surpassed everyone's expectations … including his own.

By mid-February 1979, he had been with Alpha Four for a few weeks, every night in the same spot: a bush on the corner of Whiteladies Road. He had found the first evening cold but thrilling, the second night cold but exciting, and the third night onwards just cold. The same sights every night, the same sounds every night, the same freezing-cold temperature *every* night.

Around this time, Sergeant Kelvin Hattersley held a briefing in Southmead Police Station. He had some welcome news: 'Okay, we're trying a new route tonight. Starting from Steph's flat, we're going from Whiteladies Road but through Clifton Village.'

He had a map with pins in: 'Joe, you're Alpha Four again, but you're in the stretch of green here: Birdcage Walk.'

Joe was not the quickest on the uptake, but he detected a snigger from within the room. Later, he walked through the snow-dusted pavements of Clifton Village and found a railing and a big metal gate with a sign saying Birdcage Walk.

CHAPTER TWENTY-FOUR

Sounds quite nice, he thought.

Behind the gate was just black. He slid the gate slightly; it made a gentle scraping sound, metal-on-metal hinge, and he slipped inside. The only light was behind him from the streets of Clifton Village.

He reached into his pocket and pulled out a torch. After fumbling for a moment, he found the switch and flicked it on.

Shit.

He dropped the torch.

It clattered to the ground, but the beam of light thrown up showed the marble crosses and broken tombs of a grave-yard.

He swore again. Picking up the torch, he placed his hand over it to reduce the light. He needed to find a spot near the edge of the graveyard, so he could watch the decoys on the road but far enough from the main street to keep hidden.

Joe climbed over a low rail separating the pathway from the graveyard and picked his way between tombstones, grave plots and burial slabs. It was overgrown and the snow hid brambles and thorns. He kept cutting his legs in the undergrowth. Finally, he managed to find a spot between a tombstone and a broken Celtic cross, where he turned off his torch, hunkered down and kept a watch.

After about a half an hour, he heard that WPC Cathy Holbrook had been deployed and she had made her way between Alphas One and Three. He heard a click-clicking coming from his right but even he could tell that this wasn't the decoy: two pairs of feet, neither sounded female. Sure enough, he heard two voices, both men. He couldn't make out what they were saying, but the tone was conspiratorial. Then he heard a creak.

The gate, thought Joe, *they've come in through the gate. I've got two blokes in the graveyard with me.*

Before he could consider his next steps, Joe heard another pair of feet on the pavement. As he tried to concentrate on his breathing to slow his heart, he noticed beads of sweat trying to freeze as they trickled down the back of his neck. He held himself back from the rails and saw Cathy Holbrook sweep past.

'Alpha Four, subject in view,' he said in his microphone.

'AM I IN VIEW TOO?'

He spun around to see a white spectre looming above a tombstone: a sheet with a head and a pair of arms waving about underneath it. The head was also wearing a policeman's hat and someone had drawn a face on the sheet. Somewhere to the right, a torch was playing on this DIY-phantom.

'Fuck off, fuck off!' shouted Joe.

'Woooo, woooo! There are some scary things in the big city, Slow-Joe. Not like this in the sticks, is it?' said the ghost.

'Get the fuck away!'

'Can I be your Alpha Five?'

Then it disappeared. Joe heard a rustling, a patter of steps and a cackling.

PC Joe Harford continued in the same position for three more weeks. He never discovered which of his colleagues had performed as the ghost. Part of him wondered if they had chosen this route just so he would have to spend hours in a cemetery. He tried to make the best of what he called 'The Graveyard Shift', studying the names of the people who had been laid to rest in this quiet spot in Clifton. Sometimes he would make up stories about what they had done in their lives. There was no way of knowing, but what he lacked in policing ability, he made up for with his creative imagination.

One night he did make a discovery. As he threaded through the tombstones to his observation point by the railings, he nearly tripped over a burial plate. Passing his torch over it, he saw the inscription: 'Joseph Harford, died June 26th 1881, aged 64 years'.

CHAPTER TWENTY-FIVE

Steph Whittle had now lost count of how many decoy runs she had made. It was towards the end of February 1979. The snow still falling, though more sporadically than the previous month. Five weeks had passed with no Clifton Rapist and no more attacks on women. It was gone midnight and not for the first time she wondered quite what she was doing with her life.

Her friends were in the Mandrake Club, dancing, having a good time and perhaps even meeting guys. She was walking in snow on a deserted street. There was no one around: just Steph and her observation boys.

'Alpha Three, subject in sight.'

Steph had got used to the radio traffic now.

She saw her reflection in a shop window: she looked tired and drawn, as if she had aged a few years in the last few weeks. The excitement of being a covert officer had quickly dissipated and now it was just a drag. The only thing that kept Steph going, the *only* thing, was the idea that she might catch the Clifton Rapist.

It was a quarter to some ungodly hour on a Thursday morning and she could think of a hundred places she would rather be.

'Alpha Four, subject in sight.'

Yes, Alpha Four, followed by Alpha Five, followed by the Task Force van, followed by sitting, waiting, for her next run.

I'm in the prime of my bloody life, she thought to herself.

'The only people out at this time are cops and villains,' Sergeant Kelvin Hattersley had told her.

Behind, she heard the approach of a car's engine. She looked to her right as a yellow Ford Cortina slowed and pulled to a stop next to the pavement. Steph felt a pang. She thought back to all the reports in which a yellow car had been seen in the moments after an attack.

Concentrate, she told herself. *Be careful. Try to remember everything.*

Steph saw the silhouette of a person in the driving seat lean to his left as the passenger window wound down.

'Hello there. Hi?' It was a man in his early thirties. He didn't quite look like the photo-fits, but wasn't a million miles away from them either. 'I'm a bit lost. Do you know how to get to Durdham Park?' he said.

Steph tried to place his accent. She was sure it was Bristolian but there was a tinge of something else to it.

'Er, yes,' she said. 'You go to the top of this road, turn right and bear left.'

She realised this was the first time she had spoken with anyone while out on the run. It was strange to hear her own voice again.

'Top of the road, turn left and bear right,' he said back to her.

'No, right then left, follow the Downs, head towards Westbury-on-Trym,' she replied.

'Oh, I'm not sure,' he said. 'Where are you headed?'

Steph slipped her hand into her pocket and pressed the microphone.

'I'm just heading home,' she told him.

'Hop on in, I'll give you a lift.'

'It's okay, I'm nearly there.'

'Look, it's cold – too cold to be out. Jump in.'

Steph's brain was in overdrive.

What am I supposed to do? You should never, ever get into any car.

She leaned down, trying to get a better view of the man. He was white, in his late twenties or early thirties, dark hair, clean-shaven, and she noticed an earring in his left ear.

'I'm not getting in your car,' she said.

'Please get in, I'll worry about you. Look, it's snowing.'

'For the last time, leave me alone.'

'Your loss, sweetheart.'

Steph heard a rev of an engine and the Cortina zoomed off up Whiteladies Road. She took a note of the registration plate.

'Did you get that?' she said into the radio.

'Affirmative,' came a crackle from Control.

The morning after, Steph Whittle was shattered. It was official. She had just crawled into the Police Women's Unit office and was expecting Carol Curnock to offer a degree of sympathy but she was completely taken aback by the pale look on her sergeant's face that fell somewhere between aghast and terrified.

'You okay, Carol?'

'Steph … you got a minute?'

She led Steph out from the office and into the corridor. A couple of uniformed PCs walked past. Carol waited for them to go, then said: 'You were approached by a man in a yellow Ford Cortina this morning, weren't you?'

'Yes.'

'And you took down the registration number?'

'Yes. Carol?'

Her mind was starting to whirr.

Carol looked down at a slip of paper and read out the licence number.

'Yes, that's right. What's this about?' said Steph.

'We have a woman in Redland Police Station. She said she was walking home alone in the early hours. This car pulls up and the driver pulled out a gun. He forced her in the car, told her he'd kill her and forced her to have sex with him – he raped her. Do you know how close you came?'

'Is she okay?'

'No, she's not – she's terrified. But she got the licence number and she came forward. We've located him and we've got arrest teams going to his house now.'

'Do we think he's the Clifton Rapist?'

'Not sure. Doubtful. But we're going to need you to do the ID parade.'

Hours later, Steph Whittle found herself in the Redland Inquiry office, waiting outside the line-up room. Her mind was fizzing with thoughts: 'What if I get the wrong man? Will there be a prosecution? What if I cock this up? A woman's justice is riding on me …'

'You okay, Steph?'

It was a CID detective.

'Not really.'

'The guy we arrested, he's got no previous, but when we searched his car we found an imitation firearm in the boot. We just need you to positively ID him.'

More pressure, thought Steph.

'Are you ready?'

She nodded.

He guided her into the line-up room, where eight white men stood. All in their thirties, they had a vague similarity. Steph went to the one on the furthest left, looked him up and down. She peered at him, making sure she took her time – she wasn't sure about this one.

Then to the man on his right.

My god, it was so dark, this is a light room. Everything's so different.

Then to the third man and the fourth.

It's the hardest thing I've ever done, I can't get this wrong, she thought, as she slowly made her way along the parade.

The fifth man had a little stubble. He was similar, for sure. Then she remembered the earring. Yes, he had a gold stud in his left ear. She looked into his eyes and he glanced away at the wall behind.

The sixth man was definitely not the rapist. But the seventh also had some straggly facial hair. Eight was a definite no.

Steph stood back, looked at all eight men. Then she went to the fifth man and tapped him on his shoulder. He stared down at her, daggers drawn, his stubbled face curled into a sneer.

'Fucking pig,' he growled.

'Well done, that's enough to charge,' said the detective after the seven men had been freed to go and one charged with rape and possession of an imitation firearm. Having the reg was important, but that positive identification was the icing on the cake.

'I must say, Steph, normally people doing the ID parades race up and down and then leg it as quickly as possible – I've never seen anyone spend so much time studying suspects. Good work.'

CHAPTER TWENTY-SIX

27 NOVEMBER 1963

The room is dirty and bleak and The Driver can't quite work out how long he's been here alone.

Half an hour? Two hours? Ten minutes?

Time seems to stand still here.

For what seems like the hundredth time, he counts the square grey tiles on the wall. Eight across, twelve up. One door, locked. A contraption with a hole, something that might pass for a toilet …

One bed, he's sitting on it.

One crisis, he's in it.

They had to do it in front of his wife. Do they have no class, these people?

He counts the tiles again and time passes.

Half an hour? Two hours? Ten minutes?

Two pairs of footsteps head towards the door but they pass and he can make out a metallic screech as another cell door opens. There's a gruff chatter, more metallic screeching and the steps fade away.

What did they find?

What did he have on him?

There's a clink, a screech and the cell door opens. A

uniformed officer he's not seen before says, 'Okay, son. They're ready for you.'

He gets up, perhaps too quickly – does he seem too eager? Then he follows the man out. The Driver is led down the corridor to an interview room: the door is open and two men are inside. One is the guy who arrested him, he doesn't recognise the other one. They greet him coldly by his name, but he's not thinking about that. He can't really hear what they're saying – he's just watching their mouths move, knowing that what he says in the next few minutes will change the course of his life.

He hadn't heard their names. In his spinning head, he's calling them 'Man One' and 'Man Two'.

'Okay, we can do this the easy way or the hard way. Kathleen Heathcote's murder has made national headlines, it's a big deal. You've killed her, we know that,' says Man One. 'As we speak, two detectives from Scotland Yard are on a train north to interview you.'

Man Two: 'You know where Scotland Yard is, don't you?'

Man One: 'London.'

Man Two: '*Metropolitan* Police.'

Man One: 'They deal with the biggest criminals in the country every day. You know, murderers, bank robbers, fraudsters, gangsters.'

Man Two: 'Not like us in our little force.'

Man One: 'For your sake, I'd urge you to tell us everything. We'll be kinder to you, softer. More understanding.'

Man Two: 'They'll eat you alive.'

Man One: 'Tell us where Kathleen is.'

Man Two: 'It'll be better for you.'

The Driver finds himself saying, 'I want to see my wife.'

Man Two: 'We can't go dragging her into this, not in her condition.'

Man One: 'Things aren't looking good for yer. One of our colleagues saw you with yer stuck car the day after Kathleen vanished. You told him it span off the road the night before in that rain storm. We have proof you were out. He's writing that in an official statement as we speak – he just had an odd feeling about you.'

Man Two: 'Very odd.'

Man One: 'He might be young, but he's got a bit of savvy. Took your number plate. You'll have guessed we got your address through that.'

Man Two: 'But the bigger problem for you is that your car's tyres match marks not only at Skegby Sands, where you got stuck, but also at the waste ground at Princes Street in Mansfield, where our lassie was last seen.'

Man One: 'She's just got off the bus, she were seen.'

Man Two: 'Yeah, minutes before. We've got witnesses.'

Man One: 'But the really bad news for you is what we found in your house. We searched yer car and her purse is in the boot. Bit of mud in there too.'

Man Two: 'The back seat's been cleaned. You did a good job with that, well done. But you didn't clean the boot and you left her purse in it.'

Man One: 'And we found that dry cleaning ticket in your wallet. You had a bit of bad luck with that – because the cleaner hadn't got round to doing yer trousers yet and the mud on 'em matches that wasteland. Christ, you were proper covered in that shit, weren't yer?'

The Driver can see no way out. These two guys whose names he doesn't know, with their irritating grim faces and sing-song voices, have him in a trap. He takes a breath: should he say anything, is there any way out?

'I didn't intend to murder her,' he tells them.

Man One: 'You've admitted attacking her now. That's a big step. Tell us what happened.'

The Driver finds himself talking: 'I'd been to a dance. At the colliery. And I'd had a drink – you know, a few.'

Man One is writing notes now. Meanwhile, Man Two asks: 'How many?'

'About six pints of bitter and three lagers.'

Both men raise their eyebrows and say nothing.

'I saw her as I were driving back. And yeah, I approached her. I, well, can't really remember what happened. I had intercourse with her there and then in Princes Street. When she screamed, I must've put me hand over her mouth. Must've lost control. She went limp and I panicked …

'I put her on the back seat and drove off. I was gonna take her to hospital, gonna get her some help … She were on the back seat and started groaning. I turned to look at her and the car span out. I were stuck – it were her fault. It were raining, raining hard. I needed to get home to the wife – she's pregnant – so I put her in the boot and went home.

'Next day, I went to the car, looked in the boot. It hadn't hit me whether she was dead or not. I couldn't believe it: she *were* dead. The car got towed. I couldn't go to work the next day, felt too bad. I didn't tell anyone, didn't tell the wife.'

The two men are just looking at him, impassively now.

'I thought, where can I take her? Ladybower was the first place that came into my head.'

Man Two: 'Ladybower Reservoir?'

'Yeah.'

'I drove to Ladybower, took some clothing off her. I thought, *If I'm making a job of it, I'll do it right.*'

The Driver looks at Man One's notepad and sees 'Ladybower' written in bold. He carries on with his confession: 'I didn't throw her in straight away. I drove off to Glossop and sat in the car – I was all of a shake. Then I thought, *It's no good having it in the car. I've got to get rid of it somewhere.*'

Man One and Man Two are looking at each other. Man Two says he's going to charge him with Kathleen Heathcote's murder.

'Yer wrong,' says The Driver. 'It weren't murder. How can I have killed her if she choked? She *choked.*'

Man Two: 'Did you put your hands round her neck?'

The Driver doesn't answer. Man Two charges him with Kathleen's murder, but The Driver isn't listening – he's just looking as the man's mouth moves in senseless motion.

The door opens and he's led away by a young PC. But before the door closes behind him, he hears Man One, or perhaps it's Man Two, saying, 'Fucking hell, Ladybower?! We'll never find her. And if we ain't got no body, we're gonna struggle in court. All it takes is some smart-arse defence silk to say she's still alive somewhere and we're stuffed.'

CHAPTER TWENTY-SEVEN

'No, you're doing it wrong.' The young woman looked at Chris Gould and sighed.

He was in his skirt and heels, but for once he was not out on the street but in a large, high-ceilinged room surrounded by rails of clothes and costumes. Some of the outfits were everyday, others fantastical.

'Try it again and be less flat-footed this time, use your toes a bit,' she urged.

Chris tried to glide in the shoes.

The woman leaned against the wall. Above her was a sign which read 'BBC Wardrobe Department'.

Chris had become concerned that he was still appearing too masculine as a decoy. He had met the make-up artist months earlier through a friend of a friend: she was trust-worthy, said his mate. Chris hadn't told her he was dressing up to catch the Clifton Rapist. He'd just said he'd needed to dress as a woman for 'operational purposes'.

'You need to swivel your hips a bit more. Just a bit,' she said.

Chris gave it another go.

'No, you're not a model on a catwalk. It's about balance if you're trying to look authentic. Enough wiggle to make yourself not look like a man, but not too much that you're obviously putting it on.'

Chris practised some more, and after half an hour or so the young woman gave him an appreciative nod.

'Yeah, that's better. You're getting the hang of it. What's your make-up like?'

He told her what he put on.

'Are you blending the make-up properly? Let me show you.'

She took him to a make-up room, where she applied a cream to his face followed by a powder. 'Thing is,' she said, 'if you're under those street lights, they're pretty harsh – really orange. We might need to go a bit over the top to make you look more womanly if the bloke sees you in a split-second.'

She stood back, looking at Chris approvingly.

'Are the police actually going to send blokes out dressed like this?' she asked.

He gave a non-committal answer.

'I'd like to see the rapist who tries to attack you, Chris.'

Michelle Tighe was not the only female applicant whom the superintendent had warned that the police force was not a marriage bureau. Sally Difazio had been given the same unwanted advice too. But one weekend, while playing tennis with a friend, she found herself on a court next to two other police officers.

One – Nigel – was a PC seconded to the CID. He'd been in the force for four years. He was nice, funny and charming. Soon they started dating.

'I'm sure some women secretly did join the police to find a husband, but no one I knew did,' said Sally. 'We wanted to be in the force because it was exciting. We were being active, we were doing good. We wanted to protect and serve. And a lot of the male officers were there for the same reasons. We were like-minded and if we connected, it was because of that. Not because we wanted to find someone. It'd be the same in any workplace.'

Sergeant Kelvin Hattersley knew Robbie Jones's transformation from rugby-playing police constable to female honeytrap was always going to be a tricky one. At least Chris Gould was slim and petite. No matter how much make-up, which wig or what clothes, Robbie was never going to look like a woman – not really. But the awkwardness of his appearance was matched by his determination to do the job. With the Clifton Rapist still free, nothing would keep him off the streets in drag, it seemed.

Kelvin wondered how Robbie was able to keep bearing his colleagues' tiresome one-liners with grace, how little they seemed to get at him. He also wondered what would happen if a man drank so much, his beer goggles became so powerful, that taking home Robbie in drag was a viable option.

It was the end of February now and the snow had turned to drizzle. Temperatures started to rise. The Clifton Rapist hadn't attacked again, but the city seemed to be holding its breath.

Kelvin had Robbie Jones in the back of the unmarked Task Force van. The muscular PC sat dressed in a tight jumper with a long skirt and wig. He had a new route, taking some of the eastern side of Whiteladies Road. They checked comms, Robbie smiled, leapt from the van and was gone.

Kelvin listened in as Robbie was passed from observation officer to observation officer. Robbie was in the habit of leaving his microphone on live, so for long spells, all Kelvin could hear was the clip-clop of the PC's large feet in women's shoes and the ebbing and flowing of cityscape sounds. It was the second run of the night and pubs had now shut. Whiteladies Road was busy with the aftermath of closing time.

About ten minutes in, Kelvin heard something new and that clip-clopping stopped.

'Hey, hey you …' it was a man's voice, but not Robbie's.

'Alpha Two, do you have eyes on?' asked Kelvin.

'Negative,' said the observation officer.

'You okay, Robbie? Need backup?' asked Kelvin.

'You're gorgeous,' he heard a man slur. 'Tell you what. I've got a flat just round the corner from here. Wanna come back for a …?'

There was a long silence, then Kelvin heard the voice say 'coffee?'

'You don't say much, do you? I like your hair …' The man seemed to drool that last word out. 'You know, I've got an idea: why don't we …?'

Smack!

Kelvin heard the unmistakable sound of knuckles on head and of a man collapsing to the floor. Then he heard the resumption of the clip-clop – Robbie's large feet in women's shoes on a cold Bristol pavement.

* * *

PC Chris Gould was well known as one of C-Division's hungriest, most able and most competitive PCs. His arrest rate as a decoy was staggering. So far, he had detained more than 20 men: he had stopped car thieves in action and made arrests for offences including actual bodily harm, domestic violence, indecent assault, criminal damage and hit-and-run. He was even approached by a driver in a car used in a rape the previous evening. The man was promptly arrested and charged. A dangerous man off the streets, but he was not the Clifton Rapist. What Chris was achieving dressed as a woman was outstripping even his own records set in uniform.

On a mid-February morning, he had just completed a long, tortuous walk in drag through the back roads of Clifton and was heading back towards the point where he was due to be picked up on Whiteladies Road. He was between two observation points heading south on the main street. No one was watching him.

No one was on the street: no people, no cars, no Clifton Rapist.

He saw a pair of large headlights approach and a van pulled over to where he was walking.

'Hello? Hello, miss?'

He looked across. A large black man was leaning across from behind the driver's wheel into the passenger seat.

'Can you help?'

Chris hated the idea of talking like a woman, he hadn't needed to do it yet. Walking like a woman? That was passable. Talking? Trickier.

The guy clicked open the driver's door and walked round the front of the van. He had a map in his hands.

'You see, I'm trying to find Easton. Chelsea Road. I'm nowhere near, can you show me the way?'

Chris detected a slight movement in the van. Was that a click from somewhere?

The man continued talking about directions and Easton and trying to find Lower Ashley Road but something felt wrong.

Chris turned around just before the four men grabbed him. They pulled and dragged him, trying to get him into the back door they had just opened.

'Come on, get her legs,' one of them shouted.

Chris might have been outnumbered but he had two things in his favour which the gang of abductors did not know. First, he was not a lone woman walking the streets. Second, he was a black belt in several forms of martial arts.

He now started to perform a mixture of these on his stunned would-be captors.

One man went down with a chop to the head, another was bundled over with an armlock-tumble. There was a straight punch to a third. The two extremely angry remaining men turned from trying to abduct Chris to trying to beat him up.

As he defended himself with parries and punches, Chris wondered where his observation officers had got to. He took one of the remaining men down with a karate chop; just the driver was left.

A police car screeched up and two traffic officers burst from the front.

'What's going on here?'

They looked at the four men on the floor, the astonished driver and began asking Chris what had happened. As one officer put the driver in cuffs, Chris beckoned the other to come a little distance away.

Chris recognised him as a traffic officer he had seen around. There he whispered: 'Operation Argus.'

He saw the officer's eyes widen, then take in Chris's face. 'Oh …' said the officer, nodding to a lay-by down the road. 'We were just writing up our pocketbooks when we saw this fight.'

Chris's arrest figure rose by five that night – and he had neither revealed to his abductors who he was, nor creased his skirt.

CHAPTER TWENTY-EIGHT

Michelle Tighe was in her flat having one of her twice-weekly phone calls with her parents in Dorset.

'No, Mum, everything's fine. Yes, I'm eating well.'

This was mostly true. Michelle had a good diet although she and her flatmates, Jackie and Jean, did supplement their food intake with perhaps more alcohol than was advised, particularly at their now-infamous parties or at the Mandrake Club.

'Yes, I'm sleeping really well.'

This was completely true. Michelle could be exposed to appalling cruelties, vulnerable children, care cases and even suicides, but she was somehow able to compartmentalise her mind enough to ensure a good night's kip.

'No, work's fine. Don't worry, it's not dangerous.'

Now that was a white lie. After saying goodbye to her mother, she placed the phone receiver in the cradle, looked in the mirror, put on her coat and went out to be bait in a secret operation to catch one of Britain's most wanted men. She probably could have told her parents what she was up to. No sergeant or inspector would ever have known. But she worried her mother would fret.

The weather in March 1979 had taken a dive. The nights seemed to be clear and dry in the first half of the week, when decoy operatives were not deployed. But when it came to Wednesdays to Saturdays – the nights of Operation Argus – there was rain or even snow. Tonight, Michelle was leaving Steph Whittle's flat on a route that would take her up Whiteladies Road, on to the sideroads then to another officer's property. These were the best runs because the other officer had a three-bar fire and a kettle – between runs, they could actually get warm.

Michelle attended the briefing at Redland Police Station before heading to Steph's flat.

There, Steph was on a night off.

'What do you reckon? How much longer have we got with this?' Steph asked.

'Dunno, the Chief said we'd do it until he's caught but I can't see how he can afford all the overtime the men are getting. And they can't keep us out like this – we're losing our momentum.'

'What do you think the chances are that of all the nights he strikes, it'll be one of the nights we're out, and it'll be one of us that he goes for? We have just two girls out a night. And whatever Chris and Robbie look like. Surely we need an army out for this to really work?'

'I give it a month,' said Michelle, clipping in her earpiece and covering it with a scarf.

'Look at you,' said Steph, pointing to the brick-microphone Michelle was concealing under her heavy coat. 'How are we going to go hide that in summer? In a light dress?'

Michelle shrugged and heard a crackle in her earpiece. She made her comms checks with Control and said good-bye.

Michelle was halfway along her route. There was a gentle snow that night. When the wintry snap started in late January, the streets were deserted. Everyone seemed to stay at home. But now, Bristol had grown accustomed to a gentle white carpet and the pubs, clubs and streets were as busy as usual.

Michelle had made it onto Whiteladies Road and had been passed from Alphas One, Two and Three. She was being watched by a mobile observation officer, Delta Two – she guessed he must be the silhouetted figure holding an umbrella and standing at the bus stop opposite.

A car pulled up beside her.

'Hello there, should you be out here tonight by yourself?'

Michelle looked across at a large brown Rover of some description. The passenger window was wound down. She noticed the driver was an inspector she knew from C-Division.

'Oh, alright, Dennis?' she said.

'Do you want a lift?'

'No.'

'You know the streets aren't safe at night, Michelle?'

'Yes, I know, but I'm perfectly fine.'

She slowed her walk to a stop.

'I'm not getting in your car,' she said firmly.

She glanced at him. In his early to mid-thirties, he had a brown moustache and was wearing clothes that were perhaps a bit too tight, a bit too young for a family man. She also noticed the band of white skin on the third finger of his left hand.

'Where's your wife tonight?'

'She's happy with me going out. You know, I saw a few of the boys earlier and just thought I'd have a bit of a cruise.'

Disco music was playing gently on his car speaker.

'I'm not going home with you. In fact, I'm not going anywhere with you.'

'Do you like wine, Michelle? Bet you can't afford it on your pay. I've become a bit of a connoisseur. You know, I've got a bottle of something really special in the back.'

'I've told you, I'm not going anywhere with you,' Michelle found herself saying through gritted teeth. She started walking.

The Rover started following Michelle slowly, crawling along by the kerb.

'Jump in, let's have a drink,' he persisted.

Michelle stopped again. The car stopped too. Then she said gently, while tapping her ear: 'Argus.'

It took a second for Dennis's face to switch from smooth and relaxed to pale terror. He hit the accelerator, wheels kicking up a white slush as he left.

Michelle carried on.

'Alpha Four, subject in view,' came a crackle in her ear.

CHAPTER TWENTY-NINE

29 NOVEMBER 1963

There is a television in prison, but only the inmates favoured by the screws are allowed to watch it. They think The Driver's okay. He's no problem – behaves, no backchat, no insults, no threat.

A regular guy.

So, tonight, he's sitting in the communal lounge with the television on. There's a chatter around. Men he doesn't know, still less cares about. Common prisoners …

The news is on the screen. A presenter's in the studio talking about President Kennedy's funeral in Washington. It had happened a few days before, but was watched seemingly by the entire planet – and any chance to replay the pictures was taken up.

The lounge goes quiet as the inmates watch the images of the cortège pass through Washington, D.C. The crowds, the military lines … The widow, so young, so beautiful in black. There's a bit when a boy salutes the coffin – that must be the President's son?

The Driver notices one of the prisoners starting to cry. But they stay silent in the lounge.

When the report's over, it cuts back to the presenter in the studio. He holds the moment for a beat before looking down at the papers on his desk and up again at the camera. He says: 'Now, here in the Midlands, the search for Kathleen Heathcote moved to Ladybower Reservoir in Derbyshire today. A specialist team of Royal Navy frogmen has been drafted up from Portsmouth to conduct the search. But conditions are poor and divers have told detectives that the chances of recovering the woman are slim. A man has been charged with her murder.'

The lounge inmates continue looking at the screen as an image of a wide lake appears and a team of divers is kitting up.

'Where is Kathleen Heathcote?' asks the reporter in voiceover. 'She's been missing for exactly a week and now police say they have intelligence which has led them to Ladybower Reservoir.'

A picture of Kathleen wearing black glasses appears, she's smiling easily.

The Driver flinches at the sight of her on the screen.

'The 21-year-old shop assistant was last seen getting off a bus a few hundred yards from her home in Mansfield, late on November 21st.'

An older woman with a passing resemblance to Kathleen begins to speak: 'We now accept the worst: we've been told she's been murdered. This is too awful to bear.'

The Driver notices a muttering in the room. He remains unmoved.

The screen shows the bridge. Now he feels a flutter … There's a close-up of a team of divers swimming across the surface.

'This must be one of the strangest underwater searches in policing history. Ladybower Reservoir was created 20 years ago and the whole valley was flooded, including the village of Ashopton. The small former beauty spot is exactly beneath the bridge from where Kathleen was thought to have been deposited.

'These divers must search this lost, submerged village. There are up to 18 former cottages, a pub, a church and a village hall, but the conditions underwater are proving challenging.'

A man in naval uniform is being interviewed: 'Visibility is poor – it's November, it's cold, the divers can only go for ten minutes at a time before the temperatures start affecting them. And there's every chance that the body will have floated away. Ladybower is big, 6,000 million gallons. This is a tough operation but we hope it will be successful.'

A reporter is there on the bridge, on the very spot where The Driver stood a week earlier.

'The village of Ashopton is a hundred feet below the surface, beneath where I stand. It's a ghost village, a twilight world. As I speak, naval divers are gliding through streets, looking in buildings no one has seen for two decades. Doors have rotted, walls have crumbled away, but the divers remain determined to reunite Kathleen Heathcote with her family. A man from Shirebrook's been charged with her murder – he's due to appear in court tomorrow.'

Now, the presenter's back, talking about the economy.

The driver notices a few faces looking at him. He starts to move away from the lounge – he needs to get away. A big guy passes him, the one who'd been crying at the President's son: 'You're fucking scum, mate.'

The Driver shakes it off; he starts walking back to his cell.

A tall, thin prisoner steps in alongside him. Well-spoken, he seems educated: 'Don't worry, pal. They'll not find her down there. You can come up with any old story. I've never heard of a jury convict in a bodyless murder trial – it's up to them to prove you did it. No body, no proof. You're a free man, pal.'

CHAPTER THIRTY

They were meant to carry the torches aloft, but some of the protestors kept the flames down, near their faces, to get some warmth against the freezing night. Scarves, hats and heavy coats could only do so much on a night like this. Those not holding torches gripped banners with messages including 'Anti-Rape Group Bristol', 'No means no' and 'Young or old, no escape, we all go in fear of rape'. Most of the demonstrators were women, but not all. Many of them were in their twenties or thirties, but not all. No one knew for sure how many had turned up. Some suggested 300, others said it was nearer 500 – it was a good number either way.

A woman with red, curly hair and a loudhailer was organising the crowd: 'Okay, we leave in 10 minutes, we march from here down to the Council House. There, we'll hold hands and there'll be a few speeches. We need to make our voices heard. Be loud. Don't be afraid – it's only by shining a light on the police's failure that we can show them up for what they are.'

A journalist was interviewing a couple of the protestors. A woman, twenty-something with a brown hat-scarf combo, said: 'I'm extremely concerned and so are a lot of women, that's why we're here tonight. And I'm sure that if other women who knew about this march sat down and thought about how many times they've been frightened and then turned up, we'd have had even more people.'

'What are you actually asking for?' asked the journalist.

'We're asking for the freedom to walk the streets after dark without fear of attack.'

The journalist tried another protestor, a woman in her mid-thirties with short blonde hair and rosy cheeks: 'Like many women, I try not to walk out at night. I try to use a car when I can. I'm lucky – I live with my husband and we can afford to have a car. Many women can't. When you are walking the streets, you always have the sense someone could be following you at any time.'

'Come on, let's go …' the organiser shouted and the procession moved down the hill towards the Council House. The Task Force had closed the road to cars to allow the protest to take place and there was a distant honking as drivers mixed frustration at an inability to get home with support for the crowd. It was a short walk, maybe five minutes, but by the time the crowd reached the braziers assembled on College Green, the lawn in front of the Council House, the singing seemed stronger, voices surer.

The organiser stood on a soapbox, towering above the crowd. She spoke into a loudhailer and her voice carried crisply over the chatter and the low hum of traffic.

'Thank you … Thank you for coming here. To all you women and men who have had enough.'

There was a cheer.

'For 18 months, a shadow has passed over this city. A shadow of a monster. Nine women. NINE WOMEN have been attacked. Nine lives changed forever.

'All because of one man. And enough is enough.'

There was another cheer.

'What is it that makes a man want to do this? What is it that makes society allow it? What is it that stops the police from catching him?'

There was a loud boo.

'What have the police done?' she shouted, cupping her hand to her ear.

'Nothing,' chanted the crowd.

'Where have they been?'

'Nowhere,' was the chorused reply.

'Up in Yorkshire, it's happening. They call him The Ripper. But he has murdered his victims. The only people who have seen that man are dead. This monster, here in Bristol? His victims have survived. The police have been given nine descriptions. They must know so much about him but they have failed. Failed to find him, failed to catch him, failed to protect women, failed to make our city safe.

'We are calling on the police to do something. If not, we'll take to the streets again. And again. And we will embarrass this failing force into doing something to bring this man to justice.'

There was a cheer.

None of the crowd noticed, in the distance behind College Green, a young woman dressed in wintry clothes, hurrying towards Park Street. Having finished her day shift on the Police Women's Unit, she was running up to Redland Police

Station. She was late for the briefing. And in an hour's time she would be walking streets near here as a decoy.

Chris Gould had had enough. His feet were in agony, he was only halfway through his long run, the night seemed to be stretching on forever and he was desperate for a cup of tea. Even the thought of his arrest record wasn't enough to maintain his positive attitude.

Another dark side street, another soulless night.

He had just walked four uneventful miles.

Sometimes he played the game of 'spot the observation officer'. He always knew roughly where they'd be, of course. But how they were disguised or hidden was sometimes a surprise.

Unlike the female decoys, Chris spent periods, often several minutes at a time, when he was not under the watch of a backup officer. He had developed a technique, a calculation of his pace and geography, to work out how long it would be before he saw the next observation man.

Pembroke Road, turning into Alma Road. Dave Bryant will be five minutes ahead, probably in a car, he said to himself.

This road was the Clifton Rapist's first patch. His first three victims had been attacked here. A moment ago he had passed the spot where Alice Matthews, the married woman, was attacked in July 1977. As he walked on the north pavement, he saw ahead the junction with Alexandra Road, where the man had attacked 18-year-old Patsy Delaney in a doorway three days later. Hadn't she seen a yellow Ford Capri afterwards? Now opposite was the turning to Leigh

Road. That was where he'd assaulted Denise Turner months later.

Who was she? he asked himself. *That's right, the musician.*

She'd left the city and never returned. Since then, all the attacks were on other streets around Whiteladies Road, not here.

He checked his pace, looked ahead: three minutes until he was due to see his colleague, Dave.

Chris was passing opposite the junction with Leigh Road when he saw a silhouette in the distance on the opposite pavement: a tall man with big hair. The artists' impressions flashed through Chris's mind like a slideshow.

The man emerged into the sodium light of a street lamp, then he twisted round, staring at Chris. His face was an exact match for one of the pictures Chris had in his mind.

Chris slowed, his heart racing. He was face to face with the Clifton Rapist, he was sure of it. For weeks, he had waited for this moment but he hadn't a script for how to respond in this situation.

How should he engage? What should he do?

The decoy operation was designed with the tactic of being attacked. But what if you just see him?

Thoughts raced through his head: could he call for backup?

No, the man would hear.

Could he talk to the man?

He could manage a few words, but the guy was on the other side of the road. And no woman would shout out 'hello' in a darkened back street – the communication would have to be visual.

Chris slowed his pace and stared at the man, who was looking back at him.

Come on, engage, he thought to himself. And he tried to soak up all the details he could about the man: his face, his appearance, his gait.

Slowly now.

Chris looked across again: *Yes, the man's turned around, he's coming in my direction. He's on the other side of the road. And he's looking at me.*

But the man was in the half-light, then he came up under another street lamp.

He's just like one of the original images: moustache, big black hair, tall, strong, Chris thought.

Two minutes to Dave.

He could hear a tap-tapping on the flagstones on the opposite pavement but now they were making a duller sound. Had he started to cross the road? Was he coming towards him? It sounded so.

Yes, the steps were definitely getting quicker and louder.

Here goes: get ready for an attack.

Chris braced himself, while raising his pace to try to get nearer Dave. He felt a hand on his shoulder as the man started dragging him into a doorway.

I'm just going to have to let this happen …

Now the man had pulled Chris up against the door and was starting to feel his body. He had to let this happen, he had to contain him long enough for backup to arrive.

Where was Dave?

Chris carried on acting like a woman under attack. He parried the slaps, put his hands up against the punches. And then the man opened his mouth: 'Hey you, lady. You pretty.'

Disappointment instantly hit him: the accent was all wrong, it was European. *Turkish? Balkan?*

'I wanna take you home, I wanna make love to you.'

Chris remained silent – no point in talking.

'You pretty lady. I give you five pounds, make love to you.'

This man is another attacker.

Chris had had enough, but how could he arrest this man without compromising the decoy operation? He grabbed the man's collar and spun him around. In a split second the man went from aggressor to terrified. Chris leaned back out of the doorway and looked to his left: there was Dave. He still couldn't shout – that would give it all away.

Dave, see me … he silently pleaded.

Dave glanced at Chris and started running towards him. Chris looked back at his attacker and punched him on the nose. The man slid down the shop doorway, crumpling in a heap at Chris's feet.

'Alright, my love? I'll take this from here,' said Dave. 'This must be a scare for you.'

The man on the ground looked up at Chris in drag and a plain-clothed Dave.

'I'm a detective and I'm arresting you on suspicion of attempted rape …' Chris's colleague began.

For a few, brief, violent moments, Chris Gould had believed he was about to catch the man who had eluded detectives for 18 months. This was his 36th arrest as part of Operation Argus but this attacker was not the Clifton Rapist.

He was still on the loose.

CHAPTER THIRTY-ONE

WEDNESDAY, 21 MARCH 1979

Michelle Tighe was in the briefing room of Redland Police Station. Cathy Holbrook, a community police officer drafted in for Operation Argus, sat next to her, with tonight's team of observations officers behind them.

In front of the group was the unmistakable figure of a man with a pork-pie hat and a puce face. But there was something different about Chief Superintendent Malcolm Popperwell: his shoulders were down, he looked lost.

'Okay, before we go out for the night, we've had word from the Chief. It's not good news, I'm afraid.'

Michelle noticed a change in the atmosphere.

'Operation Argus is too expensive. We haven't caught the Clifton Rapist. We've been out for nearly three months. And while we've taken a lot of very bad men off the street, we've not been successful in our main objective.

'He's given us two more nights, tonight and tomorrow. Then that's it.'

'What about the Clifton Rapist?' asked Michelle.

Popperwell shrugged.

'What about the protests?' asked Cathy.

'We've done everything we can. There've been no attacks

since December. We're out of cash. It's public money, we can't get any more. It's time to turn off the tap. The money for Argus is being taken from other frontline police work. There's nothing to say the Clifton Rapist hasn't moved elsewhere or gone to prison or died, even.

'It's over.'

There was a collective groan, Michelle included. She thought of all those nights freezing out on the streets, all the hours observation guys had spent hiding in the dark, all the backup teams in vans and offices. Yes, they had arrested a few criminals but the central target eluded them.

What a waste.

Michelle was released from the Task Force van just after 10 p.m. There was still a light smattering of snow on the ground.

Christ, it'll be April in a couple of weeks, she thought.

She turned left from St Paul's Road on to Whiteladies Road. Now she was on the main drag. The pubs were still busy, but the streets were quiet. It was too cold to be anywhere outside unless absolutely necessary.

'Alpha One, subject in view,' Michelle heard in her ear.

There was a lone woman opposite, heading south on the eastern pavement.

Michelle wondered about her: what would happen next week when the operation was called off? There would be no surveillance, no backup, no safety net. She walked past a bus shelter. Stuck to one of the panels was one of the force-issue posters: five images put together by victims over the last 18 months.

Five pictures, some photo-fits, some artist's impressions. Michelle had seen the flyer so often she knew the words by heart: 'Clifton Sex Assaults', it read at the top. Underneath was some writing: 'The following are photo-fit composite pictures and a drawing of the man wanted in connection with a number of serious sexual assaults upon women in the Clifton area of Bristol in 1977 and 1978. If anyone believes they know the identity of this man, will they please contact the incident room at Southmead Police Station, telephone 22022 extension 2137 or 2143.'

Where does this man go? Michelle asked herself. *Is he a criminal who's skipping in and out of jail? Does that explain his long absences? He's clearly a man with a double life. What does he do when he's not in the shadows? Is he married? Does he have children? Has he a criminal record? If so, what for?*

Is he like the Chief Constable said? A single man who lives around here?

Michelle looked up at the flats above the closed-up shops on Whiteladies Road.

He could be peering down at me now. Watching me walk, then noticing me again in an hour's time, round and round like a hamster on a wheel. He could be watching the observation officers casually meandering along the street, then quickly scurrying away to their hideouts. He might have made a note of the Task Force van's registration number and been watching as it loops the streets.

She tried to stop herself from thinking like this: it was pointless. But Michelle had been so lost in her thoughts, she realised she hadn't heard the observation officers pass her on the radio traffic. In fact, she couldn't hear any radio traffic.

Michelle looked around: the street was deserted. She pressed the button of her microphone.

'Hello, hello, this is Michelle. Does anyone copy?'

Silence.

Michelle kept walking and she quickened her pace.

'Hello, Alpha One? Alpha Two? Control? This is Michelle, does anyone copy?'

Nothing.

Michelle made it as far as the next street corner. When she looked across the street, she saw a man sliding out from behind the bushes. For a second, she stopped and held her breath. Then she realised she knew the outline.

'Andy, Andy?' she half-shouted, half-whispered.

Andy Kerslake tapped his ear.

She shrugged her shoulders.

Then Kelvin Hattersley came driving up in the Task Force van. He pulled over and Michelle leapt in.

'Problem with comms,' he murmured.

Michelle tried to hide her fury. *What if he'd attacked me?* she thought.

Slowly, more observation officers emerged from the shadows and started to slink quietly back to Redland Police Station.

CHAPTER THIRTY-TWO

2 DECEMBER 1963

The diver, Lieutenant Commander Kenneth Kempsell, is 32 years old and he has just won the George Cross for bravery. That was for a bomb-disposal operation at RAF Kinloss in Scotland, four months earlier. A torpedo had exploded, killing two men. The explosion had brought down the base's armoury roof, leaving exposed 24 torpedoes. Two and a half tonnes of explosives were leaking acid and hissing.

Wearing just an asbestos suit with no helmet, Lieutenant Commander Kempsell crawled through a tiny space to attach charges to the weapons, which could explode at any time. The delicate operation took 70 minutes. Then he emerged from that tiny hole, his suit covered in acid. He walked gently for a distance of three football pitches and hit the plunger.

The explosion destroyed the armoury, and it also blew out farm windows miles around.

But that had been in the middle of summer. Now, it's a freezing December afternoon in Derbyshire. They've been searching here, in this lost village, for five days now, taking it in turns: 10-minute dives at a time.

He's sitting in a tiny dinghy, floating about 15 metres from the seven-arch bridge. The stone should be golden, but on this grey day, it seems as though all the colour has been sapped from the beauty spot. On top of the bridge stands a team of four uniformed police in peaked caps and tunics, looking down. They've been waiting here for days too.

Kempsell sees bubbles rise to the side of the dinghy and a head appears.

The two men don't say anything to each other.

He looks towards the leader, dressed in a diving suit and sat on a small bench on the small boat, who puts down his clipboards and nods. Kempsell checks his breathing apparatus and the line to the boat, then falls backwards into the water.

When he started the search, days ago, the cold would catch him every time, but now part of him quite looked forward to this moment – better to be searching than waiting to search.

He passes from the surface and heads down into the black. As he descends, he checks his depth gauge. At 10 feet, any sunlight or visibility has gone: it's just a green-brown-black darkness. He carries on diving, stopping every so often to pressurise his eardrums.

Thirty feet.

Down he goes … Forty feet, 50 feet, 60 feet …

There's no life down here. He sees no fish.

It's just an abyss.

Seventy feet, 80 feet …

He stops and makes some checks; his eardrums pop again.

Ninety feet.

One hundred feet down.

There's something of a floor down here. They told him it used to be a village. He and his comrades are the only souls who have seen this road and the remains of these buildings in 20 years. He hits something hard and feels what must be a wall.

Was this a cottage? A pub, or the church?

It's cold, dark, claustrophobic. Surely there must be easier ways of earning a living?

He has just minutes left before he must return to the surface for one of his colleagues to take his place. But something in the darkened water catches his eye.

Something bright in the murk. Amid the blackness, a flash of something white.

He reaches out to grab it.

He looks at his depth gauge. It's hard to see, but it reads 105 feet down. Then he tugs at his cord and the teams above start to pull him up. He knows he will have to stop several times to repressurise on his way up – this will be difficult, clutching onto Kathleen Heathcote.

But he will not let her go.

Nothing will stop him carrying her to the surface.

CHAPTER THIRTY-THREE

Michelle Tighe shouldn't have been in the briefing room. Her friend, flatmate and colleague Jackie Clair was on rota to be tonight's decoy but she had to be in court the next morning and needed a stand-in.

Michelle had nothing else on so she said yes.

Nothing could hide the air of silent despondency in the police room. No one was really looking at each other, conversation was light. In fact, the briefings had become non-events in recent weeks whereas in January, when the operation started, the rooms had been full, abuzz with the promise of catching the Clifton Rapist. As the runs passed, the numbers dwindled like the hopes of ensnaring the target. A few people were trying to be cheery – Andy Kerslake was always good for that, Chris Nott too. But shoulders were down.

Michelle checked who else was around. No Chris Gould, no Robbie Jones tonight. John O'Connor wasn't there. Perhaps the decoys in drag were having an evening off.

'Okay, one last go,' sighed Chief Superintendent Malcolm Popperwell. 'Hopefully, we'll be a bit more successful than we were last night. I can confirm that the problem with communications was human error. Someone who'll remain nameless pulled a plug from the radio system and the whole thing went down – that person has been replaced for tonight.'

Michelle looked at Cathy Holbrook.

'Do you want to go first?'

Cathy shrugged and said she would.

'Don't worry, after tomorrow, we'll get our lives back,' said Andy Kerslake as they walked across the police station car park. He got into his car, heading off to his static observation point.

Sergeant Kelvin Hattersley met them outside his unmarked Task Force van.

'It's a shame, this,' he said. 'I thought we stood a chance. Perhaps we never did.'

Cathy jumped in the passenger seat, Michelle got in the back. Kelvin turned the ignition, threw the van into gear and headed from the light of the car park into the darkness.

The radio was on as the van drove through the dark streets. A news announcer talked of the economic legacy of the Winter of Discontent, which had started in November 1978. Some bright spark had worked out how many days had been lost to strike action. Now, school caretakers in parts of Bristol were looking to walk out. Children in the city would be staying home tomorrow.

Imagine if any of the decoys had kids. It would have been impossible, thought Michelle. She looked at Cathy, who was just a year or so younger than her. *We are barely out of our teens and look at the impossible responsibility we've been faced with.*

She thought of the thrill of those first, early runs. And now it had become a job, like any other. The rapist hadn't attacked again, like he hadn't emerged during previous operations. What if he really was a police officer? God knows, there were enough criminals in uniform. It had to be that. It was the only explanation.

The van dropped Cathy Holbrook on St Paul's Road, then Michelle moved into the passenger seat. Kelvin then started driving to the point where the run was due to end, through the back streets. Meanwhile, Cathy's progress was being broadcast on the radio channel: Alpha One passing to Alpha Two, Three, past Delta One and on to Alphas Four and Five.

Kelvin glanced at Michelle after he pulled up in Hurle Crescent.

Cathy was on Chantry Road, passing other observation guys in the darkness. The van door opened and Cathy got in.

'It's still bloody freezing out there,' she said. 'You got a cuppa?'

CHAPTER THIRTY-FOUR

DECEMBER 1963

The Heathcote family is marking Christmas, but only for the children. There's an attempt at a tree, some presents underneath. A lunch is planned, they'll play games later.

But their hearts aren't in it.

Derek Heathcote still can't get over what has happened to his sister. Kathleen didn't know her attacker – she was in the wrong place at the wrong time, police said.

It was bad luck.

His parents weren't able to cope with identifying Kathleen's body, so he'd done it. Anything for his sister. Anything for his mother.

But he has nightmares still.

He feels a tug on his trousers: it's his son. Perhaps Chris will remember this Christmas in years to come? At four, you start forming memories.

Chris wants to open his presents. Who can blame him? He's been on about them since about five this morning.

Derek smiles at his boy and goes with him to the tree. He passes Chris a small gift, wrapped in Christmas paper. The boy rips the wrapping away: it's a toy car. Delighted, he starts pulling it out of its box.

Derek picks the wrapping up from the floor and sees the note: 'Dear Chris, merry Christmas, love Auntie Kathleen'.

Kathleen had always been organised, always put her family first. She must have bought this back in November and given it to her parents.

Through his tears, Derek watches his son whizzing the car's wheels around on the sofa and carpet.

CHAPTER THIRTY-FIVE

22 MARCH 1979

Is he out here tonight?

The neon lights of clubland flashed red on Michelle Tighe's face as she passed through the city, asking the same question she had been posing for months. She leaned forward and turned up the car's heater, turned down the disco music on the radio and sank back into the passenger seat, resuming her gaze through the side window.

It would be 2 a.m soon: club closing time. A few figures were already tumbling out of bar-room doors and onto the pavements.

A thin man, maybe a student, stood on the street in a tight T-shirt and enormous flares, squinting drunkenly at Michelle's car. He put out his hand in a vain attempt to flag it down. A friend pushed him playfully.

'Better luck next time, matey,' said Kelvin from behind the wheel. Michelle glanced across at him: how many decoy operatives had Kelvin Hattersley deployed over the last month or so?

Is he out here tonight? Michelle repeated the question to herself before closing her eyes.

One more run, then bed. One more freezing run.

Kelvin hit a stretch of road where there were neither pedestrian crossings nor traffic lights, but he didn't speed up. Instead, he kept a steady 25 miles an hour, watching as he went, glancing from side to side.

Michelle turned to her left and saw the darkened side streets beyond the street lamps: this was where all of the attacks had happened. Flicking past her, the turnings into avenues which stretched off into black.

Did the man wait down these roads? Like a spider in its web, did he set a trap and wait for a woman to fall in? Or, like a predator, did he find a victim on the main street then stalk her until he found a dark corner where he knew he could carry out his attack unseen?

Michelle knew one thing: the main road was a safe space. Relatively. The crowds, the fights, kicking-out time, drunk men … She could handle all of these.

But the side streets were different.

Michelle pulled down the sun visor and tried to look in the mirror on the underside.

Her eyes were dark, her skin pale.

She thought of her friends who had done this exact same job night after freezing night. Not for the first time did she ask herself, *What am I doing?*

She remembered the latest headlines in the newspapers: 'A City in Fear'; 'The Police Should Do More'; 'How Many More Women Will Be Attacked Before He Kills?'

Michelle flipped the sun visor back up. She opened her coat and reached for the brick-shaped radio hanging from a strap around her neck and twisted the dial. As her earpiece crackled, she spasmed, found the dial again and turned it down.

'You okay?' Kelvin was looking at her kindly as he pulled up to the kerbside.

Michelle nodded.

She recalled her first walk: the flash of fear and excitement, a sense of the unknown as she left the car. But that pang of nervy adventure had dulled over the weeks. This was her job tonight – the same job she had done countless times.

She opened the car door and walked into what felt like a wall of cold air.

'Subject's left the car …' she heard Kelvin say as she closed the door. The words echoed into her earpiece.

CHAPTER THIRTY-SIX

The Driver is waiting – he's become used to that. The trial has taken two days, but it's gone pretty well. He's not a murderer and the facts speak for themselves. The post-mortem said it: she choked. The jury heard it.

He's not a murderer.

Surely they'll agree? They've only been out for 20 minutes. These things can take hours, his counsel says.

His counsel wasn't the best in the world – he could have done a better job himself. But he managed to get the right points across: he had tried to give the girl the kiss of life, he'd tried to save her life. But by then, it was too late.

Nothing anyone could have done.

The prosecution lawyer, he was a bit wily. Tugged at the heartstrings. But this is a courtroom and juries need to stick to the facts, leave emotion out of it.

The bit about the girl's mum being up all night worrying, how she called the police. How she tried all the hospitals. How the girl was engaged to be married. Really?

That bloke who was working on his car, that bit didn't go too well. How he said he saw The Driver in the rain after-wards. He was calling for help, wasn't he? Help didn't come.

The Driver is really pleased he had the chance to give evidence personally. Others might have been intimidated by that big wooden room, all pomp and procedure. But he'd said it as it was: she'd screamed and he was just stifling the scream. And the body in the lake? He just wanted to hide it for a couple of weeks until after the baby was born.

His wife ... He'd have preferred it if she and his mum hadn't been in court. He told them to stay away, he didn't want them hearing all of that. It's funny seeing them sitting there together, crying – they look almost like sisters.

Not long to go now.

One thing his defence counsel had done properly was to sum up. He stuck to the facts and the facts said that, yes, he may be guilty of manslaughter, but he's not a murderer.

The police had got that all wrong.

The door opens and a security guard looks round.

'Verdict, mate!'

He gets up and walks through the warren of corridors, which brings him to the oak-panelled room. There's the judge, his counsel, the prosecution. Behind them are those cops. He glances at his wife, who waves. His mum blows a kiss.

The jury door opens and an usher brings them in.

Why aren't they looking at him?

The foreman of the jury is asked to stand.

Oh, it's that little shit of a man. He was scribbling notes throughout. Bet he loves the power.

He keeps staring at the foreman while the clerk reads out: 'The defendant is charged with the murder of Kathleen

Heathcote between November 21st and November 23rd 1963. Do you find the defendant guilty or not guilty?'

The little man, the foreman of the jury, opens his mouth and says one word: 'Guilty.'

And everything seems to change.

CHAPTER THIRTY-SEVEN

Michelle Tighe saw a set of traffic lights ahead and she began walking towards them, then turned left onto the main road. A group of men walked past, shouting at each other. Guttural laughs. She slipped by them and started up the gentle incline before the steep stretch of Whiteladies Road.

This was the main strip: a broad road with wide pavements heading out of the city. Bars, clubs, shops and restaurants either side.

'Alpha One. Subject's past me,' Michelle heard in her earpiece. Glancing right, she thought she saw a pair of eyes near a pathway behind a bush.

Which observation guy had that been? she wondered. *Andy? John? Chris?*

The cold was starting to seep through Michelle's duffle coat, through her heavy jumper and was biting into her skin.

How many runs have we done over the months now? she wondered as she started up the steeper hill.

Then, again: *Is he out here tonight?*

'Alpha Two, subject's in view,' crackled the voice through her earpiece. She had been picked up by the next observation officer on the route.

Michelle breathed out.

Across the road a young woman walked purposefully down the hill. She looked as if she was off to work. *Was she on a cleaning shift? Or off to the hospital? Maybe a nurse, or even a doctor?*

The same thoughts flashed into Michelle's head whenever she saw someone who held any vague likeness to herself: *Do you know what you're doing out at night? Is it really worth putting your safety at risk for the price of a cab? I have an earpiece, a microphone, a backup team and self-defence training – you have nothing.*

It was then that her thoughts were interrupted by a message in her earpiece. She couldn't quite make it out, so she stayed silent so as not to talk over the repeat. But the second time she heard it perfectly.

This was Kelvin Hattersley's voice: 'There's a man on your tail. He's in a car, a Ford Capri. Repeat, a yellow Ford Capri. He's driving behind you. Looks just like the photo-fit. Repeat, there's a man on your tail.'

CHAPTER THIRTY-EIGHT

1974

'See you, mate,' says the security guard as he opens the metal gate.

The hinges screech.

The Driver walks through. He takes his first few steps outside and exhales. Somehow the air feels fresher this side of the fence.

Ten years is a long time, he thinks. But he's still young: just 33. He can have another crack at life.

He's not out of the woods yet. This is just an open prison but it may as well be a front room. Some of the guys here say they manage to go to nightclubs and no one cares. A few have jobs. He's got a trade – you'll never go wrong with a trade. Perhaps he can start a little business on the side so he's good to go when he gets his full release?

It's a short bus ride from the open prison to Bristol. He's never been here before, but he's heard it's got a good vibe. There's nothing for him up north. His wife's got another guy. His son? Well, surely the new guy's turned his mind.

Yeah, he likes the sound of Bristol. He can make a go of it here.

Another crack at life.

CHAPTER THIRTY-NINE

'There's a man on your tail. He's in a car, a Ford Capri. Repeat, a yellow Ford Capri. He's driving behind you. Looks just like the photo-fit. Repeat, there's a man on your tail.'

Okay, Michelle Tighe thought.

Her breath pulsated out of her in clouds under the orange street lamps. Cars cruised down the hill towards her, but she could focus neither on them nor on a crowd of women just yards away by the kerb.

Michelle listened for a car behind her. Was she imagining a distant chug of an engine?

Was that him?

There had been no sound in her earpiece for a few minutes. Was it working?

Speak to me. Speak to me.

Then there was a crackle. And another voice. Not Kelvin's deep tones. This was higher-pitched.

'This is Control. We've run a check on the number plate. You're not going to believe this. He's a killer. A *killer*. Out on life licence. He also raped his victim.'

It took a few moments for the words to land in Michelle's mind.

A killer?

'You can pull out at any time. If you carry on, he has to touch you. Repeat. He has to *touch* you. But you don't have to go through with this.'

Michelle breathed out again and closed her eyes. Ahead of her was the well-lit road. He would never assault her there. To catch this man, she must lead him into those darkened side streets. There, and only there, might he attack.

What he had done to these women was brutal, life-changing ... She knew this, she had read the reports. Should she put her own safety first, knowing he would almost certainly target another woman tonight? An innocent, unsuspecting woman, perhaps like the one she had just seen? Or should she put herself in the line of fire of one of the country's most wanted men? What if the backup teams didn't arrive in time? What if he had a knife? What if he took her hostage?

He had threatened to kill every single one of his victims. Now she had discovered he *had* murdered someone before.

'Do you copy?' crackled the voice in her earpiece. 'You have a killer on your track.'

Ahead of her was the well-lit road: safety. To her left were the darkened side streets: danger.

Michelle took one last breath and made up her mind.

CHAPTER FORTY

1978

The Driver sits in the grey waiting room again. It hasn't changed in three years. Same waiting room, same old routine. Same sign which reads 'Probation Office'.

Who is it going to be today?

A lot's happened since he was released on life licence. Bristol's now his home. He's found a job. He has a new wife, he has a daughter. He has a car – in fact, through the window of the waiting room he can just see the bonnet of his beloved yellow Ford Capri parked out front. He always tells the probation officer all about these: he's a family man, now, fully rehabilitated.

Except that he's not.

Because he can function on two completely separate levels. He can go to work, he can maintain a relationship with his wife. He has friends, he can be a dad. He can come in to Bristol city centre every so often and sit in a grey waiting room before going through a door that says 'Probation Office', where he tells half-truths about his life. But at night he can turn into something else. Usually after a drink. And no one knows, no one suspects. Not his wife, nor his adoring daughter. None of his friends.

Certainly not his probation officer.

Some of his mates at work joked with him last year, after the first two attacks, after the first artists' impressions were released: 'Oi, you look just like that rapist, that bloke in the papers,' one said. He was pointing to the picture of a man with big hair and a handlebar moustache.

That night, he got the razor out and shaved off his facial hair.

The images are very good. A couple were different enough to kick up some dust, though. He has wondered when he might get a knock on the door, a knock like back up north, November 1963.

But nothing.

And it's all so similar this time: he's leading a double life, the police are after him and this wife is pregnant, just like his last one was. The parallels are almost poetic.

When it became clear the cops were clueless after the first few attacks, he found it pretty straightforward: he could attack at will, he could attack at whim.

The door opens. A gorilla of a man with tattoos comes lumbering out.

He looks like a criminal, thinks The Driver. *What's he done?*

Then a small man in his early thirties appears at the door – big glasses, a flustered look.

The Driver gets up, they shake hands.

'Sorry, I'm running late. This is my first time in this office,' says the probation officer. 'Do come in.'

The Driver knows the room well – he's lost count of the number of times he's been there; also, the number of officers he's had.

The probation officer sits down and pulls out a form.

'Okay, I'm a bit all over the place today. Can you just confirm your name?'

'Of course,' says The Driver. 'It's Evans – Ronald Evans.'

CHAPTER FORTY-ONE

'His name is Ronald Evans, he's been released on life licence.'

Michelle Tighe was trying to concentrate.

Think ... think ... she told herself.

And now the electric crackle in her earpiece had stopped.

Was the radio working? Christ, what if it failed as it had the night before?

Michelle closed her eyes and turned left into Chantry Road, left towards where the observation officers were waiting, left into the trap.

Black. That was how Chantry Road seemed to Michelle after the brightness of Whiteladies Road.

Just black.

All I have to do is get under that street lamp, she told herself.

She couldn't hear him now, the footsteps had stopped. In some ways that was scarier.

Other things flashed through Michelle's head: *the double-handed throat-grip. Get ready with your fingers, try to unblock the airway if that happens.*

What if it's not actually the Clifton Rapist? It might be a convicted killer just on a night out. We only know about this guy because we're looking for suspicious people. Maybe there's an innocent explanation why a guilty man is out.

But the yellow Capri? Her heart started pounding again.

She heard the clip-clip of her boots on the pavement, saw her breath slowly brighten as she approached the street lamp. She was 40 yards away from the light now.

Where were the officers? How many were there?

She still couldn't hear him.

What was his name? Evans? What if he starts talking?

Michelle had never seen where the observation men had been placed down here. *Were they in gardens or behind pillars? Were they in cars?*

What about Kelvin Hattersley? Where was he? Was the sergeant waiting in the distance so as not to startle the attacker, to allow the assault to take place? Or was he racing through the back streets of Bristol to get there?

Thirty yards to go.

Why did I join the police? Why? I had a good job in a holiday camp – I didn't have to put up with lecherous bosses and male prejudice and headless corpses and coming face to face with convicted killers in the night.

Twenty more yards. She was nearly at the street lamp, almost at the junction of Chantry Road and Hurle Crescent.

She was nearly in the centre of the trap.

Ten yards.

She still couldn't hear him. Perhaps the whole thing was in her imagination. Maybe it was a dream?

Now, finally, she stood under the street lamp.

Silence.

Michelle turned around.

CHAPTER FORTY-ONE

And there he was.

He just looked at her, he said nothing.

The man and woman stood there under the glare of a street lamp: convicted killer and decoy cop.

In some ways he seemed to be looking straight through her, as if she weren't there. He seemed to be weighing up what to do. Then he opened his mouth and said: 'Don't scream or I'll kill you.'

Michelle felt hands around her; the man dragged her towards a garden. She screamed at the top of her voice. Then she felt a rough punch to her face. She recoiled, shouted again.

The man just pulled her faster and harder into the darkness.

PC Andy Kerslake had been watching from the darkness of a garden as the silhouette of Michelle Tighe appeared from the bright distance of Whiteladies Road. Andy had lost sight of her as she went into the shadows and then regained vision as she re-emerged into the light of the street lamp. He couldn't make out the figure behind her but as Michelle and Ronald Evans had their momentary face-off, he had a clear view.

He saw the man who stooped over Michelle drag her away.

Andy ran from his fixed observation point. He sprinted across the road, hoping to find the right garden. As he reached a stone pillar, the man came running out. Andy rugby-tackled him to the ground, falling into the middle of the road.

Andy kept a grip of the man. Just 21, Andy was only slight, but he found a strength from somewhere to pin the perpetrator down.

Is Michelle okay? he asked himself. He would have to worry about her in a second. *Where's the others? What's happened to the others?* he shouted silently to himself. He could hear a car engine and a series of shouts. At the top of the road a pair of headlamps was heading forward. It looked like a big car or van. Was that the Task Force?

He and the man were in the road, sprawled out in the middle of the carriageway in the darkness, away from the light of the street lamp.

The car was approaching, it seemed to be getting quicker.

It was coming straight for them.

It would be on him in seconds.

He was going to die, he was going to bloody die.

Andy Kerslake held on to the killer with one hand, gripping the road with another, as his short life passed before him.

Brakes screeched.

His eyes closed.

More shouting. Andy opened his eyes and saw the rubber of the tyre two inches from his face: he was actually under the car.

There were more bodies now, more shouts. Chris Nott was there, he had piled in. Two other guys too.

The man was just lying there, not moving.

Sergeant Kelvin Hattersley got out from behind the driver's seat: 'Okay, lads, who's got the cuffs? Let's have a look at him.'

The man was facing the floor. They handcuffed his wrists behind his back and the pile of police bodies got off him.

Hattersley had a photo-fit image of the Clifton Rapist.

Andy was dusting himself off; he felt shaken but somehow thrilled. He looked at the picture Kelvin was holding and then he looked at the man who had just been turned over on the floor. In the light from the headlamps of the Task Force van Andy Kerslake saw that the picture and the suspect were identical.

Yes, we've got you – you bugger, he thought.

Having picked herself up, Michelle stumbled out of the garden towards the group of people. She looked across and saw a pile of bodies on the ground, shouting.

Kelvin Hattersley asked her if she was okay. She nodded, clutching her face.

'Yeah, he hit me. Couple of times,' she told him.

'We're going to need a statement from you.'

She nodded.

Kelvin took a closer look at Michelle in the streetlight. She was utterly pale, with marks around her neck. He and Michelle looked at each other. They didn't say anything more but the look was enough to show he knew just how lucky she had been.

Michelle was put in a car and driven to Redland Police Station. On the drive, the enormity of what she'd been through started to sink in. She was shaking, but part of her mind was computing, *Have we done it? Have we really done it?*

She would have to give her account of what had happened. Kelvin knew that the only proof they had was that Evans had punched Michelle. Now, the detectives would really have to get to work.

Phone calls were being made not just to Chief Superintendent Malcolm Popperwell, but to the Head of CID, Detective Chief Superintendent Brian Theobald and the Chief Constable, Kenneth Steele.

Officers started clearing the scene. One of them noted that despite the sheer drama of the previous 15 minutes: the hunt, the chase, the confrontation, the attack on Michelle, the shouts and screams, the punches, the man-to-man scuffle, rugby tackles, the screeching tyres and the mêlée of the arrest, not one light from a nearby house had been turned on. Not a curtain twitched, not a single person opened their front door.

As the last officers were leaving, a taxi arrived and a couple got out. They were dressed as if they had been attending a ball: she was in an evening gown, he was wearing a lounge suit. The pair kissed and laughed. They looked at the last officers, frowned, then went into their home. Five minutes earlier, this street had been the scene of one of the most dramatic police operations in recent British history. Within minutes, Hurle Crescent had returned to normal.

As the team returned to Redland Police Station with Michelle Tighe or to Southmead Police Station with Ronald Evans, they knew one thing: the excitement and thrill of springing the trap might be over, but this job was just half-done. An interrogation loomed. And the detective taking the call to say Operation Argus had stopped a man called

Ronald Evans knew several things: that the prime suspect was a convicted killer and would have knowledge of police, the law and justice's unique processes. If he was the Clifton Rapist, he was capable of the most incredible deceptions. And the main proof they had was that Evans had punched a police officer.

Little more than that.

CHAPTER FORTY-TWO

etective Chief Superintendent Brian Theobald was
asleep in his home in the North Somerset countryside
when his phone started ringing. Since the beginning of
Operation Argus, back in January 1979, he had gone to bed
each night hoping to get the call, but after two months, his
optimism had waned.

Now, with the plan about to end, he was stunned to get
the call in the early hours.

After putting down the receiver, he got dressed, got his
head together and sped to Southmead Police Station, where
he was told a convicted killer called Ronald Evans was
awaiting interview.

He read Michelle Tighe's statement. Until the morning of
23 March 1979, the Detective Chief Superintendent had
never heard the name Michelle Tighe. Michelle in turn
knew Theobald as one of the Gods – but a good one.

Theobald checked in with the Argus team. No, they
didn't think Evans suspected there had been a sting operation. He didn't know Michelle was a WPC. Perhaps he
should hold that back and wait and see what happened
when the penny dropped?

Theobald read what little information the force had been able to glean at this early hour: Ronald Evans, electrician, 38 years old, formerly from Shirebrook in Derbyshire, now living in a Bristol suburb. Murdered 21-year-old shop-worker Kathleen Heathcote in November 1963. Convicted in March 1964, released to an open prison in 1974 and then on life licence in 1975.

'Why didn't we know he was on our patch?' Theobald asked a junior detective.

In response, he received a shrug and two words: 'Probation Service.'

Theobald tutted before refreshing his mind with the outline details of the attacks:

Attack 1: 16 July 1977, Pembroke Road, Alice Matthews.
   A married woman coming home from a club.
Attack 2: 19 July 1977, Alexandra Road, Patsy Delaney.
   An 18-year-old coming home from a club. Yellow
   Capri seen nearby.
Attack 3: 11 September 1977, Leigh Road, Denise Turner.
   A folk singer returning home from a gig.
Attack 4: 10 November 1977, Grove Road, Hélène Baur,
   Austrian student. This was the only 'full rape' as
   Theobald would have described it.
Attack 5: 4 March 1978, Joanna McGarry – followed in
   her car by a yellow Capri.
Attack 6: 30 March 1978, Wendy Johnson in an alleyway
   in Kingsdown.
Attack 7: 20 April 1978, 45-year-old Rachel Doulton in
   her Clifton flat.

Attack 8: 9 December 1978, Tilly Sanderson. Happened
in the dark, she didn't see him and didn't report the
assault until door-to-door police found her.

Attack 9: 16 December 1978, Anna Soltys. Polish au pair
assaulted on Durdham Down.

Something bothered Theobald about Attacks 6 and 7.
Attack 6 was in a different area to all the others. And Attack
7 was a completely different modus operandi: in a woman's
flat. He was doubtful about whether the Clifton Rapist was
behind those but if he asked open questions, perhaps Ronald
Evans would unwittingly guide him.

Evans was brought into a grey, bland interview room in
Southmead Police Station, where he sat at one side of a table.
Detective Chief Superintendent Brian Theobald walked in,
suited and smart. He was joined by a detective sergeant who
would 'scribe' what would happen. Evans didn't have a lawyer.

The interview started at 4.45 a.m.

Brian Theobald cautioned him and began with an obvious but perhaps the only open question possible: 'Do you
know why you've been arrested?'

Evans: 'I think so.'

Theobald: 'It's alleged this morning you attacked a
woman.'

Evans: 'I don't think so.'

Theobald: 'I believe that in addition to attacking this
woman you are responsible for a number of other attacks
upon women in this city in the past two years.'

He paused before adding: 'Do you want to say anything
about it?'

CHAPTER FORTY-TWO

Evans: 'No.'

Brian Theobald was struck by the similarity between the man before him and the victims' artists' impressions and photo-fit images. He smelt of drink. And he spoke with a defined East Midlands accent. Flat vowels, just as the survivors had described.

Theobald: 'Are you married?'

Evans: 'Yes.'

Theobald: 'Do you have a family?'

Evans: 'Yes, a little girl. She's about 20 months.'

Theobald: 'Are you working at the moment?'

Evans: 'Yes, I'm an electrician at RT2, down the smelter.'

Brian Theobald didn't probe further here, but he knew that Evans was referring to a chemical firm at Avonmouth Docks.

Theobald: 'Why do you attack women?'

Evans: 'I don't.'

Theobald: 'Let's talk about this morning, then. Why did you attack this woman this morning?'

Evans: 'I don't know that I did.'

Theobald: 'Why did you attack her?'

Evans: 'I was going to chat her up.'

Theobald: 'By running at her?'

Evans: 'I didn't run at her.'

Theobald offered a smile: 'Well, tell me what you *did* do.'

Evans: 'I'm not the man you're looking for, for all the attacks on women.'

Theobald: 'But it's not the first occasion you've attacked women, is it?'

Evans: 'No.'

Theobald: 'Why do you think you're here now?'

Evans just sat there and looked at him.

Theobald, quietly: 'How long have you been married?'

Evans: 'Twelve months.'

Theobald: 'Is this the first time you've been married?'

Evans: 'No.'

Theobald: 'You're in some trouble at the moment.'

Evans: 'Yes, I am.'

Theobald: 'How old are you?'

Evans: 'Thirty-eight.'

Theobald: 'Why were you out at three o'clock in the morning?'

Evans: 'For a drink.'

Theobald: 'What time did you leave home?'

Evans: 'Nine o'clock.'

Theobald: 'Where did you go then?'

Evans: 'The Duke of York in St Paul's.'

Theobald: 'How long did you stay there?'

Evans: 'I dunno. We stayed late.'

Theobald: 'Where did you go then?'

Evans: 'I had trouble with the car at Cheltenham Road – I had to fix it.'

Theobald: 'Where did you go then?'

Evans: 'I first drove around.'

There was a silence, Theobald waited.

Evans: 'I followed the girl. I went into Whiteladies Road, I thought I'd chat her up. I followed her then to cross the road, then all hell broke loose.'

Theobald: 'Did you speak to her?'

Evans: 'No, I don't think so.'

Theobald: 'Do you know what time that was?'

Evans: 'No.'

Theobald: 'It was three o'clock. What time did you leave the pub?'

Evans: 'An hour earlier.'

Theobald: 'So, people will say you left at 2 o'clock?'

Evans: 'Dunno.'

Theobald looked at Evans.

Theobald: 'I've reason to believe you are responsible for a number of attacks on women in this city. During the past 18 months seven women have been attacked in the Clifton area and I believe you're the man responsible for those assaults.'

Evans: 'No.'

Theobald: 'Is there something mentally wrong with you?'

Evans: 'I find it hard to talk to people.'

Theobald: 'I don't mean that, I'm talking about serious sexual attacks on women.' He growled the last five words as if Evans's last excuse was beneath contempt.

Evans: 'I didn't do them.'

More silence; the two men looked at each other.

Theobald: 'Where were you born?'

Evans: 'Derbyshire.'

Theobald: 'Do you have a good marriage?'

Evans: 'Yes.'

Theobald: 'What do you think your wife is going to say about this?'

Evans: 'She'll be shattered – she ought to have her mother with her when you see her.'

Theobald: 'Did you meet your wife in Bristol?'

Evans: 'Yes.'

Theobald: 'Why do you do these things?'

Evans: 'I start to chat these girls up and then I lose my confidence.'

Theobald: 'It's a good thing somebody came to her aid tonight.'

Evans: 'Yes, I suppose it was.'

Theobald: 'I understand you said to the girl, "Be quiet or I'll kill you."'

Evans: 'She's mistaken.'

Theobald: 'So, she's telling lies, is she?'

Evans: 'No, she's mistaken.'

Theobald: 'How is it she ends up with bruises on her throat?'

Evans: 'Dunno.'

Theobald: 'You see, I understand you put your arm around her throat.'

Evans: 'It was more round her shoulders.'

Theobald: 'But she wouldn't get bruises on her throat from you putting your arm around her shoulders, would she?'

More silence.

Theobald: 'Do you know who the girl is?'

Evans thought, then said: 'No.'

Theobald: 'Do you know who the men are that came to her assistance?'

Evans: 'I suppose they were policemen.'

Theobald: 'Yes, and the girl was a policewoman.'

Evans sat pale and silent.

Theobald spoke quietly: 'Now why do you think they were there when you attacked her?'

CHAPTER FORTY-TWO

Evans: 'Dunno.'

Theobald: 'Well, think about it.'

Evans sat there, looking at the desk.

Evans: 'I can see what you're getting at.'

Theobald: 'So it's not only the girl who says you grabbed her round the throat and said, "Be quiet or I'll kill you," but other police officers witnessed the assault as well.'

Evans: 'I don't remember saying it.'

Theobald: 'Well, what was your intention when you grabbed hold of this girl?'

Evans: 'Dunno. I was just going to chat her up.'

Theobald: 'And your idea of a chatting a girl up at 3 o'clock in the morning is to run at her and grab her around the neck?'

Evans: 'I didn't run at her.'

Theobald: 'Don't you think there's something wrong with you, doing this sort of thing?'

Evans: 'I don't know.'

Theobald: 'I've mentioned a number of sexual assaults on women in Bristol.'

Evans: 'On some of those I've been out of Bristol. I've been interviewed by police before – about a murder.'

Theobald: 'When was that?'

Evans: 'I can't remember.'

Theobald: 'When did you come to Bristol?'

Evans: 'May '74 or '75.'

Theobald: 'When we arrested you tonight, you were wearing two pairs of trousers. One over the other. Why was that?'

Evans shrugged.

Theobald: 'It really is very strange to be going out at night, driving in a warm car, wearing two pairs of trousers. Were you worried about getting mud on the ones underneath?'

Evans said nothing. Theobald detected him starting to close up and tried a different tack.

Theobald: 'Tell me about your wife.'

Evans said nothing.

Theobald: 'How many children do you have?'

Evans: 'I've my daughter in Bristol, a son in the Midlands and my wife is pregnant. When will you be going to see her?'

Theobald: 'As soon as it becomes a reasonable hour.'

Evans: 'Can you take her to her mother?'

Theobald: 'Yes, I'll see that your wife gets the assistance she needs. But I'll ask you again, *why* did you attack this woman this morning?'

Evans: 'We had a bit of an argument this morning about money and I suppose I was thinking about that – I thought I'd chat someone up.'

Theobald: 'Why are you short of money?'

Evans: 'Since the mortgage rates went up – I'm buying my own house.'

Theobald: 'Have you ever received any psychiatric treatment?'

Evans: 'Not really.'

Theobald: 'Do you think there's anything wrong with you?'

Evans: 'I'm insecure, I suppose.'

Theobald: 'Did the argument about money upset you?'

Evans: 'I just told her I can't afford expensive presents for Mother's Day and birthdays.'

Theobald: 'I don't understand why chatting up girls eases this pressure on you.'

Evans: 'I s'pose it just does.'

Theobald: 'But in the cold light of day it doesn't make sense. I don't understand the relation between the two. Why do you turn to women to ease this tension, or is it a combination of drink and women?'

Evans: 'Not really.'

Theobald: 'How much had you had to drink?'

Evans: 'Three pints and some whisky.'

Theobald: 'Is that the reason when you've been drinking – a combination of the two, drink and depression?'

Evans: 'Dunno. I'm only pleased that I've not hurt this girl tonight.'

Theobald: 'That's the point, that no serious injury has been caused in any of these assaults.'

Evans: 'I thought they'd all been raped?'

Theobald: 'We're talking about serious sexual assaults. But in all the attacks the women have been grabbed and held around the throat in exactly the same way as you did with this policewoman tonight. I also understand you've told them to be quiet and they wouldn't get hurt.'

Evans: 'No, I haven't done that.'

Theobald: 'Are your parents still alive?'

Evans: 'Yes, they're in Derbyshire.'

Theobald: 'Do you keep in touch with them?'

Evans: 'Yes.'

Theobald: 'What's their reaction to this going to be?'

Evans: 'Terrible.'

Theobald: 'That's the point I'm trying to get over to you, that *you have done terrible things*. Can't you see that?'

Evans: 'Dunno.'

Theobald: 'There must be a reason for you to have done these things? Don't you accept you have a problem?'

Evans: 'I've got no future.'

Theobald: 'That's a bit of a defeatist attitude.'

Evans: 'I just feel like giving up.'

Theobald: 'Well, stop thinking about yourself for a minute and think about these women and the experiences they've gone through.'

Evans: 'I don't want to hurt anyone.'

Theobald: 'Well, you've already hurt quite a number of people. Do you intend to go on causing more distress?'

Evans: 'No.'

Theobald: 'Are you violent by nature?'

Evans: 'No more than's necessary.'

Theobald: 'What's happened happened, it's done, it can't be undone. What you can do is avoid causing more distress to these women.'

Evans: 'I didn't do any of them.'

Theobald: 'On the 16th of December, just before Christmas last year, a young woman was assaulted on Durdham Down. It was three in the morning. I believe you were responsible for that assault.'

Evans: 'Don't think so.'

Theobald: 'This woman was walking from the top of Blackboy Hill towards White Tree Roundabout when you pulled up in front of her in your Ford Capri and you looked at her. A few minutes later, she was attacked.'

Evans: 'I think I'm going to be sick.'

Evans vomited over the interview desk. Detective Chief Superintendent Brian Theobald managed to move just quickly enough to avoid the contents of the murderer's stomach splashing over his bespoke suit.

The interview was suspended while a cleaner was found. When they adjourned, Ronald Evans looked sheepish. Detective Chief Superintendent Brian Theobald thought Evans looked more embarrassed by the vomit than his arrest. They sat down in the same, freshly wiped seats. Evans was offered a doctor but he said he didn't want one.

Theobald: 'So what makes Ronald Evans go from time to time and assault these women? Is the reason purely sexual or as you've tried to suggest, just for company? Do you visit prostitutes?'

Evans: 'No.'

Theobald: 'Do you know what brings these urges on?'

Evans: 'No, you've got me confused.'

Theobald: 'That's the last thing I want to do, but I'm just trying to find out why you do these things?'

Evans: 'I don't know.'

There was a silence.

Evans: 'All I've done is ruin a lot of people's lives.'

Theobald: 'I must ask you the question again: are you the man responsible for these attacks?'

Theobald and Evans studied each other.

Theobald: 'Tell me what you're thinking.'

Evans: 'I'm very confused. I'm worried about my wife – she's pregnant again, I don't know what this'll do to her.'

Theobald: 'When I see her, I assure you I'll be as considerate as possible. You don't need to worry about that.'

Theobald saw Evans looking at him. He wondered if Evans was calculating how much he could trust him.

Evans: 'Can I see her?'

Theobald: 'Of course you can. Do you think you should at this stage?'

Evans: 'Yes, I must. She's the person I must see. If I can see her and tell her exactly what's happened, I'll see you afterwards. I must see her first. Do you understand?'

Theobald nodded. He stopped the interview, got up and knocked for the door to be opened. When he got through, he was greeted by Chief Constable Kenneth Steele.

'Well?' asked the Chief in his clipped voice.

'He's our man, but we haven't got him yet.'

CHAPTER FORTY-THREE

Somewhere far away, Michelle Tighe could hear a door-bell. But it kept ringing.

It refused to stop.

Slowly, the darkness of her mind gave way to a foggy consciousness and she realised she was sleeping. She sat up and stumbled from her bed. Where were her flatmates, Jackie and Jean? Couldn't they answer the bell?

Michelle went down the stairs and opened the front door. She was greeted by a big bunch of flowers.

'These are for Michelle Tighe,' said a woman thrusting the flowers at her. She wore a burgundy apron and an impatient look.

Michelle thanked her but noticed that before she turned, the delivery woman glanced at her throat and her eyes seemed to enlarge just a little. She closed the door and pulled the card from the flowers. It read: 'To: WPC Michelle Tighe, with sincere thanks. From: The Chief Constable'.

Well, that was effusive, thought Michelle as she checked in the mirror and saw a string of bruises had started to form around the front of her neck.

* * *

Two miles away at Southmead Police Station, Detective Chief Superintendent Brian Theobald stood next to Chief Constable Kenneth Steele in a grey corridor as they watched a tearful pregnant woman leave a police interview room.

Her life will never be the same again, Theobald thought grimly to himself.

Ronald Evans had not attacked her, he hadn't crept up in the night and assaulted her. He hadn't appeared to her as a spectral figure who emerged from the shadows. Instead, he had been there before her in plain sight. He had married her, had a child with her and she would give birth to his baby in the months to come. She was a victim too, as was the daughter he had seen at the little house an hour earlier. As was the baby growing inside her.

All collateral damage in the selfish, depraved, destructive world of Ronald Evans.

Theobald looked at Steele and the Chief Constable said in his clipped, militaristic voice: 'Good. It's time, Brian.'

Theobald re-entered the room with the detective sergeant, who had been there for hours.

Ronald Evans looked impassive, blank almost.

Evans: 'I think I've caused enough people enough trouble. I don't want to cause any more distress to anyone. You can stop your inquiries and there'll be no need to call in any of those women to give evidence. I've told me wife what I've done, I'm prepared to admit what I've done.'

Theobald: 'I assume you're talking about the number of sexual attacks on women in the Clifton area of Bristol. Is that correct?'

Evans: 'Yes.'

Theobald: 'You're now admitting that you are responsible for a number of the assaults, are you?'

Evans: 'Yeah, but not all of them, 'cause there was one when I was out of Bristol.'

Theobald: 'I deliberately haven't gone into detail about any of them because I would prefer that you tell me what you remember about them.'

Evans: 'I understand.'

And then, like a book, Evans opened up. He admitted in intimate and graphic detail how he had attacked five of the nine women.

He said he was out of Bristol during attacks six and seven: those victims were Wendy Johnson in the alleyway in Kingsdown and Rachel Doulton in her Clifton flat. He denied the only attack which had been classed as rape, against Hélène Baur at the Grove Road electricity substation in November 1977. And despite his extreme physical reaction to Brian Theobald's description of the Durdham Downs attack on Anna Soltys in December 1978, he also said he was not responsible for that assault.

Theobald charged him with the attempted rape of Tilly Sanderson and actual bodily harm of Michelle Tighe. That would be enough to take him off the streets but corroboration would be needed for the other offences.

Evans was remanded in custody while detectives pieced together his whereabouts. He might yet repeat his trick from 1963: confess in a police interview but switch his plea to Not Guilty in court.

What could they prove?

Dare they believe they had the Clifton Rapist in custody?

Were the streets truly safer? And had this remarkable gamble of using young female officers as bait actually worked?

When Michelle Tighe walked into the bar at Redland Police Station that night she couldn't work out what was more heartening: the cheer that greeted her or the looks on people's faces. She was back-slapped, hugged and embraced by officers whom she had never met, as well as the many that she knew and counted as friends.

Some pointed at her throat and asked her about the injuries.

'What did he look like?'

'Did it hurt?'

'Was he like the photo-fits?'

Michelle told them everything that had happened: the walk up Whiteladies Road, the message in her ear, the car following behind, the choice she had to make – main street or sideroads.

When she described the attack, she noticed how her audience recoiled.

And what about Evans's appearance?

The similarity between Ronald Evans's face and the photo-fits and artists' impressions was something that had stunned Michelle, Brian Theobald and the few other detectives who had seen his face.

How had this monster been able to get away with it for so long?

Why didn't we know about him?

Where was the Probation Service in all of this?

Avon and Somerset Police had put out a media release to announce the charging decision, but also urged people to be careful. Two things were possible: Ronald Evans was a fantasist and there was a chance, however remote, that he was not the Clifton Rapist. The other, stronger possibility was that there was a copycat offender. Evans admitted five counts, why deny four more? There was still a risk to women.

The officers at the party talked of all of this and more. They drank together regularly and the lines were always blurred between work-talk and chat about life outside the force.

Steph Whittle, Sally Difazio, Jean Castle and Jackie Clair told Michelle she was not going to put her hand in her purse all night. As did a good many of the male detectives. And some of them were standing a bit too close to Michelle for her liking after a few hours and a few more drinks had passed.

Chris Nott offered John O'Connor a bet: a fiver to steal Malcolm Popperwell's hat.

As the numbers grew inside the police bar, bodies squashed tighter.

O'Connor found himself directly behind Popperwell. Reaching across, he swooped down, grabbed the pork pie hat and swung it over, plopping it on Chris Nott's head. Popperwell spun round, his face a darker shade of puce, and started tearing strips off Chris. Later, Chris would have to pay the £5 bet – the wording had been to steal the hat, there was no small print about where it would end up.

The whole Operation Argus team was there – well, almost.

As Michelle Tighe went to the bathroom towards the end of the night, she saw the unmistakable figure of Chris Gould in drag.

'What are you doing?' she asked.

'There's still a warning out,' he said. 'We might have the wrong man. I know Argus should have wrapped, but I want to give it one more night.'

His team of five observation men looked in at the party, shrugged and followed him out into the night.

As the evening ended, it struck Michelle that not one single member of Avon and Somerset Police's top brass had asked her how she was, questioned how she was dealing with the trauma of the attack. She knew the force didn't offer counselling services for its officers, but why not? And surely some of them should have the decency to ask if she was okay?

Michelle woke in the night. There was a sound. It was indistinct, but coming from the window. She opened her eyes and couldn't make it out at first.

Through the window she could see a clear night; the sky had a blue tinge which seemed to blend with the black. The moon was full, the stars seemed to shine a little more brightly than usual. And the light from the sky highlighted a round silhouette at the window.

It seemed from Michelle's bed to resemble a person's head.

Then it started to move.

It raised itself up to reveal that it was indeed a man.

The window's lower sash slid up and the shadow entered the room.

Michelle froze.

Now the tall, stocky figure was heading towards her, padding silently across the room. A shaft of light cut through the night, illuminating the face. It was a photo-fit of a man, white and in his thirties. He had big black hair and an impassive look above his handlebar moustache.

'Hello, Michelle,' he said in a broad East Midlands accent. 'You know me. I've managed to escape from prison, I've got some unfinished business …'

The dreams always stopped at that point for her.

But the nightmares continued for months to come.

Michelle was never offered any counselling or support. In the weeks that followed, no one of a higher rank ever asked how she was getting on. It was just part of the job, it seemed.

CHAPTER FORTY-FOUR

23 JULY 1979

Four months passed between capture and court. Detectives interviewed everyone who knew Ronald Evans. A few friends and workmates knew he had spent time in prison, but none thought he was a convicted killer. To them, he was Ron the Electrician: a family man, a loving father and husband.

His wife refused to believe her husband was the Clifton Rapist.

Michelle Tighe had not been part of the inquiry into Ronald Evans: the large investigation working out where he had been on each attack night, and with whom. As she approached through a narrow lane near Bristol Crown Court, she could hear a crowd of people: a low-level chatter, shouts and clicks.

When she turned on to Bridewell, she saw the photographers, journalists and producers carrying clipboards. The press pack outside Bristol Crown Court was three deep, the biggest she'd ever seen. Ahead of her, she could see Detective Chief Superintendent Brian Theobald and heard shouts of 'That's him, he's the SIO [senior investigating officer], get a pic of him.' There was a click-click-click as Theobald, smooth and elegant, walked through the crowd and into the building.

'Hang on, hang on, he's here, lads! He's here!' came another shout. Michelle looked behind her and a security van was speeding up the street. It swung round through a set of iron gates before pulling up by a rear door. Moments later, the van door opened and a guard wearing a blue uniform and a flat cap descended, one arm trailing behind. Cuffed to that arm was Ronald Evans.

Clean-shaven, he was wearing a jacket and smart trousers. He looked impassively at the clicking, snapping, shouting crowd.

Even though she was in uniform, Michelle noticed not one photographer took a picture of her as she walked up the steps and into the building. Inside, she made her way to the door marked Court Room One. Chief Superintendent Malcolm Popperwell was already inside, chatting with Detective Chief Superintendent Brian Theobald. They saw Michelle and called her over.

'There's a good chance the judge is going to say some nice words about you, Michelle,' said Theobald. 'I hope you enjoy this moment – you deserve it.'

Michelle thanked him.

'What do you think he'll get?' she asked.

'He'll have his life licence revoked – he won't be going anywhere for a long time. But it depends on the judge.'

'What's the maximum sentence for sexual assault?'

'Two years. And he'll get time for the attack on you.'

Michelle did the maths. Evans was pleading guilty, so he would get some credit for that, but if he got 18 months for each assault, that would be nine years as a minimum.

'Quick question,' she continued. 'What's the maximum sentence if he'd sexually assaulted a man?'

Theobald and Popperwell looked at each other.

'Two years for sexually assaulting a woman, 10 years for a man,'* said Theobald.

She was sure she noticed him blush slightly.

They made their way into the courtroom, a high-ceilinged room with stained-glass windows across the upper third of a wall. Beneath a cream public gallery was a dark, almost ebony-coloured set of benches. Men in white wigs and robes chatted. Some looked serious.

The press bench was packed. Michelle recognised TV reporters alongside others she assumed must be from the newspapers.

Notebooks ready. Pens poised.

There was a knock and a door opened. The chatter fell silent as the judge walked in.

'Okay, the case of R v Evans, Yer Honour,' shouted the court clerk.

The judge nodded, then said, 'Do we have the defendant?'

'On his way … here he is.'

There was a rattling of metal on metal and spinning around, Michelle saw Ronald Evans being led in, still cuffed to the security guard. He was brought to the dock, had his cuffs removed and was told to stand.

---

* This changed under the Sexual Offences Act 1985 when the maximum sentence for an indecent assault on a woman was increased to 10 years, in parity with attacks on men.

The judge said: 'Mr Evans, in a moment the clerk will read out each of the counts and you'll be asked how you plea: do you understand?'

Evans nodded gently.

The clerk stood and said: 'Ronald Evans, you are charged with six counts. The first being that on July 16th 1977, you indecently assaulted a woman, namely Alice Matthews, on Pembroke Road in the City of Bristol. How do you plead?'

Evans faltered for a moment, then muttered, 'Guilty.'

'Guilty?' repeated the clerk.

Evans nodded.

The clerk then repeated the process: 'That on July 19th 1977, you indecently assaulted a woman, namely Patsy Delaney, on Alexandra Road. Do you plead guilty or not guilty?'

'Guilty.'

'That on September 11th 1977, you indecently assaulted a woman, namely Denise Turner, on Leigh Road. Do you plead guilty or not guilty?'

'Guilty.'

'That on March 4th 1978, you indecently assaulted a woman, namely Joanna McGarry, in Durdham Park. Do you plead guilty or not guilty?'

'Guilty.'

Michelle glanced at the press bench, watching the 20 or so reporters furiously trying to scribble down the details of the offences.

'That on December 9th 1978, you indecently assaulted a woman, namely Matilda – otherwise known as Tilly – Sanderson on Queen's Road. Do you plead guilty or not guilty?'

'Guilty.'

Michelle also looked at the public gallery and wondered if any of his victims were here.

'And that on March 23rd 1979, you assaulted a police-woman, namely WPC Michelle Tighe, on Hurle Crescent, Bristol. Do you plead guilty or not guilty?'

Michelle held her breath for a moment.

'Guilty.'

The judge told Evans to sit down and the prosecuting barrister stood up.

'Six guilty pleas, Your Honour. The facts of the case are Ronald Evans is responsible for a series of terrifying attacks on young women in the City of Bristol. He would go out late at night, usually after a drink, and identify lone women, whom he would then threaten with physical violence and even death before subjecting them to depraved and prolonged sexual assaults. The impact on his victims cannot be overestimated. One of the attacks lasted some 15 minutes, others continued for over two hours. During these attacks his victims had no idea if they would live or die.

'Police tried everything in their powers to find the man, without luck. His victims were able to produce a set of photo-fit pictures which have an uncanny resemblance to the defendant. The attacks were high-profile and received a large amount of press attention. In 1977, police were forced to take the unique step of warning women not to go out at night.'

The barrister paused before adding, 'The Avon and Somerset force has *never* had to do that before.

'Ronald Evans was caught by an innovative police operation which had been running for many months. Now, it is unusual for police covert tactics to be discussed in court, but suffice it to say, since January a team of up to 200 officers had been working on this operation, which was codenamed "Argus".'

Michelle noticed the press looking at each other before scribbling feverishly again.

'This undercover operation involved teams of women police constables walking in attack hotspots, hoping to lure the man who had become known as "The Clifton Rapist". This is the largest covert operation in the force's history, probably one of the largest in British history. Between January and March of this year, it took up some 10,000 police man hours.'

What about women *hours?* thought Michelle.

'Your Honour will be interested to note that the force took the highly unusual step of asking some of its male officers to be deployed in drag to try to attract the attacker,' the barrister continued, a gentle smile playing on his lips as he said this.

The journalists were wide-eyed, some were scratching their heads.

'Ronald Evans was caught by Operation Argus operatives in one of these sting deployments in the early hours of March 23rd of this year. By all accounts it was a dramatic moment: the officer, a WPC Michelle Tighe, was on shift as a decoy when an observation officer noted a man who resembled the photo-fits following her. He was driving a car, namely a yellow Ford Capri, and the number plate was checked immediately with the South West Regional Criminal Records Office. It was found to belong to this man, who has a previous conviction for murder.

'This information was relayed through a concealed communication device to WPC Tighe, who then faced a choice whether to stay on the main road, Whiteladies Road, or to go into the side streets, where she might be attacked by this man, this convicted murderer. In a moment of outstanding police courage, WPC Tighe chose the latter and along Hurle Crescent at about 2.20 a.m., she was approached by Ronald Evans. He said, "Don't scream or I'll kill you," grabbed her around the throat and punched her twice.

'Ronald Evans was arrested by PC Andrew Kerslake. The defendant then admitted these counts in a later police interview.'

The judge looked fascinated. Michelle knew he would have read this submission before the sentencing hearing, but he seemed electrified by the barrister's live delivery of the account.

The press bench leaned forward in a state of disbelief.

'Your Honour,' continued the barrister, 'as I've already mentioned, Ronald Evans has one previous conviction. That is of murder. On November 21st 1963, he killed a 21-year-old shop-worker, Kathleen Heathcote, in Mansfield in Nottinghamshire.

'In March 1964, he was convicted of that charge at trial and was sentenced to life in prison. In 1974, he became a member of a Prison Hostel Scheme and started work as an electrician at a chemical firm in Avonmouth. He was released on life licence in 1975. You will be aware from the charges that he started his new series of sexual offending a little over two years after his release.

'Ronald Evans is a married man. He is a father with a very young daughter, his wife is also expecting their second child. The first of these sexual assaults happened a few days after his daughter was born.

'Despite the guilty pleas, Mr Evans is a man who poses an extreme threat to the public in general and women in particular. He was given a chance to rehabilitate into society, he was given a chance of redemption. He repaid that trust by carrying out a prolonged and terrifying series of sexual assaults which, I have no doubt, would continue to this day, had it not been for this extraordinary police operation and the bravery of WPC Tighe.'

Michelle felt herself redden a little.

The barrister continued: 'There are still two unsolved sexual assaults and one unsolved rape committed during this period, but they are not part of this case.' He then outlined what length of sentence Ronald Evans should receive and sat down.

Evans's defence barrister stood up and began his address: 'Ronald Evans has pleaded guilty to these offences. He deserves maximum credit for that. And although it may be hard to find much sympathy for Mr Evans, there are a few factors which I feel I should put forward by means of mitigation.'

He paused for a moment to allow the press bench to catch up.

'Mr Evans had something of a difficult childhood and perhaps the seeds of all of this were laid at the beginning of his life. He was brought up by his grandparents in the belief they were his parents. They were of a strict Victorian code of morality. Mr Evans's mother was only 14 years old when she gave birth to him and he spent his childhood believing she was his sister. He has expressed great shame to me and to his wife for the offences he has committed, the shame that he has brought on his pregnant wife.

'I cannot mitigate the terror these girls must have felt on the night these attacks were made. But he served 11 and a half years for the offence of murder before being released on licence and there can be no doubt that that offence from 1963 seems to loom larger in his mind than the present ones. He has described a "deep, dormant bitterness" at the way he was treated by Nottinghamshire Police.'

The barrister sat down.

The judge spoke: 'Ronald Evans, you may stand.'

Evans shuffled to his feet.

'Ronald Evans, I am primarily to ensure you will never commit these sort of offences again. For each count of indecent assault, I sentence you to 18 months in prison, to be served consecutively. For the count of assaulting a policewoman, I sentence you to 18 months in prison. You deserve severe punishment for these wicked crimes. The sentence I am passing will ensure you go to prison for at least nine years. I shall also revoke your licence for liberty on life sentence. You will go back to prison on that sentence.

'Ronald Evans, young women must be protected against you. If, after they have been protected, all well and good. It will be for others to judge if you are ever freed again. If you are ever to be freed, I trust these people have in mind what a danger you have been.

CHAPTER FORTY-FOUR

'You may go down.'

Yes! thought Michelle.

Evans nodded and the security guard led him away through a dark wooden door. It closed with a bang.

The judge turned to the prosecuting barrister: 'I have need to offer commendations to Avon and Somerset Police for this operation to bring Ronald Evans to justice, the team so ably led by Detective Chief Superintendent Brian Theobald.'

The prosecuting barrister stood: 'Yes,' he said. 'Your Honour will be pleased to know that WPC Tighe is in court today.'

'Good.'

The barrister looked around and ushered Michelle to walk forward.

'WPC Tighe, on this night you displayed very great courage. The true measure of what you did was the risk you ran. It is very well known what happened before, but you can't tell what will happen next time. You acted with the highest courage. You are very highly commended.

'May I also commend the other decoy officers who patrolled the streets at night to try to trap Ronald Evans.'

The judge smiled down at Michelle and she blushed once more. He then rose and the courtroom started to clear.

Brian Theobald came over to congratulate her. A few journalists hung around in the background.

'Later, gents, later ...' Theobald told them as he led Michelle from the front door, shielding her.

As Michelle Tighe walked from the old courtroom onto the street, every single camera lens was trained on her.

CHAPTER FORTY-FIVE

Michelle found herself enjoying the rounds of inter-views. She gave quotes to the *Bristol Evening Post* and television news crews asked to film her walking down Hurle Crescent before interviewing her about the attack.

Two days later, she was on foot patrol on the Southmead estate when she passed a couple of teenagers smoking outside a newsagent.

'Oi, smell bacon, anyone?' she heard a young voice say.

She spun around and the look on the face of one of the lads went from wide grin to abject terror.

'Eh, she's that copper on TV. I saw 'er last night. Y'alright, miss?' He was looking kindly at her.

In the police station Michelle had become accustomed to other words being said about her. She would hear whispers: 'She's so brave,' 'What a decision,' 'Face to face with a murderer.' But as the weeks passed, other things were mentioned: 'Right place at the right time,' 'Didn't do anything special' and even 'I did far more runs than she did and she gets all the credit.'

She felt that policing, like British society in general, preferred its success to be gently muted.

The Chief Constable, Kenneth Steele, ordered pictures to

be taken of all the decoy officers dressed in their Operation Argus clothes. This included Chris Gould and Robbie Jones getting into drag one last time. They stood there waiting for the force's finest photographer, a scenes-of-crime officer, to take snaps.

Word of Operation Argus was now spreading to other forces, who were taking lessons from the experience of Avon and Somerset Police to use in their own areas. A meeting of the country's chief constables was scheduled and Steele was due to give a talk about how a team of undercover officers was able to catch one of the UK's most wanted men. But despite Operation Argus's success, old rhythms were hard to change.

Soon after Evans's sentencing, Michelle Tighe arrived at Redland Police Station, 20 minutes early for her shift, as usual. But she hadn't been able to find a parking space in the station's car park.

She went into her office and started back on her work-load: care cases, looking at a repeat female shoplifter and a runaway teenage girl. At five past the hour she saw a space appear, so she raced into the street and whizzed her car from her space on the road into the vacant spot. When she returned to her office she passed in the corridor Chief Superintendent Malcolm Popperwell wearing his pork-pie hat, his face a deep shade of puce.

'You're late,' he said.

'No sir, I was early. I was just parking my car …'

'You're late. If you're 20 minutes early, you're on time. If you're on time, you're late. Stop talking back to me and get back to work,' he snapped.

Days later, she received a letter saying she had been awarded a Queen's Commendation for Brave Conduct and would be mentioned in the *London Gazette*. The officer who had nominated her was Popperwell.

The entry read: 'Miss Michelle Tighe, Constable, Avon and Somerset Constabulary.

'For services leading to the arrest of a violent and dangerous man.'

In the summer, the Chief Constable held a party to celebrate Operation Argus's success. It was three years to the day since Steph Whittle and Chris Gould had both been named Cadets of the Year. The venue was Kingsweston House, a faded north Bristol mansion used by the force for training and meetings.

The decoys had photos taken as Kenneth Steele handed out commendation medals. They posed on a set of steps, their smiles revealing a youthful exuberance so far hidden under the pressure of this police operation. Their families had been invited, there were speeches and drinks. The decoys and the observation officers knew they had taken part in something ground-breaking, something never before seen in British policing. But something occurred to Michelle Tighe later on in the day. As she sipped a glass of champagne, she watched her friends laughing, her workmates swapping stories about arrests and freezing in the shadows, and the night Joe Harford got spooked by a guy with a sheet over his head. Her mind turned to two women.

The operation had been a success: Ronald Evans had been identified and caught.

The lives of five women had been forever changed by his attacks on them, but at least they had seen justice. But what about the others? What about Hélène Baur, who had suffered perhaps the most brutal attack? What had happened to her?

Everyone called Evans 'The Clifton Rapist' but he had not been convicted of that offence.

And what about Anna Soltys, Evans's final victim? Hers was the attack which had prompted Operation Argus.

What, if anything, could ever be done for these women?

The cases weren't closed but there was a good chance they'd be forgotten.

Despite his five guilty pleas, Ronald Evans was still evading justice.

CHAPTER FORTY-SIX

AUGUST 2004

Ronald Evans was happy. The Parole Board was happy too. Evans was 63 years old now. He had been a good inmate of HMP Channings Wood in Devon. Some of the lags found him a bit arrogant but according to the screws he was well-behaved, posed no threat and had spent some of the last 25 years studying for a law degree.

The Board had agreed he could move from the Category-C jail to an open prison.

Evans was rehabilitated, no longer a threat to people, the Parole Board had decided.

He sat in his cell and awaited his transfer.

A new dawn beckoned. Just a matter of days …

Ninety miles north at a police station in a Bristol suburb, Avon and Somerset Detective Sergeant Gary Mason was blissfully unaware of the existence of Ronald Evans. He would have heard his name in passing, back in 1979, but it had been filed along with the hundreds of other criminals he had come across in the intervening quarter of a century. And, to be frank, Gary had mostly forgotten about Operation Argus.

Gary was setting up one of the country's first Cold Case Units. He had joined the force in March 1977, four months before the Clifton Rapist began his assaults. Gary had worked on B-Division in south Bristol and spent precisely no time whatsoever in the 1979 hunt for Ronald Evans. He knew there had been a decoy operation, but had never known who the undercover officers were. For the last few years he had worked on the murder squad, just a few desks away from a civilian support worker called Michelle.

Twenty-five years on, Michelle was a mother-of-two, twice-married and now had the surname Leonard. She had rejoined the force in 1995, having left after the birth of her second child. But Michelle was no longer a police officer, instead she worked in the Admin Support Unit, helping major inquiries with statements and disclosures. She and DS Mason were part of a large team kept so busy with live homicide inquiries that the past was rarely spoken about – and Michelle never said.

In 2004 Gary Mason was 46 years old. Tall, with receding brown hair, he had a greying beard and wore shirts which colleagues complained would often hang out of the back of his suit trousers. He was also a methodical, determined and relentless investigator, which was why the force had asked him to find new clues in old cases to see if anything could be done to bring justice to victims.

The force had 23 'undetected' murders but the primary aim of the Cold Case Unit was undetected stranger rapes. Domestic rapes were left to one side. Forensics could only take these cases so far before arguments about consent began. But stranger rapes could be solved with new science, the force thought.

Gary started by asking all the chief inspectors on all the divisions to gather data on their undetected stranger rapes. He also asked the Crime Management Units in each area to help. And the Home Office had more information. At the end of this lengthy process he had a list of nearly 2,000 cases, which stretched back decades.

At first, Gary's Cold Case room in Kingswood Police Station was bare: just desks, chairs and filing cabinets. But as the weeks turned to months and more information piled in, he gained both two members of staff and an organised mountain of files, forensic submission forms, witness statements and index cards. From this, Gary drew up a top ten of the most 'solvable' cases to start working on, building some momentum for the new unit.

He was successful with his first attempt.

A young woman called Kath had been raped in her east Bristol flat in June 1979. A man had broken into her apartment as she slept, raped her and then fled. Kath had given a description of the man. This included an oddity about his front tooth: it was either chipped, missing or twisted. The *Bristol Evening Post* would soon call her attacker 'The Twisted-Tooth Sex Fiend'. But there were forensic opportunities too. He'd left fingerprints on the windowsill and semen samples on her nightclothes.

Police at the time were able to get a blood-grouping but there was no match with fingerprint records. The case was left as 'undetected' and her clothes were put in police storage. It was hoped that there would be some improvements in forensic science techniques.

Gary came across the case files in October 2004. He asked for a match of the fingerprints with modern records: had the attacker re-offended and been caught for something else? And he asked the lab if they still had Kath's clothing.

Soon he had two replies – and both were 'yes'.

In the 1990s customs officers had been making random checks of a cross-Channel ferry. All staff had their berths searched. They looked in the room belonging to the boat's pianist, a man called Nigel Palmer-Batt. There, they found homemade videotapes of him on the bed in his berth, having sex with women who appeared to be unconscious. Officers also discovered boxes of sleeping tablets on a shelf. His victims, when notified, had been too embarrassed to press charges, but his DNA and fingerprints had been taken and loaded onto national databases.

The fingerprints were a perfect match for Kath's attacker, back in 1979. And a later analysis of her nightclothes found that DNA in her nightdress – semen stains – was also a hit.

Palmer-Batt refused to plead guilty but a trial was held, the force's first Cold Case prosecution. It took the jury just 15 minutes to convict him and 'The Twisted-Tooth Sex Fiend' was sentenced to eight years in prison.

Mason and his Cold Case team were up and running, but his second inquiry proved more challenging. As Gary sifted through cases and lists of possible exhibits, one in particular caught his eye. It seemed to be a one-off case: a foreign student called Hélène Baur.

A man had raped Hélène in Redland Grove in November 1977. There was nothing in the files linking it to any other cases. There was a victim's statement. Gary read of the ordeal the young student had endured 27 years earlier: she was new to Bristol, she had been walking home alone. She had turned from Whiteladies Road onto Grove Road, where she had passed a man in a phone box in the dark. Moments later, she felt hands round her throat and heard a warning, 'Don't scream or I'll kill you.' Then she was dragged more than 100 yards, pulled over a low wall into an electricity substation, where she endured a prolonged attack.

The files said a doctor had taken swabs from Hélène's body and her underwear soon afterwards. A blood grouping had been identified, but this was nearly a decade before the advent of DNA profiling in policing. And no one had reviewed the case since then.

DS Gary Mason called the same laboratory that had helped him with the case of 'The Twisted-Tooth Sex Fiend'. The following day, the lab called back. Yes, Hélène's underwear had been kept in its large industrial freezers, preserved perfectly. The scientist told Gary that he would see what forensic opportunities were available.

Gary picked up the files for his third case and started investigating that. It's seldom that anything fast happens with Cold Case work: it is slow, methodical and not for the impatient.

Five weeks later, Gary was sitting at his desk at Kingswood Police Station when his phone rang.

'Gary Mason?'

'Yes.'

'You remember that Grove Road case you asked me to look at?'

'Yes.'

'We've got a full DNA profile from it.'

'Amazing.'

Not a man known for public shows of excitement, Gary breathed out and felt his heart skip a beat.

'And more than that, we've loaded it on to the DNA Database and we have a hit, we've got a match – we know whose DNA it is.'

'Well, I've got my pen in my hand …'

'Are you ready?'

'Yes.'

'Ronald Evans.'

'Ronald Evans, Ronald Evans, Ronald Evans …? Who is Ronald Evans?'

'You don't know who Ronald Evans is?'

'No.'

'The Clifton Rapist.'

'Oh ….'

Gary Mason thanked the scientist and put down the receiver as the penny dropped: Operation Argus. The case which had gained the force so much publicity in the late 1970s, made momentary heroes of a small team of women and men, and had then been all but forgotten bar those who had taken part in it, although he was convinced that he had seen something about the Clifton Rapist in a store somewhere recently.

* * *

Days later, Gary Mason was in the attic of Southmead Police Station dusting off files and pulling out crates which no one had touched for years. He had already checked the Police National Computer and found Ronald Evans logged there. Evans had murdered Kathleen Heathcote in 1963 and had been convicted of five indecent assaults between 1977 and 1978. Details of those assaults were listed.

As he thought about what he had read, on the side Gary saw what he was looking for: a box labelled 'Detected Clifton Rapist'.

Gary opened the box to find it stuffed with piles of papers, bags and documents. He put the lid back on and struggled down the two flights of stairs before loading the box into his car boot and heading back to the Cold Case office.

As he started to work his way through the files, Gary went back in time, back to the late 1970s. There were victim impact statements from women that he had never known, descriptions of terrifying attacks: the double-handed throat grip, being dragged to dark corners and subjected to prolonged attacks.

Gary knew Evans had admitted five sexual assaults but there were six cases in the box marked 'Detected Clifton Rapist'.

Why?

The names were there and he checked them off:

Alice Matthews, Evans convicted of indecent assault.
Patsy Delaney, Evans convicted of indecent assault.
Denise Turner, Evans convicted of indecent assault.

Joanna McGarry, Evans convicted of indecent assault.

Tilly Sanderson, Evans convicted of indecent assault.

But there was also another name: Anna Soltys. Ronald Evans had never admitted this attack, nor had he faced trial. The case had been effectively dropped when he admitted the other five attacks in 1979.

Gary looked through the crime report and paperwork for Anna Soltys's case and could see the clear similarities between her assault and the others. Anna had been an au pair, walking on Durdham Down at 3 a.m. on 16 December 1978. She had just said goodbye to her boyfriend. A yellow Ford Capri slowed and turned around. Moments later, she had felt the hands around her throat, heard the threat to kill and been subjected to the sexual assault. This had been the final straw, the attack which had prompted Chief Constable Kenneth Steele to approve the whole Operation Argus campaign.

There was a lot of corroboration to show that Ronald Evans had been responsible for the attack on Anna Soltys but he hadn't admitted it and perhaps the former lead detective, Detective Chief Superintendent Brian Theobald, hadn't thought there was quite enough proof to proceed, so the paperwork had been left in the box with the detected cases.

There was also a photo-fit image. It showed a man who looked chillingly like all of the other pictures, except for one. Hélène Baur's attacker seemed to have a slightly different appearance, according to her composite image. He had a rounder face and less hair, she recalled. But Gary had a

DNA hit with Hélène's case. Now he needed to do two things quickly: find what forensic opportunities existed with Anna's case, and find Ronald Evans.

Was he even in prison still? Evans had been given a nine-year sentence in 1979 – he could be roaming around anywhere. A quick search found that he was still in jail, at HMP Channings Wood in Devon. Gary called the prison and found that Evans was due to be transferred out any day.

'Oh no, you can't do that,' he said, 'I need to speak to him about a couple of sexual assaults. What can I do to stop that?'

A frantic email from DS Mason put a hold on Evans's move. His next line of inquiry was to contact the laboratory to see if they had any samples to link Ronald Evans with the December 1978 attack on Anna Soltys. In the paperwork was a forensic statement saying the laboratory had semen samples taken from Anna – they were preserved in slides.

Gary called and asked about the slides. The scientist checked, and two days later he received a call.

'Good and bad news. Yes, we've still got the slides and there's a sample in them. But there are only five sperm heads in it.'

The detective sergeant had been working with scientists for long enough to know that this was too small a sample to get a full DNA hit.

'Can you do anything?' he pleaded.

'We can try, but it's pushing it. You can choose. If we test it, it'll destroy the sample and you may not ever be able to get a full sample. You might want to delay it for a year or two, wait until forensic science gets better.'

But Gary insisted: 'No, I don't want to ruin it. Let's wait. We'll question Evans and see what he says.'

Meanwhile the stash of boxes was producing yet more forensic possibilities. Gary found a sealed brown bag among the files for Hélène Baur's case. Ripping it open, he saw a plastic bag with plastic tubes containing swabs for sexual offences. Each of the tubes had a sticker with Hélène Baur's name scribbled on it. He knew that a defence barrister would never accept these as admissible – they had not been stored under laboratory conditions, the samples may have degraded, there was no guarantee that they hadn't been planted or contaminated. But he still sent them away.

Weeks later, he received a call from a stunned scientist: 'How cold is that attic, Gary? You know those samples, they're a perfect match to Ronald Evans.'

Gary had two separate sets of DNA linking Ronald Evans with Hélène Baur and one untested set of DNA for Anna Soltys, which may or may not be him. Could Detective Sergeant Mason and his newly formed Cold Case Unit get justice for two victims after more than a quarter of a century, or would Ronald Evans put up a fight?

It was time to see what Evans had to say for himself.

CHAPTER FORTY-SEVEN

Detective Constable Rob Callaway had spent 20 years as a police officer, mostly as a detective. He had met all kinds of criminals and seen them react to arrest and questioning in different ways. But Ronald Evans's response to being transported was a new one.

Callaway knew he wasn't on a rollercoaster but part of him felt he was. He looked at the old man next to him, gripping the seat, knuckles even whiter than his pale face. Beyond the man, through the side window of the people-carrier, the green Devon countryside sped past, trees and bushes merging into a green blur.

'What speed you doing, Phil?'

Phil Brown was their analyst, who had agreed to drive. DS Gary Mason was in the front passenger seat.

'Sixty-five,' he shouted back.

Rob glanced again at the old, white man next to him, his skin paling to a near-blue. Ronald Evans hadn't said much when Rob had arrested him on suspicion of rape and attempted rape a couple of hours earlier. He had just sat quietly in the HMP Channings Wood interview room, looking into Rob's eyes as if he were trying to work this detective

294

out. Now in the car, Rob noticed Evans appeared to be performing breathing exercises.

'Are you okay?' asked Rob in his gentle Bristolian accent.

'No. I don't like this,' Evans replied. 'Ever since I've been banged up, I've been moved everywhere in a prison van. You can't see shit. Look at it, it's so fucking fast. How long till we get to Bristol?'

'About an hour and a half.'

Evans seemed to gasp for air.

'Why the fuck are you doing this now?' asked Evans. 'You knew I was gonna move to a Cat-D, you knew I were up for parole. This a police tactic?'

'No, Ronald,' said Rob patiently, answering the question for the third time. 'We've just been reviewing the case and wanted to ask you a few questions. I can't do that now – it wouldn't be right, you don't have a solicitor – so just see it as a day out, if you like.'

'A day out at 70 fucking miles an hour!'

Callaway glanced across at Evans again: he was 63 but had a frailness which made him seem about 15 years older. He was thin, wore a bodywarmer and had glasses. Rob had seen the photo-fits from the 1970s. This looked like a different man, a shadow of the imposing figure in those photographs.

DS Gary Mason had chosen Rob Callaway for the job because he was one of the force's expert interviewers. Unlike Evans's face-off with Brian Theobald back in 1979, these days the force didn't rely on its top brass to get confessions from suspects.

It was about ability, not seniority. And Rob was an advanced suspect interviewer.

'What do you do inside?' asked Rob curiously.

'The garden, I love the garden. Spend hours there, 'ave done for years,' Evans told him. Then he added: 'You know, I'm the longest-serving prisoner in England?'

'I didn't.'

'Should never have gone down for murder. I'm no murderer. The cops, them cops up in Nottingham, fitted me up.'

'How long have you done?' asked Rob gently.

'Just done 25 years, but if you add that to the 11 before and a bit of remand, you're looking at four fucking decades!'

Rob was about to reply when the phone in his jacket pocket started ringing. Pulling it out, he said, 'Hiya, oh hiya,' before replying to the question from someone at force headquarters. As he did so, he glanced to his right and could see Evans's mouth open as he chatted. He hung up.

'You alright, Ronald?'

'Can I see that?'

Rob frowned and looked back at him, questioning.

'I ain't seen one of these mobile phones. Couple of the lads have them inside, but I ain't got no one calling me. Don't have no need for one but I've never held one before.'

Rob shrugged and passed it over, adding, 'It's called a Samsung – look, here's the news.'

Callaway pressed a few buttons and a website popped up.

'Christ, what's 'appened in the world?!' Evans exclaimed as his eyes fixed on the road ahead again. 'Does he have to go so fast?'

CHAPTER FORTY-SEVEN

'What you doing now, Phil?' asked Rob.

'Sixty-five,' Phil shouted back.

'You should see what I do on my bike,' smiled Rob, thinking of his latest motorcycle.

Evans didn't return the grin.

'You goin' to interview me?' he asked.

Rob nodded.

'I know my fucking rights. Before the gardenin', I done a law degree. I'll never forget how them cops up in Nottingham fitted me up about that girl. Fitted me up, they did …'

'You said,' agreed Rob.

He noticed a flicker of spittle at the edge of Evans's mouth as he spat out his next words: 'I were 22. No lawyer. They were there talkin' 'bout Scotland Yard detectives seein' me, sayin' it were best to confess. Them bastards are why I've been locked away.'

He nudged Rob and stared at him.

'Now I know all 'bout procedure, been studyin' it. What they did was oppression. Fitted me up. Everything … everything changed that night. You better 'ave a lawyer waiting for me otherwise I ain't saying nothing to you, sunshine.

'Can they slow this fucking van down?'

'It's okay, Ronald. We've got you a solicitor to represent you. She's very good …'

'She? A fucking woman?! You *are* fitting me up?'

Callaway thought back to the papers he'd read about Ronald Evans. How he had grabbed 21-year-old Kathleen Heathcote's throat, threatened to kill her if she'd screamed. Then he thought about what he had done after she had: the car getting stuck, a police officer trying to help and how the man now sitting next to him was able to throw his victim in a reservoir and quietly drive away.

And that was before the seven sex attacks.

'How fast are we going?' asked Evans again.

Rob stared ahead, not wishing to waste any more of the driver's time on this man.

It was a new interview suite. DS Gary Mason was outside, watching on the video. Inside was DC Rob Callaway, Phil Brown, Ronald Evans and the solicitor he had met for the first time: Stacey Rush. They had arrived from prison early the previous evening. Evans had slept, met Stacey and was waiting with her as DC Callaway arrived.

'Morning, Rob,' said Evans, standing up and extending his hand.

Rob took it, more from politeness than desire.

'Did you go out on yer bike last night?'

Callaway frowned: 'Thanks for asking, Ronald. Yes, I had a quick yomp out to Weston-super-Mare. Watched the sun go down. Look, I'd love to tell you about my motorcycle adventures, but we have other things to talk about.'

'Yes, of course. Just interested.'

'Look, Ronald. You know we've arrested you on suspicion of one count of rape and another of attempted rape. Now I want to hear your version of events …'

'Well, I'm not a rapist – you know that, I told yer. But yeah, ask away,' said Evans, sitting back on his chair.

'We have recently set up a Review Team. Some call it a Cold Case Unit. It looks at unsolved cases where we believe there are opportunities, forensically, to find out who the criminal is.'

'Good. I've got nothing to hide.'

'Gary, who was in the car with us yesterday, has reviewed two attacks which happened at the same time as the series you admitted, back in the late seventies.'

Evans nodded.

Callaway looked down at his paperwork. It was more as a prop; he knew what he was going to say: 'The attacks we're looking at now are one in November 1977 and another in December 1978.'

'I don't know nothing about no rapes, I'm not a rapist.'

'You've been convicted of five sexual assaults.'

'No rapes,' Evans protested.

'Okay, Ronald. There are big similarities.'

Evans shrugged.

Callaway continued: 'Do you know what DNA is?'

Evans nodded.

'Good. It's a science we've used for a few years now and it allows us to unlock a lot of old cases.'

'Deena?' asked Evans.

'DNA,' said Stacey Rush, his solicitor.

He flashed her a look which fell somewhere between a leer and contempt.

Rob continued: 'Yes. We all have a unique DNA – yours is different to mine and each of ours is different to Stacey's here. We can leave traces of our DNA in things like saliva, blood, sweat, hair follicles and semen.

'If there's a sample of semen at a crime scene, we can get a perfect, unique DNA profile from that. It's like a fingerprint, but better. And if we find the person whose DNA matches the sample, there is a one-in-a-billion chance that it's not that man.'

Evans looked at his solicitor: 'That right?'

She nodded.

'So what?' he continued, turning to Callaway.

'When we reviewed the cases, we found your DNA on clothing from the attack in November 1977.'

Evans snorted.

'I wonder if you could tell us about this?'

'No comment, mate. Not me. I'm sure it's not me. Put me hands up to the attacks that I did. Pleaded guilty. There're none others.'

Callaway carried on looking at his paperwork.

'This attack, it was a full rape, as you might call it. It happened on Grove Road ...'

'Didn't do it.'

'Well, we kept the victim's clothing. She was called Hélène Baur, if you're interested. We froze this clothing at the time. We know it's been stored in laboratory conditions every day since the day after she was attacked. She says she was raped and the DNA sample our scientists have been able to obtain is yours. No question, no doubt. One-in-a-billion chance it's not you.'

Evans turned to his solicitor: 'What's he talkin' about? Is he fittin' me up? Is he like them corrupt bastards who fitted me up in Nottingham?'

Stacey Rush remained impassive: 'Hear what he has to say and we'll talk, Mr Evans.'

'So, November 1977, we know it's you,' said Callaway.

'And December 1978, on the Downs. The victim was a woman called Anna Soltys. Well, we also have a semen sample from that attack. Now the sample's only small. We haven't tested it yet. We can, but we think that if we hold on for a couple of years, we will have the science to do a better job. What that means is that if you were the attacker of Anna Soltys, you can admit it now, along with Hélène Baur. Or we can come back in, say, five years' time and if it's a hit, we'll charge you then and you'll be going back inside for longer.'

'I'm no rapist.'

'Well, the charge for November 1978, for Hélène Baur in Grove Road, that is rape. That's what we're looking at.'

Evans was silent.

Callaway looked further down the paperwork.

'Hmmm ... looking at the victim's recollection, we might have grounds for a buggery charge here.'

'Buggery?!' screamed Evans, banging the table. 'Buggery?! You're a fucking fantasist, man. That girl were making stuff up. Are you tryin' to fit me up?'

Callaway looked across at Evans. Until then he'd only seen a pale, old man but now he looked younger, angrier. It was like a switch had been flicked and he was energised by fury. Undeterred, he continued: 'The victim in the second attack, it was December 16th 1978. She saw a yellow Ford Capri beforehand. She says she was attacked by this man ...'

He slid forward the last photo-fit which had been produced.

'And this was you when you were arrested in March 1979.'

301

He placed the two images next to each other, like twins. Evans didn't look down at them. Callaway noticed his solicitor took a little breath.

'No comment, pal,' said Evans, menacingly.

'Tell you what, why don't you chat with Stacey and she can explain more?' said Callaway, smiling.

He and Phil Brown, the civilian officer, left the room. Forty-five minutes later, as they sipped at their dreadful vending machine coffees, Stacey Rush came out to speak to them.

'He wants to talk.'

They went back inside.

Ronald Evans was sitting there, staring ahead with his arms crossed, a scowl on his face.

His solicitor said, 'My client has said that he would like to make a partial admission.'

Callaway sat down opposite. This was a huge relief.

'Okay, Ronald, we'd love to hear your account of things. Telling the truth will be best for everyone, for the victims and for you …'

'And for you fuckers! I hope you're not fittin' me up – I've got a law degree,' Evans repeated.

'Please just tell me.'

'Okay. None of 'em are rapes. Both girls, I gave 'em a choice. I said they could do one of two things and one of 'em, that Grove Road one, she went for full sex.'

'But she didn't volunteer to have sex,' Callaway countered. 'She was coerced into …'

'No, no, no, Sunshine! I gave her a choice: oral or full.'

'And how do you see that as consent? She didn't want to do either.'

'Don't you get fucking pedantic with me! She had a choice, she could've done either. Consent.'

'And if she wanted to do neither? If she wanted to just go home …?'

Evans went quiet.

'That is an offence of rape,' said Callaway.

Evans harrumphed.

'What about Anna Soltys? On the Downs?'

'Same thing, she opted for the other,' Evans said sulkily.

'Did she volunteer any sexual act?'

'I gave her a choice: one or other. Look, I've got a law degree and the law's changed 'bout rape. I know what I'm talkin' about. If you say that's attempted rape, I'm not sayin' nothin'. You're gonna have to prove it, Sunshine.'

Ronald Evans was duly charged with the rape of Hélène Baur on Grove Road in November 1977 and the attempted rape of Anna Soltys on Durdham Down in December 1978. Evans was taken off to a cell along with his solicitor, Stacey Rush.

DS Gary Mason entered the interview suite.

'Well done, Rob.'

'We're going to have a trial,' said Callaway. 'We're going to have to speak to the victims.'

'Yes, and we'll need their DNA too. And they're going to have to come here; we need to take the test on British soil for the courts to accept it. But it's the right thing to do,' agreed Mason. 'When you started talking about buggery, I thought he was gonna swing for you!'

'Really? I didn't clock that.'

303

'He nearly clocked *you*.'

'I was just in the moment, just concentrating on the interview.'

There was a knock at the door. Callaway opened it and Stacey Rush came in, looking flushed.

'Do you know how long I've been a solicitor for?' she asked.

Callaway wasn't expecting that question. He knew it would be wrong to guess and so he settled for a neutral shrug.

'Fifteen years. Fifteen years! I've represented murderers, child abusers, people who've slashed their granny's throats … I have never, ever felt more scared than I did when I was alone with that man in his cell.'

She didn't say it. Not in words anyway. But the look she gave the two men said exactly what she was feeling: *You convict my client, that monster, and make sure they throw away the key*.

CHAPTER FORTY-EIGHT

'You're going to have to forgive me, I've forgotten a few of my English words,' said the middle-aged woman in perfect English.

Rob Callaway was driving Anna Soltys through the streets of Bristol. He had picked her up from the airport an hour earlier. She had been warm in her greeting, had got in the car happily enough, it seemed to him. He asked if she wanted to check into her hotel first.

'No, no … I want to do this first, get it over with.'

Anna was 54 now but if Rob was being really honest with himself, she looked older. She was thin, gaunt and pale, with an edgy energy, but Rob had been expecting that; the prospect of returning to Bristol, returning to the scene of the attack, must have been terrifying.

Anna was wearing black jeans, biker boots and a T-shirt with the name of an obscure rock band, which Rob had actually heard of.

As they raced through the countryside from the airport, approaching the city, he attempted some small talk. He asked what she did for a living, but Anna remained vague.

'This and that,' she replied.

Anna still lived in the village in which she had grown up. She had a cat, no boyfriend and very bad memories of

Bristol. Rob detected a tightening in both her posture and her conversation as the car reached the city limits and the Clifton Suspension Bridge loomed into view.

'Is this your first time back in Bristol since the attack?' he asked gently, glancing at her.

She seemed to let a moment pass and then she said it: 'It's my first time out of Poland since the attack.'

'Oh.'

Rob explained that he had booked her into a hotel on the other side of Bristol but Anna told him that she wanted to revisit the scene – she said she hoped it would be therapeutic. They sat silently until Rob had driven through the lower part of Clifton Village.

'Okay, I'm going to drive up Whiteladies Road. You sure you're okay?' he asked.

'Yes, of course.'

I can arrange a chaperone if you want? A woman?'

'No. It's okay.'

He noticed with sadness what little cheeriness and bounce had been in her voice had disappeared.

They made it to the main strip of Whiteladies Road.

'It looks so different,' she observed. 'But it seems so similar too.'

'It was up the top here?'

She nodded.

Rob turned east and then north, and the expanse of Durdham Down led off to their left.

'Yes, here.'

He pulled over into a little side lane.

'You okay?'

She nodded and got out.

Cars whizzed past to their right: parents driving their children home from school, people in suits returning from the office, delivery vans clunking along the street.

And Rob and Anna stood there silently.

She looked around, her glances furtive.

'Do you remember what happened …?'

She gave him a scowl: 'I remember every second of what happened.'

'Can you talk me through it?' he asked tentatively.

'I was walking down this wide path here, from Whiteladies Road. I heard a car driving slowly behind me. I looked around. It was yellow, it drove past me just about where you are now. He spun around there …'

She pointed to a roundabout behind Rob's shoulder.

'Then it seemed to drive away the way it had come.

'As I walked further up, I just felt these hands round my neck. And he said, "Don't scream or I'll kill you."'

Anna stopped and took a breath.

'It was his smell I remember so well. Alcohol, beer … Then he dragged me over here …'

'Do you want to tell me what happened there, Anna?'

'That's why I've come all this way. May I touch you?'

Rob frowned but said yes.

Anna clasped the sleeve of his jacket and started pulling him quickly along the road.

'Imagine I'm grabbing your neck, not your arm. He pulled me from there, all along here …'

She was cantering now, holding onto his sleeve, Rob half-jogging across the grassland of Durdham Down.

'He has just told you he's going to kill you unless you do what he says … So all this time you're fearing for your life … all this time?'

Rob was still being dragged along.

'Yes …' she sighed, now almost breathless. 'Am I going to die? Will I see my parents again? Who is this man? What does he want from me?'

Still, she was dragging him.

'Live, die, rape, theft … all these things spinning around in my head. My life, how do you say it in English? My life spins before me. And I think it was around here that he did it. Yes, just here.'

'I'm going to need to write this down, Anna.'

'Yes, get your pen out. Remember, "Live, die, rape, theft …" Put that in your notes.'

Rob started scribbling.

'How are you feeling?' he asked carefully.

'You know, it's actually okay. Every day since 1978 I have come to this spot in my head. It's like it's frozen in time. And I think I have been too.

'All the cars were like what they would have been back then, old-fashioned ones. The night has replayed itself. Up here,' she tapped her head. 'But of course being here, time's moved on. All these cars are new. And the day. There is daytime here, in reality. It's only ever night-time in my head.

'This really is actually therapeutic.'

Rob knew to not second-guess how survivors would react to reliving trauma. Sometimes, like today, it actually seemed to help.

* * *

A lot had changed in Bristol in the 25 years since Ronald Evans's last Crown Court appearance, including the court itself. The ancient dark-wood building from 1979 had been closed and replaced by a new, light-brown-and-beige court block down a side street in the historic city centre.

Michelle Leonard arrived along with Gary Mason, Rob Callaway and the prosecution team, who were wheeling in boxes of court papers.

The trial was due to last two weeks.

Michelle made her way purposely through Security up a flight of marble stairs and into a side room, where the barristers were preparing the case.

'Have you done a Cold Case before?' she asked the tall man in a robe who was putting a wig on his head.

'Yes, but not this old. Twenty-six years is a long time between offence and trial. Are the victims here?'

'Yes, Anna Soltys is here from Poland and Hélène Baur's come from Austria. Neither of them wanted to be here, but they want to get him convicted so they've both made the trip.'

'What state are they in?' the barrister wanted to know.

'Well, they haven't seen Evans since the moment he attacked them. They've always thought it was him but now they know – and they're terrified.'

'All parties in Evans to Court Two, please,' rang a speaker from somewhere.

They made their way through a light-brown-and-beige door and into the courtroom. It was the largest of the building's courtrooms, with a high ceiling, big windows and a glass public gallery above.

Down in the pit, a few journalists sat on the press bench. One got up and introduced himself to Gary Mason, wanting to check a few details. He said his name was Robert Murphy and that he worked for a TV news station. The defence team was already in place and the prosecuting barrister took his place, flicking through his opening statement.

There was a knock at the door and the judge walked in. The room stood and then sat as he did.

'Case of Evans,' announced the clerk.

'Is the defendant here?' the judge wanted to know.

'Just coming up, Your Honour.'

Michelle heard the rattle of metal in metal and turned to look towards the back of the room. The first thing she thought was how frail Evans looked. He seemed sunken somehow, tiny in his large bodywarmer. He peered through spectacles, his face pale and badly-shaven.

She wondered if he had noticed her. Then she heard the clerk talking: 'Ronald Evans, you are charged with the rape of Hélène Baur on November 11th 1977 in Grove Road, Bristol. How do you plead?'

Not guilty, thought Michelle.

'Guilty,' said Evans.

Guilty?! He's pleaded guilty?

The clerk continued: 'You are charged with the indecent assault of Anna Soltys on Durdham Down on December 16th 1978. How do you plead?'

Michelle's eyes were boring into Evans now.

'Guilty.'

Christ, he admitted it. What next?

'And you are charged with the attempted rape of Anna

CHAPTER FORTY-EIGHT

Soltys on Durdham Down on December 16th 1978. How do you plead?'

'Not guilty.'

Will they have a trial now? she wondered.

The prosecutor stepped up: 'Your Honour, the pleas you've just heard have come as a bit of a surprise to the prosecution. We were expecting Not Guilty pleas and to proceed with a trial. I wonder if I might take some advice?'

'Quite,' said the judge, not looking at the prosecutor. He seemed to be studying Evans, a questioning look on his face.

He rose.

'What next?' whispered Michelle.

Gary Mason shrugged.

Michelle thought of Hélène Baur and Anna Soltys, who were in separate rooms in the building. They were in a room they didn't want to be in, a city they didn't want to be in, a country they didn't want to be in. And there had been no need for them to put themselves through the trauma of reliving their attack. They had done it because they wanted to help. And now, it was all for nothing.

'He's playing games with these victims,' said Michelle, staring at the pale, shrunken man in a bodywarmer who was leaving the dock. She was sure she could see on his face the ghost of a smile.

Anna Soltys told Detective Sergeant Gary Mason she did not want to proceed with the prosecution. He'd told her that Ronald Evans had admitted the lesser charge of indecent assault on her. If there was to be a trial, she would have to go through the trauma of giving evidence against him. Also, because he had also pleaded guilty to Hélène Baur's rape, Evans's sentence might not be that much longer anyway.

But the team had to wait five months for that sentencing hearing in Court Two of Bristol Crown Court on 13 May 2005.

Neither Anna nor Hélène was there.

But someone else was.

Michelle Leonard walked into the courtroom. She went into the public gallery and sat next to a woman who was a couple of years older than her, maybe in her early fifties. The woman was well dressed and clearly holding something back.

'Are you to do with the case?' asked the woman.

'Yes, I was one of the decoy officers.'

'Oh. Okay.'

'Who are you?' asked Michelle.

'My name's Joanna. He went for me, back in the seventies.'

'Went for you?'

'Attacked me.'

'How are you doing?'

'I just want to see him go down for life.'

Michelle nodded.

There was a knock at the door and the judge swept in. Michelle and Joanna McGarry sat down next to each other. There was then a metallic click-rattle from the back of the room and the pale, faded shape of Ronald Evans appeared.

'Case of Ronald Evans,' shouted the clerk.

'Sit down, Mr Evans …'

Michelle noticed a sharp gasp from Joanna as she craned her head, looking at the dock.

Now the prosecutor was talking about charges which had been admitted and others which had not but might still lie on file. And he began addressing the court about Evans's case: 'Mr Evans has a significant criminal history. The first being the murder of a shop worker, Kathleen Heathcote, in November 1963. He was sentenced to life imprisonment in 1964. He was released on a scheme in 1975 and set up home here in Bristol, where he lived something of a double-life. By day, he was a family man, an electrician, a reformed and rehabilitated prisoner. By night, he was the Clifton Rapist.

'Your Honour will not have missed the irony that although he was given the nickname "The Clifton Rapist", back in 1979 he admitted only indecent assaults. The count he admits today is in fact the first time he has confessed to rape. Of course, the law has changed. Had these attacks been committed today all of these offences would be classed as rape.'

Michelle glanced across at Joanna. She tried to remember what had happened to her. She had always been seen as the fifth victim, but when the charges for Hélène Baur were dropped, she became the fourth. Joanna had been working in a nightclub, had left after her shift and was driving home from work, Michelle recalled, when she spotted the yellow Ford Capri in the rear-view mirror of her car. She had parked in front of her home, walked up the path and Evans had leapt from the bushes before subjecting her to a prolonged attack.

'Your Honour,' Michelle heard the prosecuting barrister say, 'we have spoken at length to the survivors of these two attacks. And we have their Victim Personal Statements. We have an officer to read them out.'

Detective Constable Rob Callaway walked to the witness stand and opened a file.

'This is the Victim Personal Statement of Hélène Baur,' he announced. 'In the early hours of November 11th 1977, my life changed forever. I was 21 years old, I was a happy, confident, outgoing woman. I had spent my entire life in Austria but came to Bristol to study, to learn English. I wanted to be a "Woman of the World".

'I had only been in Bristol for a few months and was building a good set of friends. I had been out with these friends on the night of the 10th. We went to one of your wonderful pubs, I went back to a friend's flat and then I was walking to my own home when it happened.

'I saw a face in the night. A man. He was in a phone box as I walked past. And before I knew it, I felt hands around my neck and he said the words, "Don't scream or I'll kill you." I was dragged for about a hundred yards. It felt like an eternity. I was then bundled over a wall, where he subjected me to a prolonged, violent and traumatic rape.

'Afterwards, the man who did this just disappeared.

'I was new to the city, I was new to the country, so I had little knowledge that a serial offender was stalking the streets. Had I known that, I would not have walked home alone that night. The examination and police procedures afterwards were nearly as traumatic as the attack itself. I felt numb, used, spent, inhuman. I could not stay in the city, I had to go home. My dreams of being a "Woman of the World" were over.

'My trauma was compounded by the knowledge that my attacker had not been caught. Yes, when Ronald Evans was finally detained nearly two years later, I thought he might be the man who raped me but I didn't know for sure. Police didn't think so.

'That's been that grain of doubt which has tortured me. But now I know: you are my attacker, you are the man who took my freedom.'

Rob Callaway's voice was gentle and lilting, but Michelle felt a spasm inside from the brutality of Hélène Baur's words. She looked across at Joanna and saw a tear running down her cheek.

Rob continued: 'Since the attack and my return to Austria, I have been a different woman. I have never been able to trust a man. Every relationship I have been in has failed. My boyfriends have been nice, understanding men but they have all been unable to cope with my ongoing trauma from what happened more than 20 years ago.

'The last time I wore shoes with heels was on November 11th 1977. I wear only flats now, in case I find myself approached by a man and need to run away. I rarely go out at night. Even in the day I walk on the edge of the kerb so I can escape into the road if I need to. I steer clear of roads with hedges, even.

'While I have been able to develop as a person, I have a good career and my incredible family has helped me, my life has taken a completely different path to the one I had planned. I wanted to travel the world. Since 1977, I haven't left Austria. In fact, I have seldom left my village. Sometimes I dream about the attack and it will happen to me again and again as if on a loop in my head. My rape may have lasted more than an hour, but I have lived that attack a million times since.'

Michelle thought of her own dreams, the nights she had been woken after imagining Evans at her bedroom window. Dreams which had now faded into her memory. She felt someone grabbing her hand. Joanna clung to her, tears rolling down her cheeks.

Rob Callaway continued the statement: 'I am pleased the defendant has pleaded guilty. He has never shown any remorse but in that small action, which I am sure he has performed in self-interest, he has saved me from having to face him again.

'I will not be free, though. I do not think I will ever enjoy freedom.'

The court fell silent.

Ronald Evans looked ahead, impassive. And then he yawned.

The judge told Evans to stand. He did so, pulling the hands out of the pockets of his bodywarmer.

'Ronald Evans, the impact of the attack on your two victims has been profound and long-lasting. The public is entitled to expect that offences of this sort will be properly punished. The Parole Board may conclude that it will never be safe to release you.

'I sentence you to eight and a half years for the offence of rape and 18 months each for the two counts of indecent assault. You will serve these concurrently, making your sentence a total of eight and a half years. You must sign the Sex Offenders' Register and you will be on that for the remainder of your life. You may go down.'

Evans nodded, stifled another yawn and was led away through the dock security door.

Michelle looked down and noticed Joanna McGarry's hand holding hers still. She then heard her whisper: 'I thought I was over this man ...' Wiping a tear from her eye, she looked back at Michelle. 'But it's clear that I'm not.'

Michelle ushered Joanna out of the courtroom and away.

The re-arrest and new sentencing of Ronald Evans meant that there was a renewed interest in Operation Argus. Newspapers wrote front-page features about the team of police officers who had put their lives on the line to catch a monster – and succeeded.

Michelle Leonard was once again asked to give interviews about the moment she had caught the Clifton Rapist. As far as she was concerned, life should have meant life for Evans. Not because she was a particular believer in strong punishments but because she had seen and heard the impact his attacks had had on his victims.

She also believed he was utterly without remorse. Evans had known that he was going to be convicted, the DNA evidence was overwhelming, but still he toyed with his victims' feelings in refusing to plead guilty until the final moment. He made them travel from abroad, made them wait in a side room of Bristol Crown Court, made them feel the terror that they would have to face him once more.

Only for him to change his mind and get the maximum credit for a guilty plea.

He was no longer able to control his survivors physically, but he could still play with their emotions, it seemed.

Michelle saw him as a brute of a man who got his kicks from mind games and manipulation. As far as she was concerned, he deserved no more shots at redemption. The last time he was given the chance, he attacked seven women at night as they walked alone, vulnerable in the street.

He was hard-wired as a monster.

CHAPTER FORTY-NINE

2018

The phone rings in a neat, detached home in the West Country. Upstairs, in the office, are a few family photos in frames: Michelle Leonard with her husband, her son, daughter and grandchildren. There's a desk boasting trophies for county-level croquet competitions. Among them sits a Queen's Commendation for Brave Conduct.

Michelle tells Murphy, her whippet, to stop barking and picks up the receiver.

'Hello, is that Mrs Leonard?'

'Yes.'

'This is the Victim Support Service.'

She knows what's coming next.

'We have you listed as a victim of Ronald Evans, back in 1979?'

'No, I'm not a victim. He hit me, but I was a police officer. I keep telling you to stop listing me as a victim.'

'Okay, Mrs Leonard. Well, we have some news. Mr Evans is very old now – he's 77 and the Parole Board's decided he is eligible for release. We want you to know.'

'Thank you. What are the restrictions on his licence?'

'Well, he's not allowed to visit Bristol, he's not allowed to contact certain family members. But he is no longer a threat to society. He has to see a probation officer in London. He walks with a stick, he is very old and infirm. Did you know he's Britain's longest-serving prisoner?'

'I did. It's his claim to fame. Thanks for letting me know. I feel quite safe – I wouldn't rate his chances if he tries to come anywhere near me.'

'Thank you. Goodbye.'

Michelle puts down the phone and swears. Everything she has said is true: she's not worried about herself, she has never regarded herself as one of his victims and she does feel safe from him. But she thinks of how Evans persuaded the Parole Board to give him his freedom in 1975 and now he's done it again. She thinks of how his victims' lives were forever changed after that release and she wonders what guarantees the Parole Board and Probation Service can make to ensure a monster who is so hard-wired to attack women will not reoffend again.

And something else occurs to Michelle. It strikes her that the last time he enjoyed liberty, she was a rookie cop, just 23 years old – a mere girl. Now, she has retired from the force, she is in her early sixties, has grandchildren and only now Ronald Evans, convicted murderer and Clifton Rapist, is free again. Despite the passing of time, the passing of her career, the passing of their two lives, she wonders how safe women really are: from Evans, or from others like him.

EPILOGUE

THURSDAY, 16 NOVEMBER 2023

I am in my office in Bristol, but on my laptop screen is a live video feed to London: to both the Central Criminal Court – the Old Bailey – and HMP Pentonville. It is a right of journalists to be given access to these links to report for newspapers, or in my case, television.

A judge, Her Honour Vanessa Francis, sits silently behind a desk. Both the furniture and the panelling of the court are a sombre dark wood.

Ronald Evans sits in Pentonville's small blue-grey video suite. He is 83 years old now. Bald, wrinkled and wearing a grey sweatshirt. Earlier this week a jury convicted him of sexually assaulting a woman ... a *new* victim. I watched the trial: his victim was one of two women who had complained about him to police.

He is too slow to run after victims these days. His new method of attack is to befriend vulnerable women, groom them and get them alone. Then he assaulted them when they had no way out.

The case is simple. It is also simply terrifying.

After being released from prison in December 2018, aged 77, Ronald Evans settled in London. He joined a community group, where he started volunteering. The trial heard how Evans led an active sex life with his newfound liberty. He had consenting sexual partners and in his bedside cabinet he kept sex toys, condoms and lubricant. His voracious appetite for sex was matched by his consumption of porn, the court heard. But in 2020 he identified a woman who was half his age. Victim One was disabled and vulnerable, and twice he attacked her when they were alone, the prosecution claimed. Then in July 2022 he assaulted Victim Two. She was also vulnerable. He had befriended her, took her for a lunch of fish and chips, then brought her back to his flat, where he sexually assaulted her.

The woman was horrified, she felt trapped. She complained to the Metropolitan Police Service two weeks later. An officer looked at the Police National Computer (PNC). No previous convictions were flagged against Ronald Evans – the Metropolitan Police Service will not tell me why. Evans was listed for sure, Gary Mason found him logged there in 2004. But the Met didn't see him.

Victim Two was terrified. She was sure what Evans had done to her was *wrong*.

Then, one night, Victim Two was watching ITV News and a report promoting a four-part documentary appeared on the bulletin. The documentary was called *Decoy* and was written, presented and directed by me.

I had appeared on her TV screen talking about how a man called Ronald Evans had murdered a woman called Kathleen Heathcote in 1963, had been released in the 1970s in Bristol, where he had become the Clifton Rapist – and had been caught by an extraordinary covert trap involving young female officers.

Victim Two had felt sick and called the Met again. She complained. Why had officers been unable to find Evans on their systems and then he appeared in front of millions of people on ITV News? Detectives looked again and found Evans on the PNC.

Two days later, Evans was arrested. He had to leave his flat, his freedom and his sex toys, and was back in custody, having clearly breached the conditions of his life licence. There had been a trial earlier in 2023. Evans faced four counts: three assaults on Victim One and another against Victim Two. The jury had acquitted him of one assault against the first woman but had been unable to reach a decision on the other three counts. So, this hearing in November 2023 was a retrial, and I watched it unfold.

It had been agreed in advance that the jury would not be told Evans was a convicted murderer, but they would know he had committed seven sex attacks on women in the 1970s, as that was relevant to the new accusations. But Judge Francis ruled that revealing the murder was 'too prejudicial' to allow him a fair trial.

Evans was meant to be unwell, was meant to be frail. But when I saw him stride across the court from the dock to the witness box, I wondered if anyone was fooled by the prop of the walking stick he used. Evans was thin, tall and his voice, that flat-vowelled, deep East Midlands accent, rang across the courtroom.

He told the jury he had been a volunteer, helping the vulnerable at the community centre. The first thing that entered my mind was, *Who runs the checks on volunteers?*

Then he told the court one of his victims had been to prison before.

This was a lie.

The jury was sent out of the courtroom and the judge told him off. The prosecuting barrister argued that the picture Evans presented to the jury was so distorted from reality and the fact he had fabricated his victim's criminal past should allow her to reveal to the jury he was a convicted killer. The judge disagreed, but said that if Evans played any more tricks, the jury would be told he *was* a killer. From then on, Evans behaved, but he had muddied the waters, he had manipulated the jury and he had got away with them not knowing about his murder.

His defence barrister cross-examined both women. They were questioned as to whether they had made up their claims, had colluded with each other.

Both said no.

The jury was sent out to reach its verdicts.

I was doubtful. If jurors had known his full criminal history, I was sure they would have convicted him.

After five hours, and after the judge had offered the jury the opportunity to reach a majority verdict, they returned. The foreman stood. When asked if the jury found Evans guilty or not guilty, his words rang out.

Counts one and two against Victim One were both Not Guilty.

But then, the third charge against Victim Two was read out: 'Guilty.'

My sense of relief was overwhelming. I had waited more than a year for this moment, since I had learned of his arrest. And now, three days later, he's here on this video link for his sentencing hearing: silent, wrinkled, menacing.

Two lawyers appear in separate boxes on the screen. One is the prosecutor Lauren Sales KC. In her thirties, she has dark hair and is wearing a barrister's white wig and black gown. The other lawyer is Evans's defence counsel, Afzal Anwar KC. He's a distinguished-looking man in his forties in the same uniform. It's their job to argue what Evans's sentence should be.

Sales starts talking. She outlines that the victim was vulnerable, that now she doesn't feel safe in her own home; she is on edge and can't relax. She had been a victim of domestic abuse in the past and had noticed the warning signs about Evans, but thought she was being mistrusting because of her experience of violence at the hands of a former partner. She had joined the community centre as part of the process of rebuilding her life.

There, she had met Evans.

Seeing the documentary on the news, when the police had been unable to find Evans on the Police National Computer, had made her feel sick. She feels numb and has suffered nightmares since the attack.

Sales argues Evans should receive a maximum of two years in jail.

It's Anwar's time to talk now on Evans's behalf. He describes the assault as 'short' in duration and it's only one offence. Evans is 83, he says, and has been waiting for this trial since August 2022 – 15 months is a long time. He argues that the judge should make the sentence shorter.

Now the judge starts to explain what her sentence will be. She is scathing about Evans, telling him he had a plan to 'take any chance to satisfy your sexual needs': 'You manipulated the victim's obvious vulnerabilities and cultivated her friendship so she would feel safe in your company so you could pursue sexual contact with her.'

Now she begins talking about his previous convictions, describing how he was jailed for 'rape and murder' in 1964.

Evans starts spluttering in that gruff, East Midlands accent: 'No, no, I were never convicted of rape …' he shouts.

The judge continues: 'Although age and infirmity have no doubt impacted your ability to attack or rape or sexually assault lone women at night, it is apparent from your actions to this victim that time has done nothing to change the fact that you are a sexual predator.'

Evans is now staring blankly at the camera.

'You have sought to adapt the means by which you can continue to offend. Your previous convictions are a significant aggravating factor in this case as is the fact you were on life licence, which was first granted to you in 1975 and in respect of which you have been recalled twice for further sexual offending.

'Your victim went through the ordeal of giving evidence twice, she was cross-examined twice and it was suggested to her on those occasions that she had fabricated her account and colluded with another resident to lie about you.'

The judge now says Evans's criminal history and the fact he had been recalled while on life licence twice have elevated the seriousness of his offending to a higher category. Evans looks at her blankly as she sentences him to four years in prison – double what the prosecution had suggested.

I have *never* seen this happen.

'You are an intelligent and manipulative man,' continues the judge. 'The risk that you pose to women, not just women you are in a relationship with, but women that you target is significant.'

The judge says she is ending the hearing. The faces of Sales and Anwar disappear from my laptop screen. Now there is just the judge in her wood-panelled courtroom and Evans in his grey prison videosuite. Two images on a screen: an old, evil criminal and a judge representing justice, which has finally caught up with him again.

I think of the true legacy of this predator, the mark he has made during his time on this planet. And I think of the victims who walked up Whiteladies Road, only for their lives to change in his horrific attacks. Innocent survivors in the wrong place at the wrong time. I think of the detectives working hard to catch him, the hours put in, the doors knocked, the leads followed, the interviews with innocent suspects, the line-ups, the hope and despair involved in a large inquiry.

I think of the team of young women – some just teenagers – sent out to lure him, deployed as bait. And I think of the male officers who lay in the shadows on snowy nights, or in Task Force vans or even, in dark weeks of desperation, dressing as women.

I think of Michelle Leonard, who received that electric-crackled warning in her ear that a killer was on her track and of that dreadful choice she had to make, and the bravery of her decision.

I think of his victims at the Cold Case hearing in 2005: Hélène Baur, Anna Soltys and Joanna McGarry, three young women who, decades on, were still living with the trauma of their attacks.

And I think of Kathleen Heathcote, a young, innocent woman who had dreams of marriage and a husband. A life ahead of her, dreams which were destroyed in an instant when she got off a bus on a stormy night in November 1963 as a car followed silently behind.

And I look at the screen and see the man responsible for all of this.

The old criminal on one camera. Justice in the form of the judge on the other.

Then the judge reaches for her computer and clicks a button.

Ronald Evans vanishes.

The screen goes blank.

AFTERWORD

First, a note about the victims of Evans's assaults in the 1970s. Each is rightly given lifetime anonymity by the courts so while the dates and locations of each attack are accurate, I have changed their names and the details about them. I hope Evans's latest – and hopefully last – incarceration will bring them some peace.

While the case of the Clifton Rapist was solved, Avon and Somerset Police had mixed luck with other cases mentioned within these pages.

As we go to press, the assaults on both Wendy Johnson in a Kingsdown alleyway in March 1978 and Rachel Doulton in her Clifton flat the following month remain undetected. Police believe them to have been carried out by a different attacker or attackers, not Ronald Evans.

Inquiries continued into the murder of Susan Donoghue. A forensic review in 2016 was able to identify a perfect DNA profile of the nurse's killer at the scene. Her brother, Seamus McGeary, told the *Belfast Telegraph*: 'It was a surprise, I thought everything was gone because so many years have passed. They have made great strides in technology, so maybe they will get somebody. That is about all I can hope for. It would help bring some closure for me.' But, at present, the DNA does not match with anyone on the National DNA Database and so Susan's killer has still not been identified.

Chris Gould's 'Magic Fingers' investigation saw a Bristol mother-of-two, Rosemary Edwards, convicted of four counts of exercising control over prostitutes. Her partner, David Wakefield, admitted living off immoral earnings. They were each sentenced to six months' community service.

And what about the team of detectives and decoys who brought Ronald Evans to justice? It was always a loose connection of officers. There has never been an 'Operation Argus Club'. Some still speak, some have lost touch, others have become reunited during the writing of this book.

Sergeant Kelvin Hattersley remained in the police for his full service. He worked on many big operations including the St Paul's Riots, which were sparked a little over a year after the events in this book. He went on to be in charge of VIP visits to the force area.

Andy Kerslake, the arresting officer, was bitten by the undercover bug and spent most of the rest of his long and successful career hiding out in cars, bushes and using the shadows to conceal himself. He worked for Avon and Somerset Police, the Regional Crime Squad and the National Crime Agency.

Malcolm Popperwell became Assistant Chief Constable. He retired and became chairman of a health authority in the city before retiring again and taking various charitable roles. He died in 2020, aged 86.

Brian Theobald retired in the 1980s. Now in his nineties, he still lives in the West Country.

Sergeant Carol Curnock married a fellow police officer, Peter Miller, in the months after Operation Argus. She retired in 1990 and has spent much of her time since as an active golfer.

John O'Connor transferred to the Force Crime Squad, where he would be moved from one homicide to another. He worked on the inquiries into the murders of Melanie Road in Bath and Colin Bedale-Taylor in South Gloucestershire just weeks apart in 1984. One of these is the subject of a book, the other deserves to be. He retired to France then returned to Bristol, a city he knows so well.

Chris Gould retired in 2007 as a chief superintendent. He moved back to the country he loved, Australia, where he runs a global consultancy investigating child abuse.

Gary Mason retired from the Cold Case team he set up before returning immediately to continue as a civilian investigator. He was a key part of the inquiry which led to the killer of the schoolgirl Melanie Road being convicted 32 years after her murder. He retired (again) in 2020.

Rob Callaway retired in 2014. He divides his time between travelling, motorcycling and being an 'extra' on television shows. At one point, he worked alongside the lead actor Jason Watkins, who had previously played the title role in the TV drama, *The Lost Honour of Christopher Jefferies*. The mini-series was about how the press vilified a former English schoolmaster arrested in the inquiry into Joanna Yeates's murder in 2010. Rob informed Jason that he was the advanced interviewer who had conducted the police interview of Jefferies – and had his spelling and grammar in the statement corrected.

Michelle Leonard (née Tighe) might have been warned by the female superintendent that the force was 'not a marriage bureau', but she and several other WPCs went on to marry men in the force.

In June 1980, Sally Difazio wed Nigel Wright, the man she had met on a tennis court two years earlier. She had decided that policing was no longer for her and handed in her notice: 'I found myself hardening, I found myself losing compassion,' she said. 'You need to develop a thick skin.'

Sally went on to become a sales rep: 'The police force gave you good communication skills, you could speak with people at all levels. I used the police experience to do my new job, to build a rapport with clients. I really didn't want an office job and this took me around the Southwest. I could also carry on with all the sport I loved.'

These days, she and Nigel go on long cycling holidays, biking 1,000 miles at a time in France, Italy, Spain and Cuba. They also went to Everest Base Camp. Sally plays bowls at county level. They have a daughter and a son.

Of all the 12 decoy operatives, Steph Whittle's career was unique: she was the only one who saw a promotion. Neither Sally, Michelle nor any of the others showed any interest in moving up the ranks. Steph passed her sergeant's exams just a few months after the end of Operation Argus, when she was still a teenager, but she still needed to pass a promotion board to move up a rank.

She was waiting for that promotion when she passed her inspector's exams in 1983. But still she remained a WPC, moving to the Regional Crime Squad. She adored this job and was involved in further undercover work.

And she finally became a sergeant in 1988 in B-Division.

In 1989, Steph married a chief inspector, Pete Beardon. After her marriage came a further promotion to temporary detective inspector. Her career was growing but so too was something else.

When Steph Beardon realised she was pregnant, she handed in her notice; there was no way that she could continue being both an officer and a mother.

'I didn't think twice about it. We had no choice back then,' she said.

Steph and Pete went on to have two sons and remained married until his untimely death from cancer, aged 59, in 2004. She had a series of jobs including being a qualified swimming instructor, teaching children how to swim. She was also a teaching assistant, school librarian and worked in a supermarket food hall at an out-of-town shopping centre. As energetic as ever, Steph's favourite activities include tennis and walking holidays with her dog Flossie, a Golden Doodle. She looks back on her time in the cadets with pride and affection – for the other cadets and instructors. Some have remained lifelong friends. And she reflects on her time in the force with a sense of achievement and mostly enjoyment.

She urges people not to judge seventies policing with today's sensibilities: 'The male chauvinism was a real pain on occasions but it was of its time in society in general,' she says. 'It's very easy to look back with modern eyes and describe the time as sexist or misogynistic. I'm not excusing it, but this was the culture. And we knew what we were getting into.'

Michelle Tighe met her future husband in the Mandrake Club in 1982. He was also a police officer. They set up home in 1987 and they had their first child.

When Michelle went on maternity leave, she asked her inspector if he would make a request of the new chief constable that she could return on a part-time basis after the baby was born.

He told her: 'I can ask, but it's not going to happen in my lifetime. The request isn't worth the paper it's written on, if you ask my opinion.'

Michelle was not asking his opinion. And the Chief Constable did not approve her request.

Michelle left the force in 1989 before giving birth to her second child. Soon after that, she and her husband split up and she found herself a single mother of two, without a job. Six years later and married to her new husband, Steve, Michelle re-joined Avon and Somerset Police, eventually becoming a civilian investigating officer in the Major Crime Unit – in effect a murder detective without a warrant. She retired in 2012. Michelle still lives in the West Country, where she is a champion croquet player. Even in retirement, she remains a competitive soul. Her trophy cabinet is fully stocked with sporting awards alongside her Queen's Commendation for Brave Conduct.

These days, Michelle gives talks to Women's Institute meetings. She has a presentation about how she and a group of colleagues caught one of Britain's most-wanted men.

'Everything worked perfectly on that night,' she says. 'It's like something from a TV programme and you think, that would *never* happen in real life.

'From the time I was dropped off to when he saw me was seconds, just seconds. A complete coincidence. Had I been any earlier or later, he wouldn't have been passing by, he wouldn't have seen me. And I know he would have attacked another woman that night. He was out wearing two pairs of trousers. In 1963, he got his trousers muddy and was caught through that. He'd learnt through his mistakes – he was out to attack that night. And who knows how many more women he would have assaulted before we caught him?'

For three months, Michelle's life and those of her Operation Argus colleagues were focused on one thing: catching the Clifton Rapist. For months afterwards, she had those nightmares about him escaping prison, appearing at her window and coming into her room.

'I don't really think about him now,' she says. 'Unless I'm talking about him. He's not in my mind at all.'

Michelle has no doubt that these days a predator with the same modus operandi as Ronald Evans would be caught quickly: DNA, CCTV and telephone analytics make solving stranger rapes easier. But despite this, conviction rates have dropped.

In the days when Evans was free, if you reported a sexual assault, you had a 34 per cent chance of seeing your attacker admit the charge or be found guilty by a jury, according to research by the journalist Barbara Toner. By 2021, this fell to 1.6 per cent, according to Home Office figures. Yes, far more women are reporting assaults but for every 60 women attacked, only one will see the offender in court. A new End-to-End Rape Review has made improvements since then – a lot of innovative work has been trialled in the Avon and Somerset force – but the figures are stark and horrific.

'Why is it some men feel this need to attack women?' Michelle asks. 'It's not the 1970s anymore. We're supposed to be more civilised, better-educated. But there are still men out there attacking women.'

Monsters like Ronald Evans are rare. He was given a chance for rehabilitation and redemption, but he couldn't bring himself to take it.

How many people has this one man affected?

His survivors: women who were in the wrong place at the wrong time when he attacked them in the 1970s. They will have two parts of their lives – before their assault and after-wards.

And Evans has his own family: his two ex-wives and three children, who must live with his dreadful legacy.

Kathleen Heathcote would be in her eighties today but her chance to live her life was removed in an instant. Her hopes to marry, be a mother, be happy vanished in her short, brutal encounter with Ronald Evans.

Kathleen's family grieve her still.

As for the decoys, the risks these young police officers were asked to take were extreme, dangerous and brave. A plan like this wouldn't happen today. Neither Health and Safety guidelines nor the Regulation of Investigatory Powers Act 2000 (RIPA) would allow it – like this at least. Any of the officers could have been seriously harmed. Somehow, this extraordinary operation worked. All because on a snowy morning in March 1979, a young police officer was faced with that dreadful choice: should she stay on the main road to protect herself? Or should she turn into the darkened side streets and put her own life on the line to catch a killer?

ACKNOWLEDGEMENTS

Thank you to everyone who has helped with the publication of *Decoy*.

At HarperCollins, Kelly Ellis and Imogen Gordon Clark have been brilliant at shaping the book and challenging me – in such a supportive way. Thanks also to Ameena Ghori-Khan for all her help with images.

Jane Donovan has been responsible for so many improvements. And Sarah Foster designed *Decoy*'s beautifully moody cover.

Thanks to my agent, Clare Hulton, for believing in the project, the story, the team of Decoys and in me. Clare has been an incredible support throughout.

Thanks to everyone at ITV News, in particular Jim Stevens, Guy Phillips, Vicky Slade and Owain Meredith.

My writing collaborator, Julie Mackay, gave me a wonderful insight into being a covert police officer. If you found this book compelling, please do get a copy of *To Hunt a Killer* (HarperCollins, 2022). It's a book we wrote together about how she tracked down the killer of the schoolgirl Melanie Road, gaining justice for her family after 32 years. And another wonderful detective, Maddy Hennah, was kind enough to suggest some needed improvements – and offer very encouraging words at just the right time.

Thanks also to DC Becky Norton of Avon and Somerset Police, who deals with survivors of sexual assault on a daily basis. Through her, I have met and interviewed a number of women who have survived rape or serious sexual assaults, and this experience has informed my work in *Decoy*.

The author Susan Lewis and her husband, the journalist James Garrett, gave me brilliant descriptions of the Platform One nightclub, Whiteladies Road and the Bristol scene in the 1970s – it really sounds like a golden age.

Neil Kempsell gave a wonderful flavour of his father's life as a Royal Navy diver. Kenneth Kempsell made the extra-ordinary recovery of Kathleen Heathcote from Ladybower Reservoir in 1963.

George Kay offered great insight and huge assistance with story arcs and structure.

Lynda Kelly gave wonderful, full and forensic feedback on early drafts of *Decoy*.

Getting to know the Operation Argus team has been a joy. I have loved their company. There have been a couple of officers who I have not been able to include fully in these pages through need for brevity and simplicity. Stu Sexton was generous with his time; rest in peace, Stu. Thanks also to Steve Livings and Chris Nott.

Although not part of the book in detail, I would also like to thank the other decoy officers who were brave enough to put their lives on the line each night: Jean Castle, Jackie Clair, Cathy Holbrook, Denise Pollard, Kathy Ryan and Gillian Skinner. I am sorry one of the decoys, Diana Day,

340

died a few months before the book's publication. So too did the male decoy, Robbie Jones.

Thanks also to Brian Theobald and Carol Miller (née Curnock).

Gary Mason was instrumental in the book's genesis. He started putting me in touch with some of the officers and telling them I could be trusted. Gary has written three books about his time as a detective. Please do look them up.

Thanks to Rob Callaway, Kelvin Hattersley, Andy Kerslake and John O'Connor – each a brilliant interviewee with wonderful stories.

Chatting to Chris Gould was a turning point. It was his interview in the early days of my research which made me think there was a book in this. I am only sorry I couldn't include all of his stories of his time as a decoy. Yes, he has even more …

Thanks to Sally Difazio and her husband, Nigel Wright. Both were a joy to deal with and offered wonderful perspectives on policing in the 1970s.

To Steph Beardon for her time, help, eloquence and sense of fun.

And thanks to Michelle Leonard. She says that any of the decoys would have made the same choice as she did – to put herself in the line of fire. But it fell to her, and she was brave enough to trust in the plan and her comrades. She is an incredible woman.

I'd also like to thank Kathleen Heathcote's family for their blessing and support. Her older sister, Glenis, was so helpful, as were Kathleen's sister-in-law Annie and her nephew Chris.

I could never have written this without the backing of my wife, Ellie Barker, and my sons. Sometimes, recently, I've been at home in body but my mind has been away in the late 1970s with the Argus team. They've each been so supportive and thoughtful. This book would have remained unwritten without that sense of belief from those around me.

And thanks to everyone who has supported me on Substack, listened to my podcast and been involved with the Behind The Crimes community. You can subscribe – and watch video clips, see more images and read more about this story – at robertmurphy.substack.com.

PHOTO CREDITS

p.1 – Mirrorpix/Reach licensing

p.2 – Courtesy of Avon & Somerset Police

p.3 (top) – Mirrorpix/Reach licensing

p.3 (bottom) – ITN/Getty Images

p.4 – Reproduced with the permission of the National Library of Scotland

p.5 (top) – Courtesy of Avon & Somerset Police

p.5 (bottom) – Courtesy of Avon & Somerset Police

p.6 – Courtesy of Avon & Somerset Police

p.7 (top) – Courtesy of Sally Difazio

p.8 (top) – Courtesy of Avon & Somerset Police

p.8 (bottom) – Courtesy of Metropolitan Police Service